MATURITY AND COMPETENCE

Maturity and Competence

A TRANSCULTURAL VIEW

Douglas H. Heath

HAVERFORD COLLEGE

Foreword by M. Brewster Smith

GARDNER PRESS, INC., NEW YORK
DISTRIBUTED BY HALSTED PRESS DIVISION
JOHN WILEY & SONS, INC.
NEW YORK · TORONTO · LONDON · SYDNEY

Grateful acknowledgement is made to The University of Chicago Press for permission to quote from "Making man modern: on the causes and consequences of individual change in six developing countries," from the *American Journal of Sociology*, 1969, Vol. 75, p. 212; to Harper & Row for excerpts by Edmund W. Sinnott, pp. 16 & 17, in *Creativity And Its Cultivation*, edited by Harold H. Anderson, Harper & Row, 1959; and to Atheneum Publishers, Inc. for pp. 79, 99, 101, 112-113, 182, 194, 226-229 from *The Italians* by Luigi Barzini, Copyright © 1964 by Luigi Barzini; reprinted by permission of Atheneum Publishers.

GARDNER PRESS, INC.
19 Union Square West
New York, New York 10003

Distributed solely by the Halsted Press Division
of John Wiley & Sons, Inc., New York

Library of Congress Cataloging in Publication Data

Heath, Douglas H
    Maturity and competence.

    Bibliography: p.
    Includes index.
    1. Emotional maturity.   2. Mental health.
3. Cross-cultural studies.   I. Title.
BF710.H43   155.2'5   77-4218
ISBN 0-470-99072-4

PRINTED IN THE UNITED STATES OF AMERICA

To Harriet E. Heath

WITH SPECIAL ACKNOWLEDGEMENT TO

Dr. Gökçe Cansever
Dr. Mehmet Gürkaynak
Dr. William LeCompte
Bilge Ögun
Ulker Ilter

Dr. Maria Luisa Falorni
Dr. Filippo Boschi
Dr. Giovani Sprini
Sylvia Cassese

Contents

Foreword

The problem that Douglas Heath addresses in this provocative book is at once very difficult and very important: are objective standards of good psychological functioning attainable? The problem is central to the psychology of personality and its applications in clinical, counseling, and educational psychology, where terms like *adjustment, competence, self-actualization* and *positive mental health* have been used to evoke overlapping and often ill-defined criteria of effective functioning. But its human significance is much broader: it lies at the crossroads of ethics and empirical science. Are we inherently caught in a cultural relativism that deprives us of any critical foothold for evaluating human functioning beyond the historically given standards of the societies to which we have been socialized? Or are transcultural standards attainable and legitimate? The issue involves fundamental questions about the nature of human nature.

An earlier generation of psychologists learned from Franz Boas and his students in cultural anthropology to be skeptical of our naively received values as "culture-bound." To assume that our own evaluative yardsticks are universally applicable is to be guilty of ethnocentrism. The cogency of the relativistic critique cannot be denied: we are all too familiar with the evil done through the imposition of culture-bound perspectives outside their indigenous range. But the full implications of a self-consistent relativism are unacceptable to many of us as responsible human actors—as we

discovered when confronted with the evil of the German Nazis. Few
of us in the older generation were ready to adopt a relativist
neutrality toward the Nazi way of life, which appeared so
transparently anti human.

In the present era the sources of manifest evil seem closer to
home. In their guilt about American imperialism, contemporary
anthropologists—especially younger ones who were spared the
moral education of World War II—once more find an extreme
relativism attractive. This is congruent with the ethos of doing one's
own thing, which is an aspect of the moral disorder of our times.

For the student of personality, the implications of a radical
relativism point, paradoxically, in diametrically opposite
directions, neither of which is acceptable on pragmatic humanistic
grounds. If the norms and values of one's culture are taken as
ultimate (not as absolute, but as the only frame for evaluation that is
available to us), *adjustment* to one's social lot may appear the only
warranted criterion of good functioning. Although adjustment
(read conformity) was once a prevalent conceptualization of
"mental health," it fortunately remains in bad repute as an
evaluative criterion. So we become vulnerable to the opposite
implication of relativism: that since no standards are firm or
absolute, one life pattern is precisely as good as any other. We lapse
into anomie.

For many years, Douglas Heath has been attacking the relativist
position, arguing for a conception of psychological maturity that
embraces, in a coherent and explicit framework, the common
ground shared by many writers about personality and optimal
human functioning. What is more distinctive, he has developed his
conceptualization in close relation to dogged and imaginative
studies of Haverford College students who had been judged by their
peers and faculty mentors to be notably mature or immature.
Heath's conception of maturity not only incorporates many strands
of thought current in the "mental health" sciences and professions;
it also rests on an empirical base, and claims theoretical generality
as an account of general dimensions of adaptation arising from
universal features of the human organism in its human situation.

The challenge that Heath accepts in this book is to show that his
model of psychological maturity is transculturally applicable. In
effect, he replicates his Haverford strategy with two subculturally
divergent samples each of Italian and Turkish college students. The
results are broadly supportive of the model, although they cannot be

said to give it distinctive support as compared with other possible ways of conceptualizing effective psychological functioning. What is clear is that, within the range of cultural divergence that he has explored, broadly similar features characterize young men who are regarded as mature vs. immature by their mentors and peers. This is important to know.

These findings take an important step on the way toward a truly transcultural assessment of maturity and human potential. Eventually Far Eastern cultures need to be included in such a design, as Heath had originally intended, and the more difficult issue faced as to whether working-class subcultures or the peasant folk cultures that have prevailed in the long reaches of historic and immediately prehistoric human experience can intelligibly or fairly be incorporated in a common objectifiable, adaptational, evaluative framework. We cannot conclude from the present study whether we are dealing with convergences inherent in the common historic experience of being human, or, more modestly, with the qualities that pay off in the modern world that is so rapidly eroding and homogenizing our cultural pool of human diversity, for which colleges and universities the world over are preparing privileged youth.

Douglas Heath is an old-style individualist in his personal research program, not a creature of the era of organized research and grantsmanship. Though he has enlisted the collaboration of an impressive array of foreign colleagues in the research that underlies the present volume and found support for it from grants, the style is his own—that of the individual scholar working with small resources at his own pace. The result is that we see the problems of carrying out transcultural research at closer range than a smoothly bureaucratized study would allow. For an initial empirical exploration of concepts of positive mental health in cross-cultural perspective—a real "first"—Heath's forthright account of the research process, and his fairminded appraisal of the degree to which his exploratory findings can be built upon, are invaluable. Heath has taken the psychological study of maturity and psychological effectiveness a giant initial step beyond tolerant but paralyzing relativism. He has written an important book that deserves close reading, and should help to stimulate the further research that it entitles us to believe should yield results of great human importance.

M. BREWSTER SMITH
SANTA CRUZ, CALIFORNIA

Preface

Our society is entering an era in which psychological rather than economic men and women are becoming our dominant social concern. Goals of personal fulfillment, self-realization, equal opportunity for growth are pressing to the center of national awareness. What can behavioral scientists contribute to understanding the meaning of identity, the fulfilled life, psychological wholeness, optimal functioning? Not much. Although many complaints have been made that someone should study optimally functioning, mentally healthy, highly effective persons, most researchers study instead more accessible, troubled, unhealthy, ineffective persons. But it may be more critical to the survival, let alone wellbeing, of our planetary society to know what psychologically sound, effective, and creatively adaptive people are like and how they got that way than it is to know how to diagnose schizophrenia more reliably or discover the biogenetic factors that produce it. To not be mentally ill or disturbed does not mean to be self-actualized and well-integrated. To know what produces pathology is not to know what nurtures emotional maturity and adaptive effectiveness.

Remarkably few intensive and sustained studies of optimally functioning persons have been done. Why? Of the many reasons, certainly one is that researchers prefer to study well-defined, easily manipulated, precisely controlled and instrumented, elegantly analyzable, and neatly packageable bits and pieces of a person.

Unfortunately, such bits and pieces that fill the technical journals of fields like psychology do not tell us much about what a psychological person is, and how he or she can become more fully functioning.

To begin to study mature, well-integrated persons is to immediately stumble into a vague terminological, perhaps tautological, quagmire. Researching psychologically healthy, adjusted, competent or mature persons is like trying to lift oneself by one's own bootstraps. To seek to free, even if only part way, the concept of maturity, for example, from its entanglement with cultural values is, in Maslow's word, "bullheaded." Such an effort seems to be inextricably enmeshed in logical and methodological circularities. How can one scientifically examine such value-laden concepts? There is simply no way to identify competent and mature persons except by the judgments of others or by tests that have been validated by some person's judgments. Such judgments involve personal bias, societal standards, and cultural and religious values. So the task seems hopeless, if not foolhardy.

·This book explores the problems involved in trying to lift the concept of maturity out of its embeddedness in personal bias and cultural values. Its strategy is straightforward: use judgments of persons of different cultures to identify groups of mature and immature exemplars. Determine how such groups differ by using a large number of diverse tests and procedures that assess different levels of personality organization. Discover if mature and immature persons do differ *consistently* from one cultural area to the next. If replicable differences between exemplars of maturity and immaturity *within* a culture are found, then we can be more confident that maturity may have a common meaning irrespective of either personal biases or cultural values. This strategy is deceptively simple and not easy to implement. The studies this book reports are frankly exploratory. No other studies have been done crossculturally on positive mental health. So this book seeks to clarify the issues and suggests ways to proceed. To study mature and immature exemplars in depth necessarily limits us to very small selected samples; large randomly representative samples from the cultural areas were impossible to obtain for the supportive studies; adequate measures of the dimensions defining maturity were not always available. So the findings are tentative, the conclusions only suggestive.

The transcultural research is only one phase of a larger ongoing study of maturity. Since the book focuses only on the issues provoked by its theme, the research should be placed within the framework of this larger program. The program was initiated by the observation that clinicians, theorists, and researchers of different persuasions seem to identify similar developmental dimensions when talking of growth, maturing, self-actualization, and psychological health. Might maturity, the term I prefer for theoretical reasons, be defined by a limited number of universal dimensions? This question was initially explored by intensively studying maturely and immaturely organized college men who were found to differ in many of the ways a dimensional model of maturing predicted. *Explorations of Maturity* (1965) reported these initial studies. Since that probing beginning, the research has flowed very naturally in several directions. One direction led to longitudinal studies of college students to determine if they actually matured as the model predicted. *Growing Up in College: Liberal Education and Maturity* (1968) confirmed the broad outline and utility of the model of maturing, as well as identified specific determinants of growth on each of the dimensions of the model. This intensive study of development in college suggested that the process of becoming educated could be understood in terms of the model. *Humanizing Schools: New Directions, New Decisions* (1971) described how more powerfully maturing educational environments could be created, particularly at the secondary school level.

Concurrently with the application of the model of maturing to practical educational problems, the more formal research program took two other directions. I returned to examine the men originally studied in *Explorations of Maturity*, who were now in their early thirties, to ask, "Do persons continue to mature throughout their twenties as the model would predict? What are the adolescent predictors and adult determinants of maturing and competence?" (Heath, 1976a,c,e).

The other direction the program took is reported in this book. The writings of M. B. Smith had convinced me that the key issue was whether a "science of psychological health" ("of maturity" in my terms) could be generated *independently* of a culture's values. My original intent was to study the relation of maturity, and its related idea of competence, to cultural values by replicating precisely the original American studies reported in *Explorations of Maturity* in two different regions of a predominantly Catholic (Italy), Moslem (Turkey), Buddhist-Confucian (Japan, Taiwan), and Hindu

(India) country. It was not possible to extend the study to the Far East for financial reasons. This book therefore compares the differences found between mature and immature men from central (Pisa) and southern (Sicily) Italy, and eastern (Ankara) and western (Istanbul) Turkey. College educated men were studied to maintain the comparability of the samples with the initially studied men of the most reliable American (Haverford) group. Some of the findings of the Haverford group differ from those first reported in *Explorations of Maturity*. To maintain similarity in scores, the Haverford group's results were rescored and reanalyzed. New data are reported, more extended analyses made of other data from this group, and the results are reorganized in a different and, I hope, clarifying way.

To test the generality of the model of maturity by precisely replicating experimental procedures and tests in different cultures is fraught with danger, as crosscultural researchers will quickly point out (Brislin, Lonner, and Thorndike, 1973: LeVine, 1973; Triandis, Malpass, and Davidson, 1973; Werner and Campbell, 1970). Because no crosscultural studies have investigated selected mature-competent and immature-incompetent persons with the depth necessary to encompass the potential meanings of concepts like maturity and competence, the study I report must of necessity be considered exploratory. It may make clearer the types of problems future researchers will want to consider if they wish to study positive mental health transculturally. Many of the methodological strictures now known to be applicable to typical crosscultural studies do not apply as forcefully to the research strategy I used. Rather than compare directly the level of ability, type of value preference, or extent of field-dependence behavior of randomly selected Japanese with Greek or Tunisian adolescents, I compared mature Turks with immature Turks, and mature Sicilians with immature Sicilians as identified by judges from each culture. It is the similarity in the pattern of differences of selected groups *within* a culture, and not the differences in absolute scores *between* cultural groups, that is my focus. This focus mutes the importance of some of the factors, like randomness of selection, cultural differences in test-taking experience, and others that bias direct cultural comparisons (Brislin, Lonner, and Thorndike, 1973; Campbell and Stanley, 1966).

To create a developmental transcultural model of emotional maturity, mental health, or self-actualization that is related to ideas like competence and modernity is to enter, some might say trespass upon, the domains of psychiatrists, sociologists, cultural anthropologists, psychologists, possibly even of educators and religionists concerned about healthy growth. To reach such a range of readers, as well as my own students for whom such issues are of immediate personal concern, I have tried to simplify and clearly highlight the issues, themes, and findings of the study by confining more technical discussions and results to appendices. Researchers and students interested in abnormal psychology, mental health, culture and personality, psychological anthropology, sociology of illness and health, developmental issues, educational philosophy, and the psychology of religious traditions may secure the extensive tabular data, samples of nonpublished test materials, and a technical summary of the data on which Chapter 7 is based from the National Auxiliary Publications Service[1].

Chapters 1 and 2 examine the relation of psychological health, self-actualization, competence, and modernity to a model of maturing. Chapters 3 and 4 describe how the three cultural areas differed, the selection of the mature and immature men, and the procedures used to test the model's hypotheses. Chapters 5 and 6 report how the mature and immature men, selected by adult and student judges, actually differed. Chapter 7 asks what differences would have been found if the mature and immature men had been selected using existing test indices of maturity rather than using the judgments of local judges. Do the ideas that American psychologists have about healthy and adjusted persons, as measured by MMPI scores and Rorschach clinical ratings, for example, hold for other cultures? Using the data generated by the research, Chapter 8 examines which tests might be most useful for future research on maturing. Chapter 9 summarizes the principal arguments of the book and the response to them that the findings permit. A reader may wish to read this argument and response first for an overview of the book and its findings. The chapter then returns to the issues raised in Chapters 1 and 2 to reassess the relation of competence to maturity, the adequacy of the model of maturing, and the relation of maturing to cultural and religious values.

---

1 See NAPS Document # 02956 for 54 pages of supplementary material. Order from ASIS/NAPS. Microfiche Publications, P.O. Box 3513, Grand Central Station, New York, N.Y. 10017. Remit in advance $3.00 for microfiche copy or $13.50 for photocopy. All orders must be prepaid. Institutions and Organizations may order by purchase order. However, there is a billing and handling charge for this service. Foreign orders add $3.00 for postage and $1.50 for a fiche.

Of the numerous persons with whom I have discussed issues about maturing, I am grateful to Bernice Neugarten, Lois Murphy and Jane Loevinger for their comments. I am particularly grateful to Robert White, Robert Holt, and M. B. Smith for their thoughtful reviews of earlier drafts of this book. I also wish to thank the behavioral scientists and theologians of the Academy of Religion and Mental Health's Second Research Conference who combed through the research's concepts and findings to clarify the relation of maturity to cultural-religious values. Needless to say, only I am accountable for the book's defects.

The research was supported by a NIMH grant, #MH11227, and a Fulbright Traveling Fellowship. Haverford College enabled me to take a leave of absence to complete the research abroad, and provided some secretarial assistance.

I am indebted to the key persons who made the research possible. Dr. Gökçe Cansever, Supervisor of the Turkish studies, and Prof. Dott. Maria Luisa Falorni, Supervisor of the Pisa study, opened the way and provided wise counsel. Dr. Cansever, in particular, was drawn much further into the research than she anticipated. That she so willingly carried much of the supervisory responsibility for the research in Turkey is a measure of her generosity and dedication to the advancement of psychological research. I am also grateful to Prof. Gastone Canziani, Director of the Istituto di Psicologia, Palermo, for making the Sicilian study possible as well as to Dr. H. Boutourline Young, Director of the Harvard Florence Research Project, for providing me with facilities and advice.

The research was completely dependent upon the local psychologists who conducted the experiments and studies: Dott. Filippo Boschi of Pisa, Dott. Giovani Sprini of Palermo, and Dr. Mehmet Gürkaynak of Turkey, whose imprint on the study is the deepest. He not only assumed much of the burden of preparing the Turkish materials, and conducted the Istanbul and Ankara studies, but also helped to organize and score the data as my research assistant in America.

The research was critically dependent upon the thoroughness and ingenuity of Bilge Ögun, Ulker Ilter, Dr. William LeCompte, and Sylvia Cassese, who identified Turkish and Italian judges and supervised the selection of the mature and immature men to be studied.

Other indispensable persons were those who translated the

extensive material of, and provided secretarial assistance to, the project: Amal Abdullah, Ilker Aksoy, Adriana Chiraiotti, Ann Curiel, Tullie Dalla Mora, Ann Equino, Rowena Fajardo, Judith Greci, Carol LaMotte, Julia Lewis, Patricia Manfredi, Maria Mearnini, Meral Nayman, Lidia Restgehini, Yurdal Topsever, and Lorenna Vuilleumier. Carol Robiglio took charge of my central Italian office with great tact and an exuberant spirit that buoyed the staff during the never-ending crises and deadlines under which they worked.

Of the many others, like the judges and the participants, who contributed to the research, I want to thank Dr. Lester Alston who scored the Rorschachs for primary process and defense effectiveness; Elva Pepper who served as one of the two independent judges of the thematic material; and Mark Shimoda, Donald McClain, Russell Heath, Wendilee Heath, and Hazel Pugh. Jean Zinni and Mildred Hargreaves typed parts of the manuscript.

Few persons could be as fortunate as I to have had a research associate as capable as Emily Kingham. She supervised and organized the research with unflagging good will and great efficiency.

The book is dedicated to my wife who carried an overabundance of burdens while abroad. She supervised the office staff and provided the support that helped me to cope with the frustrations involved in doing research in four culturally diverse locales simultaneously.

DOUGLAS H. HEATH
HAVERFORD, PENNSYLVANIA

MATURITY AND COMPETENCE

CHAPTER 1

Maturity, Psychological Health, and Self-Actualization

Self-actualization, mental health, emotional maturity, normality, competence, adjustment, adaptation, coping skills, ego strength, becoming modern. What terminological richness. What theoretical confusion.

To label behavior as "healthy" or "unhealthy," "mature" or "immature," "normal" or "abnormal" is to indulge in personal whim and cultural prejudice. Szasz insists that mental illness, as well as psychotherapy, is a myth (1961, 1974); M. B. Smith claims that mental health "is inherently an evaluative term" (1961, 1972). Social and cultural values determine the meaning of terms like competence, maturity, and psychological health. We can only describe what different cultures define to be healthy and unhealthy. We cannot scientifically determine what is "healthy" or "unhealthy." Adaptation, adjustment, maturity are normative terms.

Not so, asserts Maslow.

I . . . maintain that science in the broadest sense can and does discover what human values are, what the human being needs in order to live a good and a happy life, what he needs in order to avoid illness, what is good for him and what is bad for him (1966, 125).

I believe Maslow is right. Two decades of research on effective, competent, mature men convinces me that a scientifically adequate and verifiable model of maturing is possible. It may clarify our terminological confusion. Terms like adjustment, normality, and competence are more evaluative than other similar terms because their referent is some societal norm or expectation. But terms like self-actualization, health, ego strength, and maturity are not *inherently* definable by personal caprice or societal bias. Why? Because each term in principle can be grounded on a theoretical bedrock distinct from that of cultural values. Thus, there is hope— true, very difficult to realize—that each can be progressively objectified and so increasingly freed from personal or cultural values. The model of healthy development or of maturing presented in this book describes any human being, regardless of sex, age, social class, or religio-cultural values. Maturing results in personality traits that different civilized societies have historically valued as characteristic of their "ideal" or "good" person.

Each of these convictions is debatable. Each makes a powerful claim. But each is being empirically explored. So each will in time be confirmed or disconfirmed by evidence, rather than decided by opinion and prejudice.

Chapters 1 and 2 examine these convictions. The remaining chapters empirically explore these ideas by comparing the lives of mature and immature men, selected by their peers and other adults as exemplars of maturity and immaturity, in five cultural areas: mid-Atlantic America, Northern Italy, Sicily, Eastern and Western Turkey.

To suggest that a transculturally valid model of healthy development or maturing is possible, that developmental universals do exist that can be used to assess any person's maturity, may seem to be audacious, if not indeed foolish. We have learned from cultural anthropologists, as well as from our expanding contacts with hundreds of other cultural groups, how limiting national ethnocentricism can be. This richly variegated diversity has made us self-consciously aware that we do impose our scientific view of and methodology for establishing the "truth" upon the lives of others. As a result, we have learned to be cautious about generalizing our ideas to members of other social class and cultural groups, let alone to all human beings.

Although some have hypothesized that there are genotypic, universal attributes that define terms like mental health (Cattell, 1973; Seeman, 1959) or ego development (Loevinger, 1966, 1976), I have found no *transcultural* comparative studies of selected, effectively functioning, psychologically healthy persons. To search out such possible universals no longer seems to be as misguided an endeavor as it may have been a few years ago when the culturally relativistic bias of many social scientists was so pervasive. In the last few years, however, numerous studies have demonstrated impressive regularities in psychosocial functioning in diverse cultural groups. Studies testing Piagetian hypotheses about cognitive development in more than one hundred cultural groups generally confirm that there are uniformities in sequence, though not in rate (Ashton, 1975). Based on his studies in England, Canada, Taiwan, Mexico, and Turkey, Kohlberg suggests that there is a culturally universal series of stages of moral development (1968, 1970); he also suggests that tests of such development applicable to all cultures should be constructed (1973). Studies of children in the villages and towns of six countries, including Okinawa, the Philippines, and Kenya, reveal "transcultural uniformities in the way that social behavior changes with age" (Whiting and Whiting, 1975, 182), such as the increase in bossiness of children between the ages of seven and eleven.

Cantril surveyed the personal and societal aspirations of adults in fourteen countries, including Egypt, Nigeria, Brazil, and India. Despite differences in national emphasis, he found a basic core group of commonly shared aspirations, and concluded that all human beings are built so as to make similar demands upon their societies (1965). American, Japanese, French, Belgian, Norwegian, and Swiss adults agree remarkably well about the rank-ordered degree of severity that different types of life adjustments, like the death of a spouse, make upon a person's social adaptation (Harmon, Masuda, and Holmes, 1970; Masuda and Holmes, 1967; Rahe, 1974). A comparative study of coping styles between different-aged preliterate Mexican Indian, American Indian, and Middle Eastern adult males showed that regardless of culture, increasing age is associated with a shift from active to passive, even magical, forms of mastery (Gutmann, 1975).

Partly on the basis of factorial personality studies of Americans, Japanese, and Austrians, Cattell hypothesizes, as do I, that there is a "common core to all forms of maturity or adjustment" (Cattell, 1973, 17; Cattell, Schmidt, and Pawlik, 1973). Pervasive commonalities in the identification and definition, though not frequency, of different forms of maladjustment or mental illness, have also been reported among diverse cultures. Though the methodological issues are treacherous (Draguns, 1973; Draguns and Phillips, 1972; Plog and Edgerton, 1969), considerable professional agreement exists that the traditional psychiatric categories are universally applicable (Dowrenwend and Dohrenwend, 1974); that meaningful comparisons of mental health can be made between persons of different cultures (Beiser, Benfari, Collumb, and Ravel, 1976; Leighton, 1969, 1972; Murphy, 1972, 1976); and that universal criteria defining mental illness may be obtainable (Opler, 1969; Kiev, 1969). Of the many other transcultural studies of psychological functioning, Osgood's analysis of the affective meanings of 23 different cultural groups is the most sophisticated with respect to the theoretical and methodological issues involved in establishing transcultural universals. He concludes his own study by asserting that "human beings, regardless of locus or culture, not only tend to utilize the same kinds of semantic features in characterizing their environments, but also tend to order them similarly in salience" (Osgood, May, and Miron, 1975, 354). Is it unreasonable to expect that all human beings utilize similar core components for defining maturely functioning persons?

A Model of Maturing

Why talk of a model of maturing rather than of self-actualization or mental health? For several reasons. I seek to understand how a person becomes a more effectively functioning human being, which one learns to do as a consequence of longterm accumulative experiences. *Maturing* implies dimensional continuity and makes it possible to draw upon evidence from the entire age span. *Mature* and *maturity* are used here for expository purposes, but should be understood to refer to the process of maturing. Neither *mental health* nor *self-actualization* has as clear developmental connotations. In fact, Maslow claims he would not even look at adolescents, let alone children, if he were selecting self-actualized persons to study. *Maturing* does not imply some preadapted or achievable end state that suddenly looms over the psychological horizon. The handful of researchers studying healthy adult development assume that maturing continues throughout the life span (Block, 1971; Cox, 1970; Gould, 1972; Grinker, 1962, 1974; Levinson, *et al*, 1974; Vaillant, 1975).

Furthermore, *maturing* is the only term that can be readily anchored to a vast body of research and theory. It refers to adaptive processes that have been studied in a large variety of situations by observers of very diverse theoretical and value orientations using many different methodologies. Although there is much terminological confusion and theoretical argument about terms like *mental health* and *adjustment*, psychologists agree much more than they disagree about the dimensions that define a maturing person (Heath, 1965, Ch. 1). Whether they are psychoanalysts like Freud (1923) or Hartmann (1939) retrospectively reconstructing the ego development of a patient; psychologists like Rogers formulating empirically the direction that therapeutic movement takes when a client is becoming more congruent (1959); Piaget studying the development of children (1947); Lois Murphy following the social and emotional development of nursery school children (1962); Kohlberg plotting the sequential development of moral values (1964, 1973); Werner comparing the mental development of children, primitives, and schizophrenics (1948); biologists like Sinnott conceptualizing the growth of biological systems (1959); social psychologists like Doob comparing the personality effects of societies ranging in degree of civilization (1960); educational psychologists describing the process of becoming educated (Chickering, 1969); or sociologists like Inkeles studying the effects of factories on modernity (1969; Inkeles and D. Smith, 1970, 1974)—whatever variety of researcher observing how persons change over time when adapting to new demands, there is a remarkable similarity in the way all these diverse observers sketch the broad dimensional outlines of an evolving, developing person.[1] It was out of this rich matrix of observations and reflections that a model of maturing was induced. I return later to the relation of maturing to psychological health, competence, and other terms connoting effectiveness of functioning.

Maturing is also preferable because it is less encumbered by value assumptions than *self-actualization* and *mental health* (R. W. White, 1973). Why? Because it can be placed within a broad ranging and multifaceted matrix of observations and data, and idiosyncratic and cultural biases that shape the model of maturing are much less apt to

1 *Explorations of Maturity* (1965) summarizes the concepts of these and other observers, as well as the confirming research on selected personally sound, healthy and competent persons that had been completed prior to 1964. *Growing Up in College* (1968) extends these ideas to the process of becoming educated. A selected summary of other views about mental health is available in Offer and Sabshin (1974).

be operating in the work of diverse and disinterested observers who frequently study problems other than maturity or mental health. Maslow, however in contrast, induced his characteristics of self-actualized persons from exemplars whom *he* selected—Abraham Lincoln, Eleanor Roosevelt, and personal acquaintances. Self-actualization may therefore not be much more than a projection of Maslow's values and vision of the good life, even of body type (M. B. Smith, 1959, 1974b). At one point he unabashedly wondered why most of the exemplars he selected were ectomorphs like himself.

The embroilment of the term *mental health* in controversial value assumptions is too well known to need discussion. Kingsley Davis many years ago charged that mental health was only a psychiatric rationalization justifying the values of the Protestant ethic (1938). And more recently, Thomas Szasz has claimed that our notions of health and illness are basically ideological preferences (1970).

What is this model of maturing? It is a classificatory map, a working set of categories, which orders the principal hypotheses that theorists claim distinguish mature from immature persons. The model is provisional; it is not a perfected, tidy, theoretical system, but is still evolving in response to accumulating data; some of its components have not yet been adequately defined and measured; it is probably incomplete. Figure 1 summarizes the principal outlines of the model used to organize the cultural research.

What is the theoretical status of this model in the research program? The independent antecedent, so to speak, are the groups of maturity and immaturely organized exemplars selected by local

Figure 1
The Model of Maturing

PERSONALITY	DIMENSIONS OF MATURING				
	Symboli-zation	Allocen-tricism	Integra-tion	Stability	Autonomy
Cognitive Skills					
Self-concept					
Values					
Personal Relations					

judges of each cultural area who know nothing of the model of maturing or the research. The dependent consequent to which we are predicting is the model of maturing as defined by tests and experimental procedures designed to measure its hypotheses. Later, I shall examine how this procedure avoided circularity in definition.

The person is a maturing system who can be described in terms of five interdependent dimensions in the four principal sectors of his life. He increasingly becomes more able to symbolize his experiences as well as more allocentric, integrated, stable, and autonomous. When theorists talk of psychological maturing, they talk primarily of the maturing of a person's cognitive skills, concept of himself, values, and personal relationships. Figure 1 generates twenty basic hypotheses about how more mature persons differ from less mature ones. The model predicts, for example, that in contrast to the values of an immature person, the values of a mature person are more symbolizable—that is, accessible to awareness—allocentric, integrated, stable, and autonomous. A more mature self-concept is one that is more accurately symbolizable, allocentric, integrated, stable, and autonomous.

I shall first briefly define each dimension in isolation from the others, and its linkages to some other theoretical concepts, as well as some methods used to study the model, and supporting research. I shall then return to the systemic interdependent assumptions of the model to draw out their implications.

Increased potential for symbolization. Man's capacity for putting his experience into symbolic form, whether into words, art, music, dance, or gesture, is one of his most distinctive adaptive potentialities. To be able to represent reality imaginally, as well as to label feelings and hunches, provides man with extraordinarily powerful tools for coping with the problems of his existence.

Symbolization provides the basis for so many of man's adaptive skills, such as the development of a shared language system, that when a person's symbolizations are inaccurate or disorganized, as occurs in schizophrenia, he no longer can survive independently in most societies.

Cognitive skills. The model of maturing stakes out four sectors of personality in which to identify how well a person symbolizes. To distinguish symbolization from cognitive skills is theoretically untidy, since the ability to symbolize is basic to cognitive functioning. But, as Shoben (1957) has insisted, man's capacity to symbolize, and so become aware even of his own cognitive processes and structures, is so uniquely characteristic of man that it becomes a touchstone for more generally describing his maturing. To be able to symbolize permits man to "learn from not only his own personal experience but from that of other men in other times and places, to forecast the consequences of his own behavior, and to have ideals" (Shoben, 1957, 185). A cognitively mature person is able to make more discriminations, and to reflectively monitor his own ongoing thoughts better than a less mature person can. He has more of his memories available to awareness, and is more open to different levels of awareness.

Freud sensitized us to the relation of maturity to symbolization. He described different degrees of accessibility (1900, 1915). But not until psychology repudiated the behavioristic *animus* against consciousness did researchers begin to study more diligently different types or levels of symbolized experience (Fischer, 1971; Singer, 1975). Today, much research exists that utilizes dreams, drugs, meditation, and even yoga to understand imaginal processes and our accessibility to them. And recent psychological analyses of Zen Buddhism (Goleman, 1975, 1976; Owens, 1975), and of the relation of its form of meditation to Western models of behavior self-management (Shapiro and Zifferblatt, 1976) have deepened our understanding of the relation of different levels of symbolization to healthy growth.

I have never found any tests that adequately measure how individuals differ in their ability to reflect or to bring memories readily into awareness. Traditionally, psychologists have studied individual differences in symbolization by means of the intelligence test. Vocabulary and ability to form concepts are two central components of intelligence. Broadly speaking, these skills of making symbolic discriminations predict to mature forms of adaptation, like academic achievement or coping skills (Haan, 1963, 1965). Since their content consists primarily of impersonal objective information, they therefore do not predict effective functioning very well when motives, values, interpersonal, or other conflictual problems are involved. Other measures, like self-report items, were used in the transcultural research to index cognitive symbolization as well as the other components of the model. The Perceived Self Questionnaire (PSQ) includes items like, "I readily remember the facts necessary to analyze and solve an intellectual problem." Using this and other methods measuring actual cognitive functioning, I have found that mature persons are more reflective, imaginally productive, and less repressed than immature persons (1965, 1968). Also, interviews of freshmen and seniors, the latter presumably more mature, suggested that a principal maturing effect of a liberal education is an increased reflective ability (Heath, 1968).

Self-concept. A maturing person also becomes more accurately aware of himself. A person able to symbolize more of his experience is more mature than one who constricts his awareness, retreats into hysteric vagueness, or escapes into nonreflective forms of acting out.

Socrates began the parade of witnesses testifying to the centrality of self-insight. No major theorist or researcher since has contradicted the proposition that maturity is defined by accurate self-insight (Jahoda, 1958).

There is no way to measure the accuracy of a person's self-concept except to compare it with the judgments of others who know him well or with other sources of information. The use of these methods has amply validated that accuracy of self-concept covaries with maturity in American as well as Canadian youth (Barron, 1963; Chodorkoff, 1954; Heath, 1965; Kogan, Quinn, Ax and Ripley, 1957; Westley and Epstein, 1969). Other studies using focused interviews, objectively scored for the components of the model, showed that increased self-insight was reported to be the second most important effect of one college (Heath, 1968).

Values. Theorists and clinicians agree that mature persons are more aware of their motives and values than are less mature persons. Therapists seek to help patients become aware of their wishes and desires. Psychoanalytic therapy is founded on the premise that such awareness facilitates the control and satisfaction of one's needs.

While much clinical evidence supports the proposition that mature persons are more aware of their values, the lack of adequate measures of such awareness means that the hypothesis rests on shaky empirical grounds. Using formal interview methods, I found that college seniors were more aware of their values and motives than freshmen were (1968), but more adequate measures are obviously needed. The cultural research relied on self-report items designed to measure the maturity of a person's values, using items like, "Because I seldom reflect about why I believe and act as I do, I find these questions difficult to answer."

Personal relationships. A maturing person becomes more aware of others and of his relationships with them. Sullivan is emphatic about the centrality of sensitivity to and "understanding of the limitations, interests, possibilities, anxieties" of others to becoming more mature (1953, 310). When troubled by some conflict or when dissatisfied with his relationships, a mature person can step back from the relation to ask, "What is really annoying him?" "Why is she so irritable every time I talk about what I am doing?"

Concepts like transference, countertransference, and parataxic distortion, analyses by Berne (1964) and Perls (1969) of the games people unconsciously play in their relationships, and even school curricula newly designed to sensitize students to others attest to the importance of learning how to symbolize accurately our personal relationships. Once again, though, we confront the same methodological paradox. Despite the importance of the symbolization dimension, focused and objective measures are not available by which to determine if, in fact, maturing is associated with increasing symbolization. The little evidence that I have suggests that learning to reflect about one's personal relationships is an important effect of becoming educated (1968).

Becoming more allocentric. As a child matures, he becomes progressively more allocentric. An autocentric person is egocentric, narcissistic, unable to take empathically another's point of view. He is unable, in Van Doren's words, to "rear within himself that third man who is present when two men speak" (1943, 68). The increasing ability to take a multiplicity of perspectives toward a problem is associated with internalizing the modes of communication of one's social group, the progressive objectification of the self, the humanization of a person's values, and the development of cooperative relationships.

Cognitive skills. Those who write about maturity are in uncommon agreement that a mature person can make realistic judgments, test reality appropriately, and think objectively (Jahoda, 1958). Logical consistent thought is the hallmark of the cognitively allocentric person. The immature person cannot restrain his feelings and needs from inappropriately affecting his judgment. He misperceives reality in terms of his own biases, and fails to communicate clearly because he does not take into account how others respond to what he says. Allocentric thought refers to the accurate internalization of the grammars of one's society which provide the bases for shared communication (Piaget, 1936). One of Freud's most significant contributions was his identification of primary (autocentric) and secondary (allocentric) processes and their relation to maturing (1900).

Various methods have been used to demonstrate that mature

and immature persons differ in the allocentric quality of their thought. Robert Holt's score system, for example, detects the degree to which Rorschach images are organized by primary processes (Holt, 1968; Holt and Havel, 1960). Studies using his scores have confirmed that the thought of immature persons is less socialized and more idiosyncratically fused with bizarre or very personal fantasies and needs than is the thought of mature persons (Heath, 1965). Other methods also confirm that mature or self-actualized persons are more objective and realistic in their thought (Barron, 1963; Brown, 1960; Heath, 1965), or more able to provide a range of alternative possibilities to a task (Foxman, 1976) than immature or less self-actualized persons. When students are becoming educated, they become more allocentrically organized in their communication and thought patterns. Seniors, in contrast to freshmen, made more appropriate judgments, wrote more clearly, and were more intellectually efficient (Heath, 1968).

Self-concept. Mead says that only through the internalization of the views of others about ourselves do we create a sense of self (1934). To be able to take another person's view toward our self helps to objectify our understanding of our self. We learn, as William James said, to dispassionately evaluate our strengths and weaknesses— though not without a lot of backsliding into wish and fantasy. As we mature, we gradually expand our concepts of ourselves. We identify ourselves with our children. Their hurts hurt us. We begin to think of ourselves as citizens of a country, even of the world. We become more accepting and tolerant of our worst selves as we come to realize we are not alone in our sins and vanities. Fromm speaks of learning to respect and love ourselves (1955).

How can we discover if mature persons have more allocentric self-concepts than immature persons have? We can examine how accepting they are of themselves by measuring their self-esteem. Mature and well-integrated men and women have been found to have high self-regard (Duncan, 1966; Seeman, 1966). We can also ferret out how accurately they can predict what others who know them well actually think about them. When mature and immature persons were compared in these ways, maturity was found to be directly associated with allocentric self-concepts, However, I was unable to demonstrate that college seniors had more allocentric self-concepts than freshmen. Seniors matured much less in the allocentricism of their self-concepts than they did in other personality sectors (1968).

Values. To be able to take another person's point of view is a step toward being able to experience how he feels. A maturing person, desirous and empathically capable of understanding diverse viewpoints, becomes less authoritarian, and more tolerant and respectful.

The available evidence suggests that maturing is accompanied by increasingly allocentric values. Mature men value social, altruistic and philanthropic types of relationships more highly than do immature men (Heath, 1965, 1968). Mature persons even contribute more to charity than do immature persons (Heath, 1965; Vaillant and McArthur, 1972). They also hold less authoritarian values (Barron, 1963). Many studies of maturing in college confirm that socially the values of students become more liberal, and their personal values more humanistic (Newcomb and Feldman, 1969).

Personal relationships. Similar allocentric development occurs in personal relationships. Not only tolerance and respect, but also responsibility to and care for others mark not just the values but also the personal relations of mature persons. Mutually cooperative activity that requires accommodation of one's desires to those of others occurs. Piaget assumes that interpersonal maturing proceeds toward mutual respect. Such respect is the natural outcome of the developmental process and contributes, according to Piaget, to the maturation of other aspects of the personality (Piaget and Inhelder, 1966). Experts on mental health and maturity identify social feeling, warmth, and compassion as second in importance to realistic judgment as characteristics of mature persons (Heath, 1965, Ch. 1).

I know of no studies that have directly compared the interpersonal relationships of mature and immature persons. Psychology still has not yet developed adequate measures of a quality like empathy, though current efforts to create a developmental model and measures of empathy seem promising (Selman, 1974). Attempts to measure interpersonal maturity have relied on indices of social responsibility and ability to adapt to convention without abandoning one's autonomy. Persons high on interpersonal maturity were mature, capable, dependable, and reliable, according to a measure that differentiated among Italian, Japanese and French, as well as American delinquent and nondelinquent youths (Gough, 1966, 1968, 1974). Compared to immature persons, mature persons are more social and interested in others, and less socially introversive and interpersonally aloof

(Bonney, 1964; Heath, 1965). College seniors are more interested in other persons, develop stronger needs for close friends, and enjoy meeting and helping other persons more than freshmen (Heath, 1968). *Becoming more integrated.* Maturing also means growing coherence and integration. Increasing differentiation and synthesis, and greater complexity mark mature persons. For those not familiar with clinical methods of assessment, terms like *integration* and *coherence* may sound very elusive, even ineffable. Yet, when confronted with the facts of a person's life, garnered by different tests that tap various aspects of personality organization, one frequently discovers an internal logic or order among the person's values, temperamental and personality traits, self-concept, motives and controls that is compelling in its consistency.

Most theorists as well as researchers find some place in their work for a concept similar to that of integration (Jahoda, 1958; Loevinger, 1966, 1976; Mowrer, 1973; Seeman, 1959; M. B. Smith, 1950). Concepts like ego synthesis, individuation, hierarchic structures, efforts after meaning, and self-actualization connote a progressive differentiation and integration of the personality. Mental health researchers have used criteria like, "An ideal state of complete functioning integration" to define the end point of a highly reliable and valid Health-Sickness Rating Scale (Luborsky, 1962; Luborsky and Bachrach, 1974).

Cognitive skills. Mental development proceeds toward increased differentiation as well as toward more generalized hierarchic modes of problem solving (Piaget and Inhelder, 1966). Secondary process thought is organized and relational. Thought becomes less syncretic, more deductive, coordinated, and flexible. Elements of a problem can be correctly articulated and related to more complex logical patterns. Coping and defensive modes become more differentiated and flexible with increasing psychological health (Haan, 1965; Offer, 1973).

Some studies suggest that mature persons are more cognitively integrated than immature persons. The thought of immature men is illogically ordered, and marked by condensations and arbitrary and unrealistic coordinations. Such men are judged to be erratic and inconsistent (Heath, 1965). Self-actualized persons gave more differentiated, complex, and integrated descriptions to emotionalized material than less self-actualized persons (Wexler, 1974). Studies of maturing in college consistently identify increased cognitive flexibility to be a major growth (Chickering, 1969).

Cognitive integration was a principal effect of becoming educated in three different colleges (Fieselmann, 1973; Heath, 1968).

Self-concept. Considerable research confirms that maturing is directly related to increasing integration of the self-concept. Efforts to evaluate the effects of psychotherapy led to studying the discrepancy between the ideal and the private self as one measure of lack of integration. Successful therapy reduces the discrepancy, primarily by modifying the ideal self (Rogers and Dymond, 1954). Poor integration, similarly defined, is associated with maladjustment and anxiety (G. M. Smith, 1958; Turner and Vanderlippe, 1958). Self-actualized persons, defined by the Personal Orientation Inventory (Shostrom, 1964; Tosi and Lindamood, 1975), have more congruent private and ideal selves than less self-actualized persons (Mahoney and Hartnett, 1973).

The measure of integration I prefer is the degree of agreement between the social and the private self. A person who believes that others think differently of him than he does of himself is conflicted about conforming to others' expectations at the expense of his own integrity. Such persons have less accurate self-concepts, are more maladjusted, and react to stress less adaptively (G. M. Smith, 1958; Funkenstein, *et al*, 1957). My studies confirm that increasing lack of integration of the self-concept is directly associated with increasing anxiety, obsessionally rigid and projective trends, and social aloofness. Well-integrated persons do better academic work, and are judged to be realistic, planful, and well-coordinated (1965).

Values. Many theorists assume that the integration of a person's values is indicative of maturity, but few have actually tested the assumption. Allport claims that a mature person has developed a workable philosophy of life (1964); Freud and other analysts (Fenichel, 1945) insist that a mature person has integrated partial or pregenital instincts under the dominance of the heterosexual instinct. Lecky assumes that each person strives for consistency or integration in his attitudes and motives (1945). Psychologists from James through McDougall to Rogers and Maslow assume that personality integration occurs as a consequence of master sentiments like the actualizing tendency.

Yet few means are available to measure the integration of values. Kohlberg has measured the developmental maturity of the values of persons from the principal religious groups in Taiwan, Mexico, and Turkey. He found that maturation of values follows an invariant sequence, even though educational, class, and cultural values affect their rate. He describes the dimensional maturing of a person's values in terms of increased differentiation, integration, and universality.

> Each step in development then is a better cognitive organization than the one before it, one which takes account of everything present in the previous stage, but making new distinctions and organizing them into a more comprehensive or more equilibrated structure (1968, 30).

I have used other indices of the integration of a person's values. Mature persons, for example, are more consistent than immature persons of the same age in their conscious value orientations, as measured by the Study of Values, and their less-conscious temperamental preferences, as measured by the Strong Vocational Interest Blank. College seniors have more differentiated and crystallized values than do freshmen when measured by the Strong. And seniors agree significantly more than do freshmen to questionnaire items like, "I have found a way of life that integrates most of my values and desires and that gives me some direction," and "I don't often feel torn and divided between several inconsistent and conflicting values, beliefs, and desires" (1968).

Personal relationships. As a person becomes more aware of the needs of others as well as his own, his relationships become more discriminating, differentiated, and mutually accommodating. Words like *trust, reciprocity, mutuality, we-ness,* and *openness* describe progressively integrative relationships in which one risks "being all there" when in the presence of another. The image of two ballroom dancers, each of whom is subtly, and frequently not consciously, sensitive to the bodily position and intended movement and mood of the other, and who gracefully and effortlessly coordinate their movements expresses the meaning of interpersonal integration.

Theorists like Jourard rhapsodize about the centrality of interpersonal trust, love, and mutuality to healthy development. He believes the key to developing such trusting "I-thou" relationships is to be self-disclosing and open in one's relationships, for then one's partner knows how to respond appropriately to one's needs and feelings. More well-adjusted persons are more self-disclosing (1974). A study of American, Japanese, and New Zealand college students found that personal adjustment, as determined by questionnaire ratings and friends' ratings, was directly related to increased preferences for intimate relationships with others (Scott and

Peterson, 1975). Mature and psychologically healthy men have more close friendships than do immature men (Heath, 1965; Vaillant, 1975). Developing more integrative relationships with both men and women was one of the three most important effects of one liberally educating college. And seniors more than freshmen agreed that they could be very much themselves with others, and that they hid very little of themselves in such relationships (Heath, 1968). Unfortunately, no economical and objective observational or behavioral measures were available for use in the cultural research to verify the integrative hypotheses. So we relied on self-report items supplemented by ratings of others about the men's interpersonal relationships.

Becoming more stable and autonomous. D. B. Harris summarizes the views of many psychologists that a model of maturing must consider an "(1) organism . . . as a living system; (2) time; (3) movement over time toward complexity of organization; (4) 'hierarchization' . . . of parts or part-systems into larger units or 'wholes'; and (5) an end state of organization which is maintained with some stability or self-regulation" (1957, 3).

The fourth and fifth dimensions defining maturing are progressive stabilization and autonomy. Stable structures provide the basis for autonomous self-regulation. I discuss these dimensions together, not because they cannot be theoretically distinguished, but because I have not been successful in separating the two in researching the maturing of a person's cognitive skills, the most carefully researched of the twenty hypotheses about maturing.

The consequence of successive adaptations is the acquisition of a stable schema, habit, skill, or value. Such stable structures make up the warp and woof of personality. A measure of the stability of a habit or skill is its resistance to change or disruption, as well as its resilience in recovering from disorganization. Such stable structures can enormously facilitate efficient adaptation. To be able to concentrate, read quickly with comprehension, organize information accurately while under the stress of a critical examination is very adaptive.

Habituation releases energy for other adaptive tasks. The habit also moves to the periphery, if not outside, of consciousness. I can no longer recall the location of the keys of a typewriter without much embarrassing effort. Stabilization leads to the automatization of skills and habits.

Many talk of the increasing autonomy of a mature person

(Angyal, 1956; Clausen, 1968; Erikson, 1963; Loevinger and Wessler, 1970; Loevinger, 1976; Luborsky and Bachrach, 1974). Neugarten identifies as a distinctive quality of middle-aged persons a "conscious self-utilization" and a sense of command of self (1970). Despite differences in the definition of autonomy, most psychologists agree that the mature person is self-regulating. His habits, skills, and motives have become independent structures, freed from the initial learning conditions which spawned them, as Allport proposed many years ago with his concept of functional autonomy (1961). An indication of the autonomy of a person's reading skill is its use in situations very different from those in which it was mastered. Stabilization does not guarantee autonomy, as many transfer of training experiments demonstrate. Many students who learn the calculus are unable to apply it when faced with nontextbook types of problems.

Cognitive skills. What are the cognitive skills that facilitate adaptation to the widest range of situations? Freud identified secondary-process skills as the core regulating processes of the ego (1900). Piaget identified the ability to form logical concepts, to analyze and synthesize information, and to make realistic judgments (1947) as the principal secondary-process skills mediating adaptation. We know such skills have become stable and autonomous when they can be effortlessly and efficiently adapted to a wide range of situations, when they are not readily impaired by stress, and when a person can rapidly recover their use if they are disorganized.

Mature men should have more stabilized and autonomous cognitive skills than immature men. This hypothesis is critical for understanding maturity, and also provides a link to the idea of ego strength. Measures of cognitive skill when applied to impersonal, nonconflictual, objective problems do not predict a wide range of different adaptive competences (McClelland, 1973; Vaillant, 1974). Mental health-like terms that do refer to a range of adaptive competences apply to the management of personal, conflictual, and subjective problems that involve strong emotions, values, interpersonal relations, and attitudes toward one's self. Freud identified as the essence of the secondary process a "concern . . . with the connecting paths between ideas, without being led astray by the *intensities* of those ideas" (1900, 602). Other theorists similarly identify the ability to resist or to recover rapidly from the emotionalizing of one's thought when reasoning with personally threatening information as a central property of a strong ego (Hartmann, 1960). The task of therapy, one might say, is to help a patient stabilize his cognitive skills so that they can be autonomously and efficiently used in whatever conflictual and disturbing situations may arise. Adaptation may be immeasurably facilitated if a father maintains his judgment and capacity for analysis in an argument with his daughter about how late she may stay out for the night.

The concept of a strong ego, or ego strength, is very popular though it has never received the theoretical analysis its popularity demands. Characteristics attributed to persons with strong egos invariably emphasize autonomy or self-control. Fenichel writes that ego strength includes the abilities to tolerate the frustrations involved in renouncing short for longterm pleasures, to form "valid judgments about reality and [carrying out] . . . intentions even in the face of obstacles" (72), to master and direct instinctual energies as well as the demands of the superego, to maintain one's self-regard independently of the opinions of others, and to integrate or unify conflicting trends in the ego itself (1938). An autonomous person is not driven by unresolved childish wishes, tyrannical "shoulds," ungovernable instincts. His judgment and will remain unimpaired. He is in charge of his own powers (Ezekiel, 1968; Neugarten, 1970; Rotter, 1966), and perceives himself to be his own "origin" (De Charms, 1968). Maintaining autonomy of judgment when confronted with opposing, and false, judgments of others is related to greater ego strength, intellectual effectiveness, and social maturity (Crutchfield, 1955).

How does one measure the stability and autonomy of cognitive skills, that is, strength of the ego, in the face of disturbing conflictual information? Barron has a questionnaire, Ego Strength (Es), which reputedly measures resilience in recovering from stress. But critiques of the research using the Es suggest that it indexes the absence of pathology rather than the ability to cope with and recover from stress (Frank, 1967; Stein and Chu, 1967). My results with the Es scale confirm this critique (1965, 1968). I have also found that Holt's scores indexing the effectiveness of a person's defenses against threatening Rorschach images consistently predict maturity as well as recovery in cognitive skill stability after disruption (1965).

No other measures of cognitive stability in response to disturbing information were satisfactory. Special experimental measures designed to assess cognitive stability have shown that mature, in contrast to immature, persons not only are more cognitively efficient in solving personally conflictual problems, but also are more resilient in recovering from disruption of their efficiency. Persons whose cognitive skills were more stable were more proficient academically, imaginally productive, interested in others, and had more accurate and stable self-concepts than those whose cognitive skills were unstable (Heath, 1965).

When the autonomy of a person's cognitive skills is measured by Witkin's field-independent tasks, and maturity by a measure of self-actualization (Shostrom, 1964), we find suggestive though not definitive evidence that persons who cognitively resist external influences are more inner-directed and self-actualized (Doyle, 1975). Such persons have also been found to be more mature and have higher self-esteem (Witkin, *et al*, 1954). The demonstration of the cross-cultural generality of field-independent relationships provides indirect evidence for the transcultural universality of the relation of cognitive skill autonomy to maturity (Witkin, *et al*, 1974; Witkin and Berry, 1975).

Self-concept. Erikson has written about the importance of a sense of identity or fittedness to a socially recognized role that is personally integrative. Identity implies stability of the self-concept and furthers its autonomy. Certainty about one's strengths and weaknesses, motives and values, ability to be effective, means that a person can be his own self-reinforcer. R. White identifies two sources of self-esteem: the opinions of others about one's self, and the evaluations that one makes about one's self based on knowledge of one's effectiveness. Competence provides an independent basis for becoming more autonomous of others' definitions of our worth (White, 1963). A person with an autonomous self-concept can be more selective in deciding what opinions of others to assimilate (Tippett and Silber, 1966).

The stability of a person's self-concept is easily measured by the extent that it fluctuates over time. Increasing maturity has been found to be directly associated with increasing stability of the self-concept. Persons with unstable self-concepts are more maladjusted, insecure, and poorly controlled (G. M. Smith, 1958); think of themselves less favorably (McGehee, 1957); and also have less integrated, accurate, and allocentric self-concepts (Heath, 1965). Their thought is dominated by primary processes, which may account for their poor academic performance (Heath, 1965). I found that the effect of becoming educated is to further stabilize a youth's self-concept, an effect that the alumni of the college reported to be one of the principal enduring effects of their education (1968, 1976e).

The autonomy of a person's self-concept can be determined by challenging his view of himself with discrepant evaluations, and measuring the degree to which he subsequently changes his ideas. In principle, the procedure is straightforward; in reality, I have had difficulty developing adequate experimental measures of autonomy. In contrast to college freshmen, seniors report that their opinions about themselves are not as readily influenced, particularly by their parents (Heath, 1968).

Values. Maturity is directly associated with stable and autonomous values. From his developmental studies of normal adolescents, Robert White identified deepening, presumably stabilizing, of interests to be one of four significant types of growth during this period (1952). Klein cites strength of character or the willingness to sacrifice self-interests in behalf of a conviction as a cardinal characteristic of maturity (1960). Enduring values provide purpose and direction which, I expect, a mature person will maintain in the face of hardship and opposition. Loevinger identifies autonomy, shown by mastery of one's impulses, as characteristic of more mature development. However, her other criteria of autonomy—tolerance of others' values and of impulse solutions, and acceptance of mutually interdependent relations— seem to be more characteristic of interpersonal allocentricism than autonomy (1966, 1976).

Little research has been reported confirming that maturity is related to the stability and autonomy of a person's values. Psychologically healthy men value making autonomous judgments (Duncan, 1966), but some evidence suggests that this finding may not hold for similarly healthy women who did not differ from randomly selected women in their scores on an internal locus of evaluation scale (Seeman, 1966). I have found that college seniors, in contrast to freshmen, report that their values are more stable and crystallized, as well as less susceptible to outside persuasion. But no direct test of the autonomy of their values was made (1968).

Personal relationships. A mature person establishes stable relations that persist. Clausen identifies interpersonal stability to be an important characteristic of maturity (1968). A mature person's relations are not compulsive repetitions of unresolved transference reactions; his relationships are free, determined more by the demands of the present than by those of the past. His relationships stand on their own feet, so to speak. The psychologically healthy adult male is less passive, suggestible, and dependent in his personal relationships (Vaillant, 1974) than one who is not healthy.

Psychologists have not studied the stability and autonomy of interpersonal relationships very extensively across the age span. We know that sociometric preferences become increasingly more stable with increasing age in children (J. D. Campbell, 1964). A forty-year study of interpersonal styles found that seventy-year-old women who were interpersonally distant and autonomous had been that way when young adults (Maas and Kuypers, 1974). Men independently rated to be well-adjusted had more stable marriages and close friends than poorly adjusted men (Vaillant, 1975). But I have found no studies that relate such developmental trends to changes in the psychological health of persons.

My own research on relationships has produced equivocal results with respect to both the interpersonal stability and autonomy hypotheses, particularly the latter. I have not found good measures of interpersonal autonomy that reflected the complexity of the kinds of relationships established by young adults. It may be more maturing for a heretofore self-sufficient and emotionally independent youth to become emotionally dependent upon another peer and be deeply influenced by her than it is to retain his self-sufficiency. Allocentric maturing in adolescence may be necessary before interpersonal autonomy can be maturely established. Increasing stabilization of personal relationships may also occur as a consequence of declining moodiness, a principal developmental change found in college males (King, 1973).

Some Assumptions of the Model of Maturing

The model of maturing that I have just sketched is bareboned when matched against the overpowering fullness, for example, of Maslow's discussion of self-actualization (1962a,b, 1967a,b). R. White would say that it is too abstract, and does not deal with the different life patterns that describe individual uniqueness (1973). But it will be only by creating general, though hopefully operationalizable, abstract dimensions that we will transcend the manifest particularities within and between cultural groups to form a transculturally general model (Triandis, 1972a). In any case, the model needs flesh, connective tissues, nerves—and a heavy dose of spirit. A person is not just a collection of dimensions and structures, though that is where we were when the cultural research began. Let me flesh out the model a little more by making explicit some assumptions and their implications.[1]

We need to keep in mind some obvious properties of human beings. A person is a constantly changing, open, organized system dependent both on his means of adaptation to others and on the environment for his fulfillment and survival. Because of psychology's powerful reductionistic bias, we ignore the organizing *systemic* properties of the person in most personality research. We break up the system into components whose development we then study, usually in isolation from their relation to each other and to the functioning of the total system. The presence of a behavioral "symptom" like homosexuality, for example, has until recently been routinely taken as a sign of "illness," without evaluating its relation to the strengths and systemic organization of the person. Clausen has justly criticized epidemiological studies of mental illness on this account (1968). My own studies show that highly mature and effective young American males are as conflicted about homosexual information, the most threatening type of information for them to deal with, as are very immature and ineffective men. Their symptom of anxiety is the same, but its significance for the healthiness of the two groups is vastly different. The mature men recover from their anxiety to the homosexual information much more rapidly (Heath, 1965). M. B. Smith found that psychiatric judgments of the potential effectiveness of Peace Corps candidates did not predict their actual effectiveness in the field. The psychiatrists ferreted out pathology in the volunteers, but failed to identify strengths that altered the significance of specific symptoms for each person (1966). Haan's study of ego functioning showed that MMPI indicators of defensiveness did not predict effectiveness unless complemented by measures of coping skills (1965). Allport has consistently and rightly insisted that we keep the person always in view (1964). It is a person's systemic organization that is the touchstone for understanding the meaning of his specific traits and "symptoms."

1 Detailed discussion of the model's assumptions and implications are to be found in *Explorations of Maturity*, Chapters 2 and 14, and in Chapter 9 of *Growing Up in College*, where I also evaluate the adequacy of the model.

What implications do these comments have for the model of maturing and the test of its validity? I am studying maturing systems. The arbitrary structural and dimensional categories are not independent of each other. A person's self-concept is organized around values that concern his personal relations; involved in its formation are cognitive skills like analysis and judgment. To be able to reflect about an issue depends upon having internalized realistic representations that maintain and recover their identity while being imaginally rearranged in different integrated patterns. In other words, the dimensions are not independent of each other. Each is one facet on a multifaceted, complexly organized, and, let us say, living crystal. Each is intrinsic to the unity of the crystal. Alteration in one facet affects the structural relations of the entire crystal. Hence, change in the allocentric facet alters the others, though not in any simple, linear, additive way.

One implication is that development on one dimension of maturing may become excessive *relative* to development on other dimensions and so distort the system (Holt, 1974; M. B. Smith, 1950). Too extended symbolization may result in obsessive introspection and indecisiveness that paralyze the system's ability to adapt. Overextended allocentricism *relative* to integration and autonomy may describe Loevinger's conformist stage of development or Fromm's marketing personality. Overdeveloped integration *relative* to the neglected dimensions may represent the overorganized machine or automaton that has little spontaneity. Too much stability turns into rigidity depending upon the level of development of the other dimensions. And excessive autonomy breeds a self-sufficient or individualistic narcissism.

The methodological implications are clear, but troubling and perplexing. Neither a linear nor a curvilinear method of analysis is really appropriate for testing the extent of maturing on a particular dimension. The meaning of a particular score on a test of stability of self-concept depends upon the maturity of the larger system. The same score on a dimension may not mean precisely the same thing for two different persons—a fact we know from work with IQ tests but which we consistently ignore in using their scores. A stable self-concept for one person may be achieved at the price of the flexibility that is associated with comparable integrative development. The same score for another may mean an easy openness to new experiences just because of the certainty that comes with a stable identity. Scores indexing stability of self-concept, therefore, will only moderately predict scores indexing the maturity of a person.

Some will criticize the way I shall deal with these issues statistically. I remain unconvinced that complex statistical corrections for systematic interdependencies, like multiple regression, partial correlations, or covariance analyses, are really appropriate for representing nomothetically what is inherently an idiographic problem. So I must be content with lowpower methods of analysis that produce moderate relationships. I rely on (hopefully) disciplined intuition to organize and interpret recurrent patterns of findings from replicating groups. It will be the context of the findings, not specific results, that will be compelling. I am not making an apology. I am stating where I am after many years of being wedded to traditional experimental and statistical, as well as holistic clinical, methods. Although I use reductionistic methods and statistical procedures, the more deeply I enter the lives of the effective men I study, the more convinced I become that such methods are just not appropriate for representing the complexity of systemic patterns.

I also assume that every viable living system has an intrinsic equilibrating or self-regulating principle that preserves its structural integrity. This is an abstract way of saying that a person is like a rubber band. If he is stretched, tension is induced that "resists" the stretching. A complexly organized system, even an infant's, has a "natural" form that resists too great distortion. Even a relatively formless amoeba has a form that has its breaking point.

In contrast to Neill (1960) and Fromm (1947), for example, I do not imply that a person is like an acorn, so preformed that he just needs moisture, oxygen, minerals, and a little manure once in a while to develop into some predestined shape. I accept Sinnott's more complex biological view about how living systems develop.

> Development is not an aimless affair . . . through all this alteration . . . [the organism] maintains its own particular identity, its own organized unity. Each organism has its particular series of norms, its special cycle of progressive and creative development. Continual change is the keynote of this cycle; not unguided change but change that moves toward a very definite end—the mature individual and the completion of the cycle . . . The unity of the organism seems to inhere in the end toward which it is moving rather than in any fixed course for reaching that end, for the end may be gained not in any single linear progression but in a variety of ways (1959, 16–17).

I phrase the regulating principle this way. Overdevelopment in one sector begins to induce resistance within the system to further development in that sector until maturing occurs in those more immaturely developed sectors. The system must maintain some semblance of its given organizational unity while changing. This is very abstract. Some examples: Doob studied how less civilized societies differed from more civilized societies in their psychological effects (1960). The personality data from representatives of societies of different degrees of "civilization" indicated that increasingly civilized societies induced more self-control in their members at the expense of emotional spontaneity. Doob asked if a society may become too civilized and so produce distortions in interpersonal maturing. Jung's wellknown, successful, but neurotic middle-aged persons illustrate how development of an attitude like extraversion can go awry. Further individuation requires the development and integration of the opposite function of introversion. Another example may be the excessive, in my judgment, development of symbolization in some contemporary American youth relative to their allocentric and integrative maturing. Their use of drugs may be one of several ways by which they try to retain their systemic unity or wholeness. Drugs aid some to get over being so uptight by blowing their minds—that is, their hyper self-consciousness—at the same time deinhibiting their allocentric relationships, thus helping them, so they believe, to get themselves together (1971).

Maturity and Psychological Health

We are now ready to turn to the relation of maturity to "psychological" or "mental health," terms that still remain unclear after decades of discussion. I agree with R. White (1973), with the implications of Szasz's attack on the term "mental illness" (1960, 1970), and with others who find such terms and their assumptions to be vague, not useful and misleading. Maslow (1959) and Shainess (1973), for example, claim that psychological healthiness means maturity. Srole suggests that psychiatrists are beginning to replace traditional diagnostic categories by dimensional ones (1976), though the issue of whether the major psychoses qualitatively differ from less severe forms of maladjustment remains in dispute (Dunham, 1976).

Studies suggest that the reliability of the traditional psychiatric health-illness categories may be primarily the result of diagnoses being made in terms of "general maturity level" or the *healthiness of the system*, rather than in terms of specific symptoms that reliably distinguish manic-depressives from schizophrenics (Phillips, Broverman, and Zigler, 1966). Researchers have been developing scales to measure systemic healthiness. On the Health-Sickness Rating Scale (Luborsky, 1962) and the Global Assessment Scale (Endicott, Spitzer, Fleiss, and Cohen, 1976) healthy or mature poles are defined in terms remarkably similar to some dimensions of maturing: integration or integrity; resiliency in the face of stress (stability); autonomy; realistic judgment; and interpersonal warmth (allocentricism). Such scales are quite reliable. They also validly predict other indices of psychological health, like ego strength, maturity of defensive orientation, Rorschach measures of interpersonal maturity, and reality testing (Luborsky and Bachrach, 1974). Lichtenberg has empirically demonstrated that different types of manifest pathologies can be ordered in terms very similar to several dimensions that define maturing. He has shown that decreasing mental health, running, for example from situational neurotic to schizophrenic reactions, is associated with decreasing symbolized intentions to initiate shared, cooperative, and integrative personal relationships (Lichtenberg, 1955; Lichtenberg, Cassetta, and Scanlon, 1961).

Another promising alternative to the traditional psychiatric categorical approach is a hierarchical model of the developmental maturity of defenses, ordered on the basis of psychoanalytic ego psychology. A measure of the maturity of a person's defenses was inversely related to psychopathology and directly related to various measures of adult adjustment (Vaillant, 1971, 1974, 1976). Following Haan (1963, 1965), if defenses can be understood as less symbolizable, more autocentric (unrealistic), less differentiated and integrative, and less stable and autonomous, then the model of maturing may offer a more systematic theoretical basis for deriving types of defenses in the future. More generally, might not an adequate, transculturally-valid model of maturing provide the criteria for more reliably describing deviations from healthy systemic functioning in the future?

The most thoroughly researched model of ego development is that of Loevinger who, relying on sentence completion results, proposes that development begins with presocial and symbiotic milestones and ends, for a few rare persons, with autonomous and integrated stages (1976). Although accepting that the integrated stage comprehends the principal traits that Jahoda (1958) used to describe positive mental health and Maslow (1962) self-actualization, she suggests, somewhat inconsistently I think, that ego development is independent of psychological adjustment, e.g., a conformist may be as well-adjusted as an autonomous person. However, Loevinger has no systematic view or independent measures of psychological health to test this hypothesis. She accepts that there may be "several more or less independently variable dimensions encompassed in ego development" (1976, p. 188) and in discussion mentions, for example, increasing symbolization. Might not the model of maturing identify such genotypic ego dimensions? Our measures may provide the independent indices necessary to determine the relation of psychological health to her ideas about ego development. Since she organizes her scoring system in terms of structures similar to cognitive skills (cognitive style), self-concept (conscious preoccupations), values (character development), and interpersonal relations, it may be possible to reorder her specific scoring criteria in terms of the dimensions defining maturing. Since more autonomous and integrated, in contrast to self-protective and conformist, persons possess traits more facilitative of adaptability, e.g., objective, tolerance for ambiguity, and adaptability is certainly related to psychological health, it is reasonable to expect that ego development as she defines it should covary with dimensional maturing.

What might be the implications of using the dimensions of maturing as criteria for assessing psychological healthiness? An astute critic will note that no manifest behavior in and of itself can be identified as unhealthy or immature. It is the systemic maturity of the person that is the referent by which to understand the "healthiness" of a specific act. Failure to understand this assessment principle has led to the identification of persons who participate in homosexual acts as "ill." If an adult who participates in such acts is as maturely developed as other adults who participate in heterosexual acts, as is suggested by one study using the model of maturity and its tests as indices of healthiness (Fineman, 1976), then unless we labeled the latter psychologically unhealthy, I would not label the former unhealthy, even though some aspects of his behavior are maladjusted to the value system of his society. This is not to deny, as some assert, that being so maladjusted to one's societal values creates a different adaptive problem that may make it more difficult for him to maintain his level of maturity (Gove, 1975b; Sagarin and Kelly, 1975).

Wise clinicians have always diagnosed in terms of the configurational context in which a specific symptom occurs. Failure to observe this holistic principle leads to unreliable diagnoses and much fruitless controversy (Crown, 1975; Farber, 1975), as Rosenhan has provocatively demonstrated (1973). Sane psychologists playing the role of patients complaining of hearing voices were admitted to mental hospitals with provisional diagnoses of schizophrenia. Once the staff came to know them as persons, they were released. If we had a clearer understanding of the criteria defining healthiness or maturity and not just of psychopathology, it might not take as long to make more reliable contextual assessments. But it does take time to "know" a stranger.

A skeptic might say, "Well, I can accept that a psychologically healthy adult is mature and a mature adult is psychologically healthy. But on your dimensions of maturing we can speak of a child whose systems are go, who is learning in school, and who is adaptable, as psychologically healthy *but* immature. So we need both terms: *psychological health* to refer to a system maintaining itself while developing; *maturity* to distinguish different levels of development."

I believe this argument is terminologically deceptive. We fall into the trap of using terms like *healthy* and *immature* categorically rather than dimensionally, and evaluate level of maturity in terms of an adult's rather than a child's age norms. A child who is educable, resilient, adaptable, and has energy available for playful enthusiasms—criteria frequently used to define psychological health—would test, I suggest, dimensionally more mature than a child who was less educable, rigid, not very adaptable, and constricted. And more mature children would be more educable, resilient, and adaptable than less mature children.

Until a systematic, logical, researchable model of psychological health is developed that is applicable for any age, that successfully overcomes such linguistic difficulties, and that contributes more to our understanding than does a developmental systemic one, I continue to equate maturing with becoming psychologically healthier. I reserve the term *healthy* for colloquial use; by *healthy development* I mean "maturing"; by *unhealthy* "immaturing."

Theorists like Sanford will vigorously disagree (1962). The issues, he would assert, are more than just terminological. He cogently argues that we must distinguish between *health* as the potential for maintaining stability; *maturity* as the predominance of adult over childlike processes that make for efficiency, differentiation, and realism; and *development* as increasing complexity. He may be right. The model of maturing is incomplete; it is not a systematic theory of personality; it may not lead to theoretical clarification. I take the heuristic position at this time that it will take much more research before we can construct such a systematic theory. The model of maturing provides a practicable scaffolding by which to operationally deal with some of the issues Sanford raises.

Maturity and Self-Actualization

Self-actualization is another popular, but confused and confusing term. I distinguish between naive self-actualization, popularly conceived, and the more sophisticated assumptions proposed by persons like Rogers and Maslow.

Naive self-actualization proponents have never satisfactorily dealt with the central issue raised by William James' inimitable analysis of the self.

> I am often confronted by the necessity of standing by one of my empirical selves and relinquishing the rest. Not that I would not, if I could, be both handsome and fat and well dressed, and a great athlete, and make a million a year, be a wit, a *bon-vivant*, and a lady-killer, as well as a philosopher, a philanthropist, statesman, warrior, and African explorer, as well as a "tone-poet" and saint. But the thing is simply impossible. The millionaire's work would run counter to the saint's; the *bon-vivant* and the philanthropist would trip each other up; the philosopher and the lady-killer could not well keep house in the same tenement of clay (1890, 309-310).

What does a person actualize? His potentials. But what are a particular man's potentials? What determines which potentials are to be realized? Are we to live only in the here and now, making life a spontaneous happening, impulsively living out whatever fancy and wish dictate? Naive self-actualization becomes narcissism, a justification for sloth, greed, and every form of polymorphous perversity—unless one makes some very powerful assumptions that the "real" nature of the self is good, social, loving, just, and beautiful.

Psychologists are aware of these questions. Both Rogers and Maslow have a conception of the potentials that define humanness, of the ideal end point of development, that guard their theories against license for narcissism and justification for evil. Rogers constructs his model of the actualized and fully functioning person on the basis of growth trends his clients regularly demonstrated in therapy as they were becoming better, healthier, mature (1959). Maslow induced his model from his well-known study of the most actualized mature persons he knew (1954). But Maslow's methodology was so feeble that the potentials cited must be primarily projections of his own values (M. B. Smith, 1973). He equates self-actualization with maturity and psychological health—an equation supported by the inverse relation between the Personal Orientation Inventory (POI), constructed to measure self-actualization, and indices of neuroticism (Knapp, 1965; Knapp and Comrey, 1973; Raanan, 1973; Shostrom, 1964, 1973; Shostrom and Knapp, 1966; Tosi and Lindamood, 1975; Wills, 1974).

Both Rogers and Maslow assume that there is a given direction to development, that there is a "structure of being," a ground plan that defines any human's "particular series of norms . . . (his) special cycle of progressive and creative development" (Sinnott, 1959, 16). Each assumes that there are fundamental, general potentials that define humanness, that must be actualized if the person is to be psychologically healthy or mature. More clearly stated by Maslow (1967a) than by Rogers is the principle that the realization of man's developmental potentials is regulated, organized, harmonized not only by the hierarchical integration of man's more basic needs, but also by the systemic unity of the person.

Each, like other theorists, differs in the details of the lists of potentials he proposes. Their failure to anchor their models to a systemic developmental or some other theory gives neither Maslow nor Rogers a basis for deriving a comprehensive, systematic model of fundamental human potential. The model of maturing can be viewed as systematizing the principal developmental potentials that define self-actualization for Maslow, and the fully-functioning person for Rogers. Maslow talks of integration, identity, autonomy, increased objectivity, ability to love, clearer perception of reality (allocentricism), and openness to new experience (integration) (1959). A factor analysis of the POI revealed a number of factors, among which the following could be easily ordered by the model of maturing (Wright and Wyant, 1974) (because some factor labels seemed arbitrary, I give either of the two highest loaded items for some factors): Allocentric self-concept (Identity with mankind); Integration of values ("The truly spiritual man is sometimes sensual"); Integration of self-concept ("I am able to risk being myself"); Stability of values ("I feel dedicated to my work"); Autonomy of values ("I live by values which are primarily based on my own feelings"). No factors related to the dimension of symbolization or to cognitive skill maturation were reported, suggesting which aspects of maturing may be neglected by the POI.

Rogers talks of symbolizing experience accurately; of congruence or integration; of experiencing oneself as the *"locus of evaluation"* (autonomy); of openness to experience, regard for others, and positive self-regard (allocentricism); and so on (Rogers, 1959, 234).

So do we need the term *self-actualization?* No. Because there is the possibility that a more systematic, scientifically verifiable, developmental model of maturing can be constructed from a broad theoretical and research base that includes most of what Rogers and Maslow have induced from a narrower observational base. A maturing person is a self-actualizing person; a self-actualizing person is mature.

I have now described above a model of maturing, as well as some assumptions about how a maturing person maintains and extends his organizational unity while adapting. I assume that *in principle* psychological health, self-actualization, and maturity can be derived from a developmental conception of the person as a system. The concepts should be relatively free of personal bias and sociocultural values.

I have focused thus far on issues concerned with the developing person and his self-organization, and kept to the periphery the question of adaptation and the sociocultural matrix within which maturing occurs. It is now time to shift this focus to the relation that the environment bears to the maturing person, and I enter this complex problem by way of the concept of competence, the issue of social evaluation, and the relation that cultural values bear to maturity.

CHAPTER 2

Maturity, Competence, and Cultural Values

In Chapter 1, I presented a culture-free developmental-systemic model of maturing or healthy growth. However, maturing takes place in a ceaselessly changing physical and social environment that varies remarkably from one region and culture to another. To survive, a person must continuously create equilibrating interactions with such changing environments, effectively adapting to new information and resiliently recreating his organismic integrity when disorganized by the necessity of new adaptations. How can a universal conception of healthy growth comprehend the manifest variety of cultural differences? Just what is the theoretical relation between the model of maturing and the effectiveness with which a person adapts? These questions are critical, both practically and theoretically, to the creation of a valid transcultural model of maturing.

Practically, identifying mature and immature persons to study must ultimately be based on some social evaluation of their effectiveness in adapting. Reliance on such judgments immediately opens the research to influence by idiosyncratic and sociocultural biases and values. Theoretically, the question is at the center of several contemporary storms. Can value-free transcultural universals be established? Is the definition of mental-health like terms only an ethical-legal value choice, as psychiatrists like Szasz (1961, 1970) and Laing (1967), and social-labelling theorists like Scheff (1972) have claimed? Our entry into the issue of the relation of maturity to adaptation begins with an analysis of competence, the technical concept referring to adaptive effectiveness. I will then examine the relation of maturity to competence and propose that the model of maturing identifies the core traits that define adaptive effectiveness. Following a brief analysis of the related sociological concept of modernity, I will discuss the issues involved in the relation of maturity, adaptive effectiveness, and cultural values.

The Concept of Competence

R. W. White's clarifying critique of psychoanalytic ego psychology (1959, 1960, 1963) triggered an expanding interest in the concept of competence. He proposed an effectance motive to "explore the properties of the environment; it leads to an accumulating knowledge of what can and cannot be done with the environment; its biological significance lies in this very property of developing competence" (1963, 186). He defined *competence* as an "organism's capacity to interact effectively with its environment" (1959, 297). "Competence . . . is a cumulative result of the whole history of transactions with the environment, no matter how they were motivated" (1963, 39). White insists that a distinction must be drawn between competence as a biological fact and as a social ideal:

> Learning to reach and grasp, crawl, walk, climb, push others around, and later more complex skills do not in principle require any socially defined goals, however much they may eventually become caught up in them. At its roots the concept could hardly be more purely biological and less related to societal standards . . . (however) competence as an ideal of life is socially defined (1974).

White prefers to restrict competence to its ethically neutral or biologically based meaning. From his point of view, competence refers to those skills and knowledge that are instrumental to adaptation.

Others, however, who are more typical, use the term *competence* more evaluatively. They seek to identify general traits and skills associated with effective functioning in complex types of environments. Their preferred route for studying competence is to rely on judges to identify effective and ineffective persons as they function in a defined situation. B. L. White, for example, studied small groups of competent and incompetent three-to five-year-olds selected by fifteen observers, their teachers, and psychological tests (1971). M. B. Smith studied competent and incompetent Peace Corps volunteers, relying on the evaluation of judges in the field for determining effectiveness (1966). Assessing competence in relation to the demands of progressively more complex environments inevitably involves personal and societal values about what superior coping or adaptation is. The use of *diverse* judges, however, does dilute the effect of idiosyncratic biases in assessing effectiveness.

Perhaps because the concept of competence has not been located within a systematic theory of adaptation, researchers of competence as a complex personality variable have not tested specific hypotheses about traits defining effectiveness. Actually, studies of persons labeled competent only seem to confirm what studies of persons labeled mature, healthy, sound, ideal, and optimally adjusted seem to have already demonstrated. M. B. Smith has penetratingly analyzed and summarized the theoretical positions and research he identifies to index competence (1969a). The traits he informally cites are also those generally ascribed to psychological health: self-confidence, self-esteem, assertiveness, self-reliance, self-control, buoyancy, affiliativeness, realistic openness to experience, tolerant, principled responsibility, initiative, feelings of control over own destiny, reality-orientation, control over impulses, clarity about identity, persistence in face of failure, determination, problem-solving attitude, strength of interests, risks disapproval "to master a task on one's own terms," capacity to resist inner distraction, native and intrinsic curiosity, "ability and disposition to make use of others' help on one's own terms" rather than just self-sufficiency, and so on (1961, 1968). Central to the concept of competence, so Smith believes, is a constellation of attitudes toward one's self based on the belief that one has control of one's own life, that one is an "origin" and not a "pawn," to use De Charm's distinction (1968). Others who write about competence also seem to be talking about maturity. Clausen says, "I . . . expect that highly competent persons would, in general, be characterized as self-confident, dependable, and responsible, open to experience, and tolerant and understanding" (1968, 130). B. L. White identified competent preschool children as those who anticipate consequences, plan, and take the perspective of another, traits similar to those predicted by the model of maturing (1971).

Maturity and Competence

To clarify the relationship between maturity and competence, I restate some obvious points. A person can be a competent surgeon, watchmaker, lover, gambler, father, thief, and winetaster. He can be a most competent accountant, but also a most incompetent husband and almost everything' else. A highly creative and competent mathematician I know has periodic psychotic episodes. Another highly competent scientist is severely maladjusted to his society. Gauguin was judged to be a not very good painter until after his death. Competence is to some degree in the eye of the beholder. Nixon was a superbly competent president to some— including himself; the epitome of incompetency to others.

The theoretical issue each statement illustrates scarcely needs to be made explicit. A person has many different types of competences, which may range broadly or be highly focused. Competence may be independent of pathology or of social adjustment; competence may be socially defined; its criteria may change over time; a person's evaluation of his own competence may not be confirmed by the judgments of others.

Maturity is certainly not equivalent to competence as R. W. White, but perhaps not as others, use the term. Maturity refers to universal genotypic developmental dimensions. Theoretically, we could identify persons as more or less mature in terms of the level and pattern of their dimensional development. If adequate measures were available, we could even ignore manifest effectiveness or competence when assessing a person's maturity. Practically, however, we must infer maturity from the type and range of tasks, roles, and situations in which a person functions effectively. We can make such an inference with some confidence because, as I shall show shortly, effectiveness in adapting to complex environments involves maturity.

Competence refers to effectiveness in relating to some specific environmental expectation or task. To identify competence requires that we evaluate a person's level of skill in relation to what is required by the task. The assessment of competence, therefore, cannot be divorced from the demands of the task or situation in which it is being assessed; maturity can be in principle, though not in practice at this time.

Maturity as determinant of generalized competence. While not equivalent, maturity and competence are not exclusive of each other, either. To function competently requires some developed skills, motives, ideas about one's capabilities, and/or interpersonal skills. Different roles and tasks differ widely in the degree to which they require different levels and patterns of maturing for their effective accomplishment. Maturity may not contribute as much to packing herring in a sardine factory as it does to functioning as a Peace Corps worker in Uganda. Researchers have been more interested in assessing competence in complex situations that demand types of skills and traits more generalized than technical, and more central than peripheral. Effectiveness in dealing with such situations increasingly depends upon greater maturity (Cross, 1971; Haan, 1965; J. G. Harris, 1973; Lanyon, 1967; Rasmussen, 1964; B. L. White, 1971).

Smith talks of the competent self, a core of interrelated traits that mediate effective adaptation over a very wide range of different tasks and roles that, he proposes, may be transculturally universal (1969a). What Smith calls a "core" competence factor will, I believe, for empirical and theoretical reasons, turn out to be what I have defined as maturity. Empirically, the best predictor of the rated competence of men in their early thirties, whether as husbands, fathers, or workers, was their psychological maturity as defined by the model of maturing (Heath, 1976a,c). Confirming this relation between maturity and adult competence is the finding that men in their late forties who made excellent career and marital adaptations were psychologically healthier than men who did not (Vaillant, 1974). Studies of the competence of Peace Corps volunteers in the field identified not narrowly defined task-specific or technical competences, but more general traits characteristic of maturity as the *primary* determinants of their effectiveness: self-reliance, inner strength (autonomy), perseverance (stability of values), realistic goals (allocentrism), judged "general maturity" (J. G. Harris, 1973), and the ability to make complex anticipations about future consequences (cognitive symbolization) (Ezekiel, 1968). Finally, a factor analytic study of various measures of competence resulted in the first factor being most heavily loaded on tests measuring the model of maturing (Jensen, 1971).

Why is maturity a consistently powerful indicator of a wide range of adult competences? The answer involves the theoretical relation of the model of maturity to the adaptive process.

Maturity as a model of the adaptive process. I suggest that because the model of maturing identifies the traits that define effective adaptation, it provides the model of the adaptive process that competence theory has lacked to date—a lack responsible for the fact that this research has been fragmented and atheoretical. I have already mentioned, for example, how Haan's criteria defining coping skills could be reformulated in terms of the dimensions of the model: potentially symbolizable rather than unconscious, reality-oriented rather than reality distorting, differentiated rather than vaguely developed, stable rather than rigid, and autonomous rather than compelled (Haan, 1963, 1965).

We need to clarify some terms. By *adapting* I mean responding in a way that optimally satisfies and is integrative of the demands of the environment and of one's organismic integrity. Adaptation does not necessarily mean adjustment, which is the accommodation of one's values, needs, and talents to fit the demands of others. Adjustment to such demands may not integrate a person's values and talents, and may inhibit his maturing, as it does in some men who conform to a culturally defined *machismo* expectation that does not integrate their more dependent and emotional needs (Heath, 1976d). High competence may represent an effective adjustment, but not a mature adaptation, if the societal definition of competency includes more immature types of adjustments. Generally, though, it is reasonable to expect that competences in fulfilling complex adult roles, such as parenting, are congruent with mature forms of adaptation.

I suggest that there is an optimal sequential set of dependencies among the dimensions of maturity that mirror the process of effective adaptation. Therefore, the personality traits found to be associated with each dimension are the qualities required to make effective adaptations. How does a person adapt? And what is the evidence that supports the hypothesis that there is an optimal sequence to the adaptive process?

The process of creating a new adaptation is initiated by a difficulty for which no immediate response is appropriate. The person is brought up short. Awareness is heightened. Efforts to figure out the problem are intensified. Symbolic adaptive skills are focused on the issue. The situation is rehearsed imaginally. One's motives are re-examined. Interpersonal frictions are mulled over and *symbolized* more accurately. Different viewpoints and alternative solutions are sought. Books are read. Advice is sought. Efforts are made to understand how others may or will react.

Perspectives are broadened. Following this *allocentric* phase in adaptation, links are formed. Tentative relationships are made. *Integrative* syntheses are examined for inconsistencies. Cooperative teams are formed. Action is initiated to test tentative preferred solutions. New skills, ways of doing something, or relationships are tried out. What fits is tried again; what does not is dropped. Gradually a new approach begins to *stabilize*. Self-consciousness about a relationship or new skill diminishes. Self-confidence increases. Emotional involvement is less intense. The new skill, habit, or motive is so stable it has become routine and *automatized*. We easily use such a skill in new situations. We feel more in control. We laugh about the previous difficulty, and wonder why we got so uptight. "Why didn't I ask her earlier?" We have more energy. We relax, become more expressive, less serious, more playful, more hopeful.

What evidence, other than the logical compellingness of the sequence, supports the idea that such dependencies describe the process of adaptation? The insight that there might be an ordered sequential dependency to the dimensions came from my studies of how students changed during and after college (1968; 1976e). In their first weeks as freshmen, most students became deeply introspective in order to comprehend their own confusion, as well as their euphoria (symbolization). Bull sessions, behavioral rehearsal of more "adult" activities, confrontation with other people's views and values socialized their symbolizations (Coehlo, Hamburg and Murphy, 1963). Through argument, communication became clearer (allocentricism). Efforts to get themselves together followed the initial shake-up. The college's demand that an academic major be selected was one tentative adaptive route (integration). When the identification with the major was nonintegrative, resistance to becoming involved academically in the major occurred. Those whose identity with the major was a good fit (stability) frequently showed marked spurts in independence and self-direction (autonomy). But not until the students tested their evolving identities in the world outside of college did they learn how genuinely integrative, stable, and autonomous was their provisional way of life. Only as the research was completed supporting this formulation did I discover that John Dewey had used the same adaptive sequence as the basis of his theory of habit formation (1922). Other researchers, notably Perry (1970), have identified a similar sequential ordering to the intellectual and ethical development of students. Students moved from an unexamined dualistic mode of thought, through an awareness of multiple viewpoints, to the formation of an integrative and stable commitment that became the basis for autonomous decision and action.

Vocational theorists like Ginzberg *et al*, (1951) and Tiedeman (1961) talk similarly about the process of vocational decision-making: imaginative exploration of self and world (symbolization), crystallization of alternative patterns of choice (allocentricism), their provisional organization into sequential possibilities (integration), followed by their tentative implementation (stabilization) that produces increased self-assertiveness and feelings of control (autonomy).

Since this book is about maturity and cultural values, I take two examples from crosscultural studies. In one, commenting on cultural change in the Harvard southwest study on values, Kluckhohn and Strodtbeck (1961, 45) said, "that the better integrated a value-orientation is, the greater will be its power of resistance to the effects of impinging forces." Their insight is that stabilization of a society's values is enhanced by increased integration among its values. A structure cannot become maturely stabilized, in other words, until it has become integrated.

The second cultural example is the work of Cantril, who studied the changing aspirations of 14 countries in different stages of national development (1965). He proposed that there was an irreversible, regularized order describing national development that remarkably parallels the adaptive sequence. Not until a country's people become psychologically frustrated, as had not at that time yet happened in rural areas of India, for example, do they become more aware of their national potentialities. They or their leaders create dreams and hopes of what their country could be like, as occurred in Panama at the time of the study (symbolization). This initial stage is accompanied by the dissolution of former controls and traditions, and the occurrence of anxiety and tumult. New alternative institutional or other more realistic ways are sought to fulfill the emerging dreams. Cantril saw this in Nigeria, a country that viewed the acquisition of technology as the means of raising its standard of living. A nationally shared goal produces an intense sense of patriotism that replaces former narrower loyalties, as occurred in Cuba (allocentricism). Leaders who articulate and coordinate realistic ways to achieve the goals of the people unify the nation's values and establish faith (integration). As goals become realized, faith is confirmed, confidence increases (stability), and there is a "heightening of the feeling that self-direction is possible through responsible action" (308) (autonomy). The studies of modernity (Inkeles and Smith, 1974), and, as I shall show shortly, the model of maturity identify the adaptive traits that emerge out of such national development, traits which, in turn, facilitate subsequent adaptation to new challenges and frustrations.

This adaptive sequence, beginning with symbolization and culminating in autonomy, takes many forms. Frequently it is short-circuited, occurs at different levels of awareness, may be almost instantaneous, or persist for years as in some personal relationships and problems, or occurs simultaneously with respect to different types of problems. A maturing person becomes more able to use the adaptive sequence self-consciously—that is, his own potentials for adapting—not only to accelerate his own growth, but also to make his interactions with the environment more effective.

Let us take the list of terms Smith attributes to competence and reorder them in terms of the adaptive sequence:

Symbolization	clarity about own identity; problem-solving attitude
Allocentricism	affiliativeness, reality-orientation, self-esteem, tolerance, principled responsibility
Integration	openness to experience, curiosity
Stability	identity, strength of interests, persistence in the face of failure, determination
Autonomy	assertiveness, self-reliance, self-control, initiative, feelings of control over own destiny, capacity to resist inner distractions, control over impulses, risks disapproval to master a task on one's own terms, and (combined with allocentricism) ability to use others' help on one's own terms without meaning self-sufficiency.
Consequence	buoyancy

The ordering is crude and in some cases not far from being arbitrary. But it does suggest which aspects of maturing are more central to the concept of competence, and also which aspects of effective adaptation are being ignored in theory and research about competence. Smith's emphasis on autonomy may neglect the importance of values as well as types of mature adaptive skills. But the point should be clear. The process of adapting effectively that defines competence may be systematizable, deeply general, and hold across many different tasks as well as situations and cultures. The model of maturing, therefore, may provide a systematic basis for Smith's idea of a "competent self"; and the research I will report shows evidence for his idea of a universal transcultural model of effectiveness. An important implication is that to further a person's competence, one should find ways to enhance his maturity. I have illustrated elsewhere how the model of maturity can be used as a rational way to diagnose and prescribe change in educational systems, *if* there is a commitment to furthering student maturity and therefore eventually enhancing subsequent adult competence (1971, 1974, 1976e).

Competence as a determinant of maturing. We have seen that maturing may enhance a person's competence. Reciprocally, increasing competence may encourage a person's maturing. Robert White has noted that competence enhances one's self-esteem as well as facilitates the shift in dependence on others for approval to one's own (autonomous) judgment or self-approval. To believe in one's own ability to create effective adaptations produces confidence and a willingness to risk initiating problem-solving efforts in increasingly novel situations. Self-esteem provides a resilient buffer against failure. Since a primary determinant of maturing is confrontation with a difficult problem, confidence that one can master it becomes a very critical spur to seek out and master, rather than to avoid, those opportunities that could stimulate maturing (M. B. Smith, 1974a).

Maturity, Competence and Modernity

Comparative cultural studies of the process of adapting to the demands of increasingly complex societies, and of changing from being a "traditionalist" to a "modern" person support our belief that the creation of a transcultural model of maturing is a reasonable hope. Such studies also provide the opportunity to examine from sociological and anthropological perspectives the relationship of maturity to competence (Doob, 1967; Inkeles, 1966, 1969; Inkeles and Smith, 1970, 1974; Kahl, 1968; Rosen and

LaRaia, 1972; D. H. Smith and Inkeles, 1966). Inkeles and Smith have studied the modernization process in Argentina, Chile, East Pakistan, India, Israel, and Nigeria. Assuming that adults can continue to adaptively change their values, needs, and modes of thought throughout their lives, they propose that

> men from very different cultures . . . respond in basically the same way to certain of the relatively standard institutions and interpersonal patterns introduced by economic development and socio-political modernization (1974, 12).

However, "modern" man is not necessarily contemporary man; modernity is a state of mind that could equally apply to a Periclean Greek or an Elizabethan Englishman. Change from a traditionalist to a modern personality presumably reflects increasing competence in adjusting to more differentiated complex societal demands. If maturity is the principal contributor to effective adaptation, and, reciprocally, if the process of adapting furthers maturing, then we should discover that the qualities that define modern man are comprehended by the model of maturing. Such, in fact, is the case. The person who becomes more modern is increasingly able to anticipate and plan (symbolization). He becomes more trustful and tolerant of greater diversity, his identifications and interests expand beyond immediate familial ones, and he participates in a wider range of nonfamilial activities (allocentricism). He becomes more cognitively flexible, curious about, and open to new experiences (integration). He also becomes more confident in his ability to adapt (stabilization of self-concept), as well as less passively and fatalistically acceptant of traditional authorities from whom he becomes more independent (autonomy). As measures of modernity less cumbersome than three-hour interviews (Gough, 1976), and as valid transcultural measures of maturity become available, we should discover if the assumption about the relation of maturity to adaptation is correct—in other words, whether or not modern man is also more mature man. Might not the model of maturing provide the theoretical personality framework that modernization research lacks to date? Might it not suggest other traits that distinguish modern man, the person who can change and adapt, from traditional man, the person who is rigidly and passively imprisoned in his own autocentricism?

On the basis of his extensive crosscultural sampling, Inkeles rejects, as do I, the culturally relativistic biases of many social scientists when he asserts that

> . . . what defines man as modern in one country also defines him as modern in another. It argues for the actual psychic unity of mankind in a structural sense and the potential psychic unity of mankind in the factual sense. . . . the nature of the human personality, its inner "rules" of organization, is evidently basically similar everywhere. . . . the association of the elements or components of personality which increases the probability that those individuals—whatever their culture—who have certain personality traits will also more likely have others which "go with" some particular basic personality system. . . . this structural unity provides the essential basis for greater factual psychic unity of mankind. Such a factual unity, not merely of structure but of *content*, can be attained insofar as the forces which tend to shape . . . the modern man become more widely and uniformly diffused throughout the world (Inkeles, 1969, 212).

Issues About the Relation of Maturity and Competence to Cultural Values

I have argued that *in principle* it may be possible to establish universal developmental-systemic criteria by which to identify one person as more mature than another. Such a definition could then be freed of idiosyncratic and societal values. However, to define a person as *competently* interacting with his environment does depend upon personal and societal values. The criteria of effectiveness vary as a function of the demands of the particular setting to which a person is responding. The issues implied by these statements are more complicated than I have suggested, and many will disagree with my position. Both terms, Szasz (1970) would say, represent norms evaluated by a "psychosocial and ethical standard." Scheff, a social labelling theorist, has written:

> . . . mental health is . . . a value choice about what kind of values should be encouraged in our society. Whether one selects a notion like aggressive mastery of the environment, traditionally a Western ideal, or the more inward turning goal like self-actualization, more akin to traditional ideals in the Orient, is not dictated by the natural

order of stably reoccurring regularities in nature but by human choice (1972, 402).

The central issue is, to what extent do evaluative personal and sociocultural values *inherently* affect the meaning of maturity once the value choice that maturity should be one's goal or standard has been made? The social-labelling controversy (Broadhead, 1974; Clausen and Huffine, 1975; D'Arcy, 1976; Gove, 1975a,b; J. Murphy, 1976; Sarbin, 1969), as well as other analyses of the meaning of "mental illness" (Devereaux, 1956; Edgerton, 1969)—one pole of a dimensional view of effective adaptation—help clarify some issues about maturity. I shall avoid the complex epistemological and ontological questions that hover on the edge of my comments here, since others more qualified than I have examined them (Moore, 1975; Szasz, 1961, 1970).

Much of the discussion about values and mental health is ambiguous, partially because of a failure to anchor comments like Scheff's in specific defining operations. At least five meanings, for example, have been educed for Szasz's polemical phrase, "the myth of mental illness" (Moore, 1975). Here I will discuss first the relation of values to the scientific study of maturity; then the empirical process of objectifying the concept of maturity; and finally, the cultural differences in valuing traits of maturity.

Values and the scientific study of maturity. The issues on which I believe most theorists would agree are the more obvious ones. To choose among health, maturity, competence, creativity, adjustment, happiness, or death is to assert a preference, a choice based on personal and/or cultural values. Such choices are fair topics for scientific study. We can ask, why was this choice made? what are its consequences? In principle we could even establish which choice is "better," if we had an external independent criterion by which to compare the consequences of the two choices. If we agree to apply the scientific method, certainly we also commit ourselves to particular values, such as objectivity, truthfulness, and public verifiability, even though scientists themselves do disagree about some of their value assumptions (Maslow, 1966; Tart, 1972). Our values determine the problems we study, as well as the methods we prefer. And probably most definitions of mental health, maturity, and self-actualization that have been selectively induced from a clinician's rich experience reflect his, his profession's, and his society's values to some extent. If we assume that maturity cannot be defined relatively independently of someone's, or of a society's values, then this present book must be considered primarily a study of the values that judges from five cultural areas have made about the meaning of maturity.

Objectifying the concept of maturity. Once the value choice has been made to study maturity, the central issue emerges into the foreground: how to purify it as a concept from personal and cultural values. Let us first examine some issues involved in the strategy of relying on local judges to identify mature and immature exemplars—the only *practicable* way to begin the empirical definition of maturity. Then we shall examine a more ideal way, given unlimited resources and time, to determine which stages in the empirical process of defining maturity are most vulnerable *in principle* to the influence of personal and cultural values.

The transcultural study of maturity began with the effectiveness of a person's adaptation or competence. All procedures used to separate mature from immature persons at this time are based on some evaluation of their effectiveness in adapting. Typically, judgments of judges have been most frequently used to identify maturity or its related concepts. Judgments of mental health are apparently no less reliable than those made of other complex human phenomena (J. A. Davis, 1965). College personnel have judged "personal soundness" (Barron, 1963; MacKinnon, 1960), "ideal" student (Brown, 1960), and degree of "successful living" (C. W. Heath, 1945). Peers have nominated those outstanding in "normal personality" (Bonney, 1962, 1964), effectiveness (Rasmussen, 1964), and rated qualities of mental health (Duncan, 1966; Seeman, 1966). Clinicians have identified traits most characteristic of "optimal adjustment" (Block, 1961), or identified academic, marital, and vocational effectiveness from interviews (Coelho, *et al*, 1962, 1963; Vaillant, 1975). Even questionnaires like the MMPI, used to identify well-functioning persons (Golden, Mandel, Glueck and Feder, 1962), or the California Personality Inventory to identify social maturity (Gough, 1966, 1968, 1974), or combinations of questionnaire and projective tests (Westley and Epstein, 1969) have been validated against judgments of effective adaptation.

Personal bias and societal values must surely affect the judgment of judges identifying "personally sound," "optimally adjusted," or mature persons in the *beginning* phases of such studies. Such bias and values are not necessarily capricious; they may have been shaped by much experience with and cultural wisdom about persons who recurringly have been very effective in adapting to a wide variety of situations. Despite the intrusion of such values upon the operational definition of maturity, we can, as M. B. Smith has recommended (1972, 1974b), progressively objectify our understanding of such terms—much as has been done with evaluative terms like intelligence, aggression, and conformity. For example, intelligence was originally defined by the evaluations of teachers of the academic effectiveness of students. Some seventy-five years later, "The assessment of intelligence," Wechsler says, "inevitably . . . [remains] a value judgment . . . necessarily consistent with the value criteria of the time" (1975, 138). His stance is more understandable when we consider that he thinks of intelligence in *adaptational* rather than developmental terms: intelligence has "to do primarily with the appropriateness, effectiveness, and worthwhileness of what human beings do or want to do" (135). As terms like intelligence come under the cloak of science, their referents become specified more objectively and precisely; they become defined by increasingly reliable measures; their idiosyncratic attributes are distilled out by the work of many observers; and they become located within some network of results and theory—though controversy still exists about the cultural boundedness of intelligence (Vernon, 1969). The objectification of a term gradually purifies it of particularistic values associated with individual judges and unique cultural situations.

Complex, holistic terms, like *maturity*, that refer to less specifiable adaptive criteria than school achievement, for example, increase the opportunity for the biases of judges to shape their definitions. We can take steps, however, to make the maturity concept "relatively less vulnerable," R. W. White's phrase (1974), to personal whims by using, as we did, numerous and diverse judges in the five cultural areas to identify mature and immature exemplars for us. The model of maturing used to organize the study may also reflect in subtle ways both cultural biases and my implicit assumptions about personality. That this model was induced from the experience of diverse observers of different-aged persons functioning in varied situations and coping with different problems helps to "universalize" it to some extent. If a core group of maturing processes can be discovered in different cultures that predict effective adaptation in a range of situations, then we begin to free the concept of maturity even more from its particularistic cultural embeddedness and seeming value determinants. Only by so doing can we avoid the tautological trap of defining maturity in terms of the particular values of local judges who select mature exemplars to be studied (Kluckhohn and Strodtbeck, 1961).

Our hypothesis is that a culture-free model of maturing can be constructed *in principle*. To pursue the hypothesis further, I examine an alternative research strategy which, while impractical today, would have several steps.

1 The first step would be to identify a reliable battery of tests that measure a wide range of the principal behaviors and personality traits listed in cultural dictionaries and reported in the research literature. Include in the battery measures of the dimensional hypotheses of maturing. The tests should be transculturally equivalent and tap different "levels" of personality organization.

That a culture does not differentially react to, or have a term or construct like "stability of self-concept" obviously does not mean such behavior does not objectively occur, a point some social labelling theorists seem to ignore, as their critics have pointed out (Broadhead, 1974; Clausen and Huffine, 1976; Gove, 1975a,b). A culture may not recognize or have a term for megalomania even though behavioral indices of it are present in a group. Of some interest is the fact that most cultural groups have terms for "deviant" behavior, and many share similar criteria for defining it (Draguns and Phillips, 1972; Dunham, 1976; J. Murphy, 1976). Systematic lexicographic-like studies of positive mental health terms have not been reported (Soddy, 1961). The fundamental issue is, however, whether similar behavior or patterns of behavior occur in diverse cultures regardless of whether the behavior or pattern has or has not been labeled by each culture as indicative of a higher-order construct like "maturity" (Leighton, 1969; Leighton *et al*, 1963).[1]

To what extent are such descriptive observations and measures of behavior influenced by personal and cultural values? We may label them as "evaluative" if we wish, but then the implications of the term become trivial: all scientific description is evaluative. Or we can assert that our values affect not only what we perceive but

1. This distinction becomes confused in practice, when we rely on judges to select exemplars of labels signifying mature personality organization. Ideally, we would prefer to use nonjudgmental measures of maturity, like those to be reported in Chapter 8, to identify exemplars of maturity. Such measures could then be used in any culture, even one that did not have a label referring to maturity or psychological health.

also every choice that we make, such as what behavior to study and what methods to use. To so equate "value" with such methodological choices is to say nothing that is more *uniquely* discriminating about mental health than about any other concept that one studies.

2 The second step would be to use such a descriptive battery to study randomly selected persons in every culture throughout their life span and under any transculturally general conditions—becoming educated, married, entering the work force, or encountering death—that induce disequilibrium requiring altered adaptation. This step does not seem to pose unique or inherent evaluative judgments except that the selection of the conditions under which to study the persons is a value judgment, an issue I examine in the next step of the research procedure.

3 Determine which childhood, adolescent, and adult measures are both *conjointly* sensitive to developmental changes over time *and* predict personality change in adapting to disequilibrium.

The decision to use developmental and systemic criteria to which to predict is a personal but not a cultural value judgment. We can make such a study without any reference, moreover, to higher order mental-healthlike terms. The issue to determine is, are there universal culture-free developmental and systemic criteria? It seems reasonable to assume that there are universal dimensions that define human development, and in Chapter 1 I cited pancultural evidence that such might be the case. All human beings are systems capable of change in response to new information, and resilient in recreating their organismic integrity when disorganized by such change. So it seems reasonable to also assume that there are such universal systemic criteria like maintenance of cognitive efficiency or its recovery in face of stress. Cultural values may shape the manifest but not the underlying structure of the developmental and systemic criteria (Draguns and Phillips, 1972).

4 Establish independent reliable measures of effectiveness in the principal adult roles found in all cultures—spouse, worker, parent, and friend—and determine what traits identified in Step 3 predict the widest range of effective adaptations. At this stage of our knowledge, this step certainly involves, either directly or indirectly, personal and sociocultural values. However, their influence may not have to be as decisive as it seems. Since humans are partially open systems, dependent for survival upon creating certain stable interactions with their environments, there may be universal,

culture-free criteria that describe adaptive effectiveness. There is a growing acceptance of the idea that pancultural adaptive criteria may be obtainable, associated with efforts to free the definition of mental illness from its medical, ethical, and legal implications— though, quite frustratingly, no one systematically describes what such criteria might be (Plog and Edgerton, 1969). Ausubel says mental illness may be defined by "seriously distorted or sufficiently unadaptive" behavior (1961, 72). Opler claims

> mental disorder ... represents impairments in functioning destructive of the individual's integration in his adaptation to a context. ... cultural evolutional processes induce stress systems that are comparable and ... forms of psychopathology [occur] that can be found transculturally (1969, 98).

Sarbin proposes a "new metaphor" for understanding mental illness. Its postulates are that

> man as social creature must confront and solve certain ongoing problems ... [and acquire] modes of solving problems that may be successful under some conditions and not successful under others (1969, 22–23).

Cattell asserts that there are "objective standards and demands for adaptation and adjustment" that in all cultures require similar adaptive qualities, such as the capacity to control impulses, foresight, and the ability to work for remote goals (1973). If such adaptive universals were discovered, then we could expand our developmental-systemic criteria of maturity to include adaptive ones.

Transcultural criteria of adaptive effectiveness might be generated in terms of the functional demand requirements of each type of role. They might limit the *direct* effect that cultural values have on the criteria. For example, competent parenting requires specifiable attitudes and skills *if* maturation of a child, defined by empirically generated norms like cognitive stage standards, is identified to be a primary value (Heath, 1976c, 1977a). Vocational adaptation depends upon fulfilling task requirements and vocational satisfaction, both of which can be specified by general criteria only indirectly influenced by cultural values (Heath, 1976a). As research increasingly identifies what behaviors and traits covary to contribute to and describe role "effectiveness," the direct effect of idiosyncratic personal and cultural values may be moderated, and more objective measures of effectiveness substituted.

If the model of maturing actually does provide a rationale for specifying the traits that predict effectiveness transculturally, then we could dispense with the adaptive criteria, since they could be subsumed under the developmental-systemic ones.

5 The last step is to conceptually order and label the patterns of covarying traits that predict developmental-systemic change and resiliency (and adaptation).

I believe that much of the argument about the label "mental illness" is terminological. No one disputes that behaviors like "hearing voices" or "social withdrawnness" occur, or that such symptomatic traits covary regularly among cultures (Draguns and Phillips, 1972). At issue is the higher-order label used to "explain" such covariation. For Szasz, the use of "mental illness" as a label connotes assumptions about etiology that have not been validated, refers to subjective ethical and legal, rather than objective, standards, and contains implied prescriptions for action that are false. Because he hypothesizes that patterned traits of traditional psychiatric categories refer to socially learned "patterns of living," that cultures vary in valuing such patterns, and that changes in such patterns involve communication rather than medical procedures (1970, 1974), he is able to claim that mental health *qua* mental health terms are essentially ethical-legal evaluations.

In principle, our "ideal" definitional study avoids these pitfalls. If successful, we will have empirically generated patterns of traits that predict objectively determinable developmental-systemic differences, and possibly adult effectiveness, transculturally. We can order and identify such patterns as our definition of maturity.

Cultural differences in valuing traits of maturity. Other important issues are involved in discussing the relation of maturing to cultural values (Allinsmith and Goethals, 1956; M. B. Smith, 1950; Soddy, 1961). In many cultures, maturity and psychological health are defined by terms that have the status of values. Some cultures highly prize gentleness and tolerance; others harmony and autonomy. For example, Triandis empirically found that an ideal person for Americans would be one who is highly motivated,

seeking to improve himself, a good planner, easily adjusted to others, intelligent, curious, and experienced. According to the Greeks, the important characteristics are patience and will power, followed by diligence, honesty, ability, motivation and courage. . . . according to the Japanese, the ideal individual is achievement oriented, concerned with "being right," highly motivated, enthusiastic, courageous, faithful; he also has a pleasant personality and shows respect for others (1972b, 258–259).

Different cultures thus nourish or suppress different potentials of the maturing person. The Japanese culture, for example, may encourage allocentric more than it does autonomous maturing. Japanese students rated themselves to be significantly more dependent on external controls (Rotter I–E scale) than students of six other countries (Parsons and Schneider, 1974). In comparison with Americans of similar age, Japanese men are described as more dependent on their mothers (Norbeck and DeVos, 1961), a dependency that Caudill suggests begins to be culturally learned during the early infant months when Japanese babies are carried, rocked, and lulled significantly more than American infants are (Caudill, 1972; Caudill and Frost, 1974).

Excessive cultural nourishment of some potentials at the expense of others, according to the systemic assumptions about maturing, may be nonintegrative and induce resistance to fulfilling the cultural definition of "ideal" healthy persons. Those youths who blow their minds with drugs, seek more experiential forms of education, or flirt with communes may be overdeveloped in abstract symbolic modes of functioning, and underdeveloped in the integration of their emotionality and social needs with their intellects (Heath, 1971).

If the hypotheses of the model of maturing and its systemic assumptions are valid, then they will be validated only partially by studies of mature and immature representatives of any *one* culture. Furthermore, the model may be more comprehensively and validly tested in some cultures than in others. As M. B. Smith has pointed out (1950), cultures that are highly restrictive, suppressive, and authoritarian may not provide the expectations, opportunities, or social routes by which to mature "freely" in any number of potentials. Some cultures create more stress than others, and so can impede healthy development (Naroll, 1969). The typical "paranoidal" Douban Islander had little opportunity to develop allocentric interpersonal skills and values (Benedict, 1934). The typical communal Hutterite had little opportunity to develop an autonomous self-concept and values that could protect him from the guilt and depression that stemmed from the overriding socio-religious expectations of his community (Eaton and Weil, 1953). Nor does the typical American youth, living in a rapidly changing, impersonal, competitive, technological society, have the same opportunity to form integrative, allocentric, and stable personal relations (Heath, 1971, 1976b) as does a typical Chinese youth, living in a more caring, coherent, stable, (though suppressive) small community, who, however, may not have the same cultural opportunity to grow autonomously. One study, for example, identified Americans as "cold . . . frivolous, closed to strangers," unable to form mutually intimate relationships because of a fear of losing their autonomy (Klein, Miller and Alexander, 1974, 218). Chinese students, on the other hand, were found to value friendships marked by "complete trust, unswerving reliability, mutual obligation, mutual anticipation of needs," (Klein, *et al*, 1974, 230), but they are not noted for individualistic self-assertiveness and interpersonal independence (Yeh and Chu, 1974).

Theoretically, then, the most mature, not necessarily the most "civilized" (Doob, 1960), culture provides the most favorable condition for systemic maturing to occur. That is the culture where the model of maturing should be tested. But what culture is that? I do not know, and I know of no reliable way to answer the question, though researchers are beginning to seek out such ways (Naroll, 1969). To test the model's validity requires that I find ways to at least measure differences in "cultural values," as well as in the socialization expectations of the cultural areas studied. Such measures were necessary not only to demonstrate objectively that the cultures, the independent variable so to speak, did differ in fact, but also to secure data by which to interpret the relation of maturing to specific cultural values and expectations. Some results of these methods are reported in Chapter 3 and Appendix A.

Although cultures may value different patterns of potentials as mapped by the model of maturing, I expect to discover a similar genotype core defining maturity in most, and especially in developed, cultures. Our systemic assumption is that maturing is an organismic process, even though some potentials develop more rapidly than others in some cultures. Exact replication of the tests of the model in different cultures hopefully will result in the distillation of those recurring potentials most frequently associated with effective functioning in those cultures. Many observers have shared this hope (Campbell, 1975, 1976; Cattell, 1973; M. B. Smith, 1950, 1969b; Soddy, 1961), and it is indirectly supported by empirical efforts to identify culture-free reliable criteria of pathological adaptation (Draguns and Phillips, 1972; Lebra, 1972; Leighton, 1969; Leighton, *et al*, 1963; Murphy, 1976; Plog and Edgerton, 1969; Wittkower and Fried, 1967). For example, a recent transcultural effort, sponsored by the World Health Organization, has successfully replicated the presence of twelve signs and symptoms reliably identifying schizophrenia in nine diverse cultures, including Columbia, Nigeria, India, China, and the USSR (Carpenter, Strauss and Bartko, 1973).

This completes our theoretical mapping of the meaning of maturity and competence, and their relationships to terms such as psychological health, self-actualization, and modernity. It is now time to discover if our map accurately sketches how mature and immature persons differ in five different cultural groups. We shall return to the issues of Chapters 1 and 2 in the final chapter. First, however, we must consider the details of the *empirical* relationship between maturing, competence, and cultural values.

CHAPTER 3

The Study of Maturity: Selection of Mature and Immature Men

D o different cultures define maturing similarly? Our problem is to confirm or disconfirm that mature persons, in contrast to those who are immature, are better able to symbolize their experience, and are more allocentric, integrated, stable, and autonomous *regardless of the culture from which they come.* Our problem is *not* to compare the level of maturity of persons of one culture with that of persons of a different culture.

Research in different cultures demands frustrating compromises that may limit the power and generality of transcultural comparisons. For example, our research involved thirteen university presidents, directors, and deans; four European professors; three psychological supervisors; four experimenters; over four hundred faculty and students canvassed to be selection judges; two hundred and thirty-six friends who rated the one hundred and thirty men who actually participated; many hundreds of volunteers who participated in peripheral, smaller concurrent studies; seven research assistants, eight secretaries, ten translators; and a host of others on whom the research depended, such as *portiers* with the keys to the offices on weekends, or registrars who had never made up lists of their students before. This was research that involved hundreds of persons, each of whom had some power of decision (if only the decision not to cooperate or not to keep an appointment), and therefore some control over the whats and hows of the research; research that had to be completed in nine months and take into account student vacations and examination periods; research run in countries where intensive personality studies of this scope had never been done before—well, such research risked the temptations of expedient compromise, and we must therefore pay particular attention to the necessary compromises and errors that were made.

What different cultural areas were studied? How were mature and immature exemplars selected in each cultural area? Did the American, two Italian, and two Turkish groups differ in ways, like intellectual level or socio-economic backgrounds, that might confound the interpretation of their findings?

Cultural Areas Studied

The generality of the model of maturing was tested with Protestant and Jewish (America), Catholic (Italy), and Moslem (Turkey) mature and immature men.

The research had been initiated with several groups of mature and immature men attending Haverford College near Philadelphia. Considerable work had confirmed the reliability and usefulness of many of the procedures designed to test the model's validity, as well as the feasibility of the research design which guided the Italian and Turkish studies (Heath, 1965).

Why study Italians and Turks? In addition to their different religious values, a number of other factors affected this choice. Groups of mature and immature men had to be identified who were comparable in intelligence, background, and education to the American men. Otherwise, differences in any of these ways between the cultural groups might cloud the meaning of the results. The principal characteristics of the Haverford men determined the sub-population to be studied: highly intelligent, very well-educated males predominantly from the middle and upper-middle social classes.

The selection procedure required a residential college setting. To make reliable judgments, the judges needed to know well the members of the population from which the mature and immature men were to be selected. Numerous and diverse judges who had contact with the men in a wide variety of activities had to be available in order to dilute the effect that a particular judge's idiosyncratic biases might have upon the selection process.

Other practical reasons for selecting the cultural area to be studied required the existence of a viable psychological research tradition, the availability of psychologists and other trained persons to supervise and conduct the research, the feasibility of creating comparable translations of the eight hours of tests and experiments, the probability of completing the entire research program within a nine-month period, and the receptivity of the universities to intensive research with their students.

As it was, more than a year was spent canvassing, communicating, and negotiating with psychologists of different countries before Italy and Turkey were selected. Of the Catholic countries, Italy readily met the requirements. Because northern and southern Italy differ markedly, universities in Pisa and in Palermo, Sicily, were used. The choice of a Moslem country was more troublesome. The limited number and availability of psychologists, as well as the absence of a strong psychological research tradition in most Moslem countries made Turkey the most practicable choice. The research took place in western (Istanbul) and central-eastern (Ankara) Turkey. Each of the universities had national reputations and drew students from all parts of their countries.

How do the three cultures differ? The question is important to consider. Let us assume that the three cultures are found to define maturing similarly. How do we interpret the finding? A skeptic might claim, "Turkey, Italy, and America are really not very different. You have not shown me that they differ. You have not made a very powerful test of the generality of your model if the cultures aren't very different."

I dared not risk opening a Pandora's box of tangled and entangling issues too far in trying to respond to this possible complaint. Theoretical issues—for instance, "typing" of a culture (Benedict, 1934; Triandis, 1972b; Triandis, Malpass and Davidson, 1973), "national character" (Inkeles and Levinson, 1969), or meaning of "cultural difference," as well as problems of measurement and sampling (Abel, 1974; Brislin, Lonner and Thorndike, 1973; Meade and Brislin, 1973) were far beyond the focus and resources of the research. But I could not avoid the fact that the "subjective culture," and its values and expectations Triandis, 1972a,b), affect the socialization and hence the maturing of a youth; nor ignore the fact that judgments of judges about who is and who is not mature are affected by knowledge of how effectively a person has adapted to his society's expectations.

To provide a workable context in which I can later interpret some of the results, I will sketch here quite impressionistically some of the principal values that distinguish the three cultures, and then summarize more objective information. In Appendix A I report in greater detail the exploratory methods used, as well as their suggestive data, about how the three cultures may differ.

I will not describe, since most of my readers will know it well, the American culture's historic Protestant work ethic, or its meritocratic and democratic traditions, competitiveness, restlessness and rebelliousness, practicality and pragmatism, materialism, skill in getting "the job done," and repressive distrust of affection and sexuality (Heath, 1976b; Hsu, 1961).

Turkey is a Moslem country. It still is in continuing and divisive conflict about Atatürk's 1923 "opening to the west," which was an effort to move away from the cultural values and practices associated with Islam. Islam's fatalism about the future, passivity toward the present, and idealization of the past do not nurture values of civic responsibility, social awareness, or interest in social betterment and change. Nor does Islam prize the typical American values of controlling and directing one's physical environment, or of striving energetically and persistently for success. When something goes wrong, a Moslem says, "*Incha' Allah*," God willing. An American says, "Damn! What can we do about it?" The wise Moslem lives for today, not expecting much out of life. A man is born to success. Why fight what is going to happen anyway? "Let things be, particularly our past way of life," Muslim Turks will say. Change may lead to worse things. Strict enforcement of the religious laws, obedience to authority and custom, and authoritarian parental discipline of youth still define the ethos of much of Turkey, particularly the rural areas from which many of the Ankara group came. In some peasant villages, a man's wife dare not look at a strange man for fear of retribution by her husband against her. Marriages of many young Turks are still arranged. The parents of some men at Roberts College, the most westernized of Turkish schools, had picked their sons' fiancées before they entered college. Although legally banned, polygamy is still condoned in Anatolian villages.

The heirs of Atatürk have been trying to change these deeply entrenched values and customs for decades. The resulting divisions between the conservative Eastern and liberal Western Turks persist. Such divisions were always on the fringe of the awareness of modern young Turks when I was there. I was impressed by the number of men who were driven to tell me about their conflicts with their parents and society, and their sense of futility that much fundamental change would ever come. Many were in profound rebellion against their conservative parents, who controlled the power in a country where job opportunities and advancement were still largely dependent upon political and parental influence. The Turkish research groups contained some of the country's rising socialistic and communistic youth leaders who were intensely committed to radical social and political change.

The Turks differ in other ways as well from the Americans. The Turkish men have separated the expression of affection and sexuality. The men are demonstratively uninhibited in their relations with each other. Middle-aged men walked hand in hand through the Ankara airport. Men at Robert College casually sprawled, leaned upon, hugged, and walked arm in arm with each other. Turkish males are expected to assert their sexuality around fifteen with a prostitute, but not with their girl friends—though this value is changing. This custom is an important rite of passage. One evening I discovered an entire street not far from the principal shopping center of Istanbul that had been blocked off by the police, to prevent too-young adolescents from entering. Hundreds of men milled through it silently, peering at the barely dressed women in the open houses who were seductively displaying themselves and enticing the men to pay, in those days, their seven lira. Any unescorted woman discovered on the Istanbul streets in the evening is considered to be a prostitute.

Italy differs dramatically from both America and Turkey. Barzini, a perceptive, but acerbic and perhaps too cynical writer, says of his native Italy that "everything is seen but nothing is understood." Using this insight, I will offer here a collage, a kaleidoscope of impressions, contrasts, and contradictions, rather than try to explain the silent but persistent power of the Catholic Church, or pervasive familial allegiances, or the instability of Italy's central government.

Barzini's key to the Italian character is that

> . . . a good show makes a man *simpatico* to powerful people, helps him
> get on in the world and obtain what he wants, solves many problems,
> lubricates the wheels of society, protects him from the envy of his
> enemies. . . . Behind the turbulent and picturesque agitation of

Italy, behind the amiable, festive, and touching spectacle, behind the skilful performances, real life is something else. It can be sordid, tragic, pitiless. It is often an anguished, sometimes a mortally dangerous game. . . . The first of the evil spirits is poverty (1964, 99, 101).

An Italian student who had visited America said:

Life in the States is somehow easier. The students there don't really have to fight for life. Students here have to work because their families can't support them. The Italian boy is more used to fighting for what he wants. He's more prompt to face difficulties in living. He always tries to get around, to see what the score is. He'll be more diplomatic at school because he faces the problem of failing. What could he do? He fears to offend the teacher; he tries to behave the best way. He has to learn how to be diplomatic, smart, clever and changeable to act according to the situation.

Barzini's rule for survival is that:

. . . one must cultivate one's family, entertain as many useful friends and . . . perfect the art of being obliging and *simpatico* at all times and at all costs. . . . Above all, one should remember at all times that conflicts are not decided on the basis of the law, abstract considerations of justice or the relative merit of the contestants, but most frequently by a pure confrontation of power. . . . choose the right companions . . . choose the right protectors (1964, 226–229).

An Italian doctor at dinner:

I failed my medical exam and went to my professor and asked him what to do. He told me not to worry. The next time the examination was given, the first student left the exam saying he had been given an easy exam; the second came out saying the same thing. Finally, it was my turn. I was given easy questions, too. The problem was the examiner didn't know which student was to be given the easiest exam.

Barzini's law of self:

Transparent deceptions are constantly employed to give a man the most precious of all Italian sensations, that of being a unique specimen of humanity, a distinct personality deserving special consideration. An Italian considers it a duty to cultivate such illusions in fellow human beings. . . . Nobody in Italy ever confesses to being "an average man" (1964, 79).

A judge, from the Scuola Normale Superiore, trying to select mature and immature men for the study, told the Pisa experimenter: "I can't do this. We all are mature here."

Barzini's Italian way:

The Italians were also naturally impervious to most of the ideals which made the medieval world go round: unswerving loyalty to one's chief, allegiance to one's sovereign, and *noblesse oblige*, or the sense of duty towards dependents, inferiors, the weak and defenceless. Foreign words like honour, *honneur*, *Ehre* cannot be translated exactly (1964, 182).

Newspaper headline: *Sicilian Girl Balks; Suitor on Trial*

A young Sicilian was on trial today for rape because his victim broke with a centuries-old tradition and refused to marry him. . . . Since the Middle Ages, Sicily's men have resorted to rape to get the women they want. Traditionally, no one else will take the women who refuse to wed their attackers.

A Barzini contrast:

To *sistemare* all things is considered to be the foremost, perhaps the unique, mission of man on earth. . . . *sistemare* means to defeat nature . . . in the sense of "conquest of security" . . . any kind of *sistemazione*, is the dream of most Italians (1964, 112–113).

Time article:

Not long ago, a Eurofinance researcher discovered why Italian statistics on heavy electrical engineering came out three months after the French figures and usually showed about half the French total: The Italians, having no production figures, simply guessed after seeing the French reports (April 18, 1966).

Such vignettes provide a flavor but scarcely objective evidence about how the cultures are similar and dissimilar. I know of only one study that explicitly compared Americans, Italians, and Turks using the same methods.[1] American exchange teachers who had taught in thirty countries described their typical foreign students, predominantly seventeen- and eighteen-year-olds, using a sixty-five item Q-sort procedure that tapped self-attitudes and interpersonal relationships (Fawcett, 1965). Seventeen and twenty American teachers respectively described their typical Turkish and Italian male students; sixty exchange teachers (including thirty foreign teachers teaching in America) subsequently described American students. Statistical comparisons of composite portraits of each country's typical student revealed that the Italian and Turkish students were rated similarly (composite correlate of .76). They were judged to be sensitive about their personal honor and maintaining face, to be impressed by social power and prestige, and to take opportunities to test and stretch the rules. Two American composite portraits were discovered. The principal white middle-class portrait diverged considerably from the Italian (.34) and Turkish (.37) composites.

In comparison, the typical American student was rated to be a friendly, funloving, competitive person who thought highly of himself and who set high aspirations for himself. Interestingly, the second American composite, associated primarily with lower class urban students, was very similar to the Italian and Turkish portrayals. Confirming Barzini's observations, the Italian students regarded their family relationships as very important, were argumentative, uninhibited in the expression of their feelings, and concerned about the evaluations that others made about them. The Sicilian males were generally similar to Italians from other parts of Italy, though they were less reticent about their private lives and more competitive, fickle in their attachments, and inclined toward hero worship. In comparison to the American and Italian youth, the typical Turkish male was judged to be extremely nationalistic, inclined toward hero worship, opportunistic, and to have closer relations with other males.

1 Other studies that have compared the Italian and American cultures (Almond and Verba, 1963; Pearlin, 1971) provide some objective support for Barzini's observations. In contrast to Americans, the Italians view their world as unpredictable, threatening, and unresponsive to their control. They are deeply alienated socially and isolated, but they are strongly committed to traditional familial values. Of the five cultures studied, the Italians felt least obligated to participate in community and national affairs (Almond and Verba, 1963).

But a skeptic could rightly object: "Except for Barzini's observations, the descriptions of the Italian and Turkish cultures are those of outsiders like yourself and American exchange teachers. How do the members of each country describe their own cultures? Can you show that Americans, Italians, and Turks value their interpersonal relationships differently? Do Turkish males value closer relations with males more highly than do Americans; do Italians actually regard their families more positively than do Turks?"

Systematic and objective evidence from studies of the three cultures provides some answers to these questions. But these questions are methodologically too complex to be answered satisfactorily; furthermore, each provokes other questions that lead further and further away from my primary focus, the test of the generality of the model of maturing. I will therefore briefly summarize here how such questions might be answered, and leave the details of the studies and their findings to Appendix A.

Several groups of university men and women, selected randomly from the same populations from which the mature and immature men were selected, completed different exploratory procedures assessing their culture. One group of judges from each of the five cultural areas rated eleven key attributes of their culture— for instance, Mother, Religion, Sexual Practices—by checking three adjectives descriptive of each dimension of maturity. The test, called Cultural Semantic Test (CST), provides scores assessing the dimensional maturity of various aspects of the culture. Groups of other judges assessed the degree to which their culture approved or disapproved of different types of persons interacting with each other in eight different ways: a girl of eleven flirting with a married man of forty-five; a boy of eighteen arguing with his father. This test, called the Cultural Valuator Test (CVT), mapped the degree to which each culture positively and negatively valued or reinforced different patterns of personal relationships.

On the Cultural Semantic Test the American judges rated their culture to be most mature; the Turks rated theirs to be the least. The Italians judged their culture to be least integrated and autonomous. The judges confirmed the view held otherwise in each culture that the more economically backward or least "modern" section of the country was dimensionally less mature. The Italian South, for example, was consistently described by both Northern and Southern Italian judges as dimensionally immature. Interestingly, children from Southern Italy have been found to be significantly less advanced than Northern children on a variety of psychological measures (Ancona, Carli, and Schwarz, 1971). The judges agreed in identifying the mothers of each culture to be very mature allocentrically, but they disagreed about their country's fathers. Turkish fathers were rated to be the most immature on every dimension of maturity. Of all of the judges, the Turkish were most critical of the maturity of their culture's familial relationships. They were also the most critical of their religious tradition, rating it as socially unconcerned, unrealistic, unhealthy, and immature. The Italians rated the maturity of their Catholic tradition very highly.

The Cultural Valuator Test provided too rich a matrix of significant differences among the three cultures to be adequately summarized here. (Appendix A provides detailed evidence illustrating how similar and dissimilar the three cultures were rated to be.) The judges rated their countries to be remarkably similar in the degree to which their members could generally be aggressive, controlling, flirtatious, and so on with others. Every culture more strongly disapproved sexual and aggressive relations than any other type of relation. The American culture was most deviant from the other two cultures in its disapproval of dependency relationships, particularly for post-pubertal boys as well as girls. Of greater interest are the specific differences among the cultures' expectations about the specific types of relationships a boy of eleven or a girl of eighteen, for example, may have with other persons of the culture. The results were very clear. The three cultures had very diverse expectations of what was appropriate and inappropriate behavior in specific relationships.

Here are a few of the more distinctive patterns: The American culture was consistently rated as the most emotionally suppressive, particularly of sexual, affectionate, and dependent needs. The expression of such needs is limited to a very small number of relationships in comparison to the other cultures. The Italian and Turkish cultures were much more acceptant of adults being dependent upon their parental families, as well as being more dominating and controlling in a larger number of different relationships than the American culture. The Turkish judges agreed significantly less consistently among themselves about what were acceptable and unacceptable types of personal relationships, particularly among family members. As interviews with Turkish students had suggested, the Turkish family is under great stress.

Turkish young people are very uncertain about how to relate to their parents (Lecompte and Lecompte, 1973) Finally, the judges from northern and southern Italy, as well as those from western and central Turkey did not materially disagree in their ratings of their culture's patterns of approval and disapproval

Both the CST and CVT findings suggest that each culture has its own distinctive evaluation of its different attributes and its own unique set of expectations about what is acceptable behavior. The conclusion seems merited that the three cultures are diverse. If our hypotheses about maturing are confirmed among these three cultures, the findings cannot be readily explained away by the claim that the cultures do not differ in their values and patterns of interpersonal relationships.

The Selection of Mature and Immature Men

We now approach the critical moment, so to speak, of the research. How did we secure consensual judgments of maturity by judges of each cultural area that were not unduly influenced by idiosyncratic biases, personal preferences, and narrowly imposed criteria of maturity? How did we identify comparable groups of mature and immature men similar in intellectual level, education, and socioeconomic background? To answer these questions, I shall first describe the planned selection procedure we tried to rigidly adhere to in the five cultural areas, and then describe the procedure that was actually carried out.

Population criteria. Italian and Turkish educators identified the leading universities of each cultural area with student residential units. The university population from which to select mature and immature men was defined to include students of the upper three classes; unmarried males between the ages of eighteen and twenty-three who had been resident at the school continuously since matriculation; and parents who were natives of and resident in the country. Information about intelligence and socio-economic status was not available, but was secured during the research. Alphabetic lists of the 18–19, 20–21, and 22–23-year-olds were prepared to approximate the age sequence of American sophomores, juniors, and seniors. Cultural differences in the age of matriculation meant accepting some Italian students who were older than the American and Turkish men.

Selection procedure. The Italian and Turkish research assistants, who knew nothing about the research and its hypotheses, and who were responsible for the selection procedure in their cultural area, consulted with adults and respected students to identify those persons considered to have sound judgment who might know a large number of the student population. Ideally, twelve adults and twelve students were to be preliminarily selected to serve as judges in each cultural area. The judges were to represent a variety of viewpoints about and experience with the men. One of the judges was a janitor; several were priests; some were coaches and counselors; most were administrators, faculty, and student peers.

Each prospective judge rated how well he knew each student. Following the completion of the ratings, the nine adults and nine students who reported knowing the largest number of men were chosen to be the selection judges. If it was impossible to secure nine adult judges, additional student judges were used.

A week after he had made his acquaintance ratings, each judge completed the actual selection procedure. At no time during the entire procedure was any judge informed about the model of maturity, its hypotheses, or the tests and procedures to be used. I paraphrase the instructions and cite the exact selection criteria given to each judge.

> A research group . . . is attempting to discover what traits describe effective, maturely organized persons of college age around the world. . . . it is necessary to rely on the judgments of persons who are well acquainted with many youths to identify such persons to study further. . . . the enclosed criteria . . . . used to define such men are vague and indefinite, just because such persons have not been studied in the past. We are interested in identifying those most maturely and immaturely organized men . . . not just the men with the most outstanding intellectual accomplishments. A brilliant scholar may or may not be a very maturely organized person.

No explanation of the following criteria was given to any judge.

Selection criteria

Most maturely organized person	Most immaturely organized person
1 Behavior control is reliable and predictable.	1 Behavior control is erratic and unpredictable.

2   Behavior determined by flexible but firm inner controls, manifested by a sense of direction

2   Behavior determined by impulse or by pressure of social environment, *e.g.*, minimal self-defined sense of direction.

3   Unity and harmony between action, feeling and intellect.

3   Lack of integration between action, feeling, and intellect.

4   Sense of identity (accurate understanding of whom he is and what he wants).

4   No sense of identity (lacks understanding of his real self and needs).

Do not include the following

1   Rigid, highly controlled individuals whose good organization is forced and who are incapable of relaxing their overcontrol, *e.g.*, the driven, harried, well-organized person.

1   Nonconformists or "odd" individuals who do not meet the above criteria for the immaturely organized group (deviant persons may or may not be well-organized).

2   Individuals of special talents whose effectiveness may not be due to sound personal organization, *e.g.*, intellectual brilliance, good social adjustment, or athletic skill are not necessarily in themselves indices of mature self-organization.

2   Ineffective poor students, social isolates, or athletic incompetents whose ineffectiveness may be due to other determinants, *e.g.*, handicaps, than those listed above. Such ineffective individuals may not be particularly disorganized persons.

Generally, mature self-organization or immature self-organization is manifested in many areas of life—*e.g.*, social, academic, extracurricular, athletic, and personal—rather than in just one or two areas. The degree of the maturity of a person's organization may or may not be related to his popularity.

Each judge completed the procedure in private. He identified the ten most maturely and ten most immaturely organized men for each of the three lists by placing a check mark after the names in columns labeled "mature" or "immature." Since a judge might not know many men well, he was told to indicate if he believed his judgments about specific men were unreliable. From the total of thirty mature men, he then selected the twelve *most* maturely organized; from the thirty immature men, he selected the twelve *least* maturely organized. He was asked not to talk to others about the procedure or his judgments.

The number of adult and student judges who identified each student as mature and as immature was tabulated. The men about whom there was greatest adult and student agreement were selected. Only those men were selected about whom there was *both* adult and student agreement. The names of the mature and immature men were then listed on separate sheets. Other adults who knew many students, but who did not know the criteria used for their selection, judged the homogeneity of each group, indicating the men who did not seem to "belong" to each group.

Once the final groups had been "certified," each student received an invitational letter that described the purpose of the study as seeking to increase our "understanding of cultural similarities and dissimilarities." He would be given tests that "measured the rapidity, consistency, and adequacy of (his) judgment . . . as well as (his) attitudes toward himself." No students knew the study was about maturity. An attractive sum of money was offered if he completed the project. At his first appointment, he signed a sheet indicating that he understood his participation was voluntary; he could stop participating at any time; he would not make appointments that interfered with his academic work; he would appear for every appointment; all information was confidential, and no information would be released to any person without his written consent; the amount of the payment was acceptable; and he probably would not receive any results.

Selected samples. Such was the planned procedure. The actual procedure differed, though not critically, for two of the groups. It proved to be very difficult to find high-quality institutions with student houses where any more than a few adults knew more than a few men well. The research was eventually completed at the Scuola Normale Superiore and the University of Pisa; the University of Palermo in Sicily; Boğaziçi Üniversitesi in Istanbul; the Orta Doğu Teknik Üniversitesi in Ankara, Turkey; and Haverford College near Philadelphia, USA.

Pisa group. The original plan was to study the men of the Scuola Normale Superiore, Italy's most distinguished university of letters and science. After identifying the students who met the initial criteria, we discovered we had a population of only sixty-six students from which to draw the mature and immature men. Three student houses of the University of Pisa were then located which, when combined with the eligible students of Scuola Normale, gave an acceptable population of 265 men from which to select the mature and immature men.

Twelve adults and twenty-four students served as selection judges. The number of judges for each student house was kept proportionally the same. The number of mature and immature men identified was decreased to be proportional to the size of each residential unit. Fourteen mature and fourteen immature men were selected. All but three of the immature men accepted and completed the studies. They were replaced by three additional immature men.

Sicily group. The Sicilian was initiated halfway through the academic year at the University of Palermo, the principal university of Southern Italy. A residence house was located that had an eligible population of eighty-three students who came from the provinces. Two adults and eight students served as selection judges. They identified thirteen mature and thirteen immature men, who completed the study. Given that the Sicilian group was drawn from a much smaller population, its mature and immature groups may be less homogeneous and extreme, thereby reducing the probability of obtaining significant differences between them.

Istanbul group. The research was conducted at Boğazici Üniversitesi, formerly Robert College, Turkey's most prestigious college at the time of the research. Of the institutions studied, it was most similar to the typical American college. The planned selection procedure was completed without any alterations. The eligible population of males was 218. Nine student and nine faculty judges, all Turks, followed the prescribed procedure. Fourteen mature and fourteen immature men completed the study.

Orta Doğu Teknik Üniversitesi group. Orta Doğu, or the Middle East Technical University, is a nationally known university just outside of Ankara. The eligible population was drawn primarily from the arts and sciences, architecture, engineering, and administrative sciences. Several alterations were made in the selection procedure. The student residences were predominantly filled with engineers. The supervisor included students who lived off campus, in order to increase the number of students in the arts and sciences in the population pool. Despite an intensive survey of a preselected group of thirty Turkish faculty from the divisions other than architecture, few faculty knew more than several students. More than fifty students, selected in consultation with student leaders, also completed the acquaintance forms, but only twelve of them knew many students. The mature and immature men were selected from two populations: one of ninety-two architectural students, and one of 209 men from the remaining divisions of the university, making a total population of 301. The architectural students were well known by their teachers and fellow students. Three faculty and eight student judges completed the prescribed procedure. Twelve students, but no faculty judges, followed the procedure for the larger population. To secure faculty judgments about the mature and immature men nominated by the student judges, the names of the twenty-six men most qualified for the study were placed on separate cards. Copies of a six-point line-rating scale designated "mature" and "immature" at either end were made. From records of the courses of each man, thirty-seven Turkish faculty who had had the men in their courses were identified and contacted. Each faculty member rated his degree of acquaintance with each student, and then rated the student's maturity on the six-point scale, if he knew him at least casually. The ten faculty who knew the largest number of the preselected students were chosen to be the selection judges. Their ratings of the maturity of the men were used if they had marked either extreme. Nine mature and nine immature men were selected based on the combined nominations of the student and adult judges. The three most and least mature of the architectural students were included to give a final Ankara group of twelve mature and twelve immature. All of these men eventually participated in and completed the study. Student political unrest and deep suspicions by some that the project was a tool of the American CIA delayed the research until the experimenter convinced them otherwise.

Haverford group. At the time of the research, Haverford College was one of America's prestigious small men's colleges. The planned selection procedure was completed without alteration. From the eligible population of 289, twelve mature and twelve immature men were selected. They all completed the study.

Table 3—1 summarizes each group, as well as the amount of judge agreement about the men who composed it. The median number of judges agreeing about the maturity and immaturity of

Table 3–1
Amount of Judge Agreement about the Identification of the Cultural Groups

Size of Population	Total Number of Judges	Size of Group	Number of Judges Agreeing on Number of Students								
			12+	11	10	9	8	7	6	5	4
Pisa 265	36	28			2	6	4	8	5	3	
(83, 66, 61, 55)[1]	(10, 9, 9, 8)										
Sicily 83	10	26				4	4	9	4	4	1
Istanbul 218	18	28	1	3	3	3	2	4	9	3	
Ankara 301	33	24	5	1	2	2	5	1	2	5	1
(209, 92)	(22, 11)										
Haverford 289	18	24	3	0	2	4	4	5	5	1	
Total 1156	115	130	9	4	9	19	19	27	25	16	2

1 Figures in parentheses refer to size of separate populations and proportionate number of judges used in the selection process.

the men was seven. That judges can agree about the more extreme mature and immature members of a population of several hundred men is reassuring, particularly when so many of the judges, especially the faculty, did not know many of the population. For example, at Robert College, which provided favorable judging conditions, the median faculty judge knew only 32 per cent and the median student judge only 56 per cent of the students. These percentages include large numbers known only by name or reputation. And one must remember that we had selected judges who knew the largest number of students. The results confirm those of other studies that have found high judge consensus about who is and who is not personally effective or mature *when* the judges know well the members of the population to be judged (Duncan, 1966; Seeman, 1966).

Some Reflections

The selection procedure is our independent operational definition of maturity. What is its relation to the model of maturing and competence, as well as to other theoretical issues involved in this type of cultural research? The procedure sought to draw a preliminary distinction between competence and maturity. Recall that the judges were explicitly told to identify maturely and immaturely organized persons. They were invited to take into account the effectiveness or competence with which the men adapted to a *variety* of situations, including academic, social, personal, and other activities. Their judgments necessarily involved their biases about what was effective and ineffective adaptation, though the amount of judge agreement suggests such judgments are, in practice, not too personally arbitrary. I said in Chapter 2 the assessment of a person's competence is where studies of maturity must begin, at least at this moment. But since the competency route does not inevitably lead to the selection of highly mature persons, the judges were specifically asked *to not include competent persons whose competence was not due to "sound personal organization."* I provided some vague clues about the meaning of "sound personal organization"—inner harmony and identity—which they were asked to infer. Judgments of effectiveness of observable behavior, like competency indicators, are likely to be more reliable than inferences about vague inner causes of that effectiveness. To be more precise, we probably have contrasting groups of broadly competent and incompetent men whose competence is determined to a considerable but as yet unknown extent by their inferred personal soundness or maturity. We undoubtedly have some competent men whose competency may mask considerable immaturity, as was discovered in the earlier Haverford groups—for example, effective compulsives with incipient ulcers. It seems unlikely we have highly incompetent persons who are as psychòlogically healthy or mature as competent persons. Our task is now to determine if such independently defined groups actually differ in the ways that the model of maturing predicts they will.

By providing criteria distinguishing mature from immature personal organization, have we not imposed our own biases and assumptions on the judges, thereby risking not securing "pure," culturally defined mature and immature groups? If we confirm that the mature and immature men of the five cultural areas differ as the model predicts, can we still claim the results demonstrate that different cultures have similar definitions of maturity? And have we only enmeshed ourselves more tightly within the grip of circularity: define maturity, select persons in terms of that definition, and discover they have the qualities that define our ideas of maturity?

I think we must distinguish between a logico-theoretical ideal and that which is operationally practical. I mentioned earlier that research on maturity and cultural values was a bootstrap procedure, trying to escape the tautological problem of merely rediscovering its own preconceptions. Yes, we risked theoretically contaminating the judges' judgments with our own ideas. Practically, it was necessary to provide such criteria because they had been given to the American judges in the initial studies on maturity prior to the time the model of maturity had been formalized, and the comparative cultural study required exact replication of these selection procedures. Earlier research had shown it was necessary to specify some broad criteria to judges (Barron, 1963). Academicians, in particular, had been found to interpret "personal soundness," a concept close to maturity, in terms of academic competence as manifested by grade average. Maturity is not equivalent to, although it may contribute to, high grade average (Brown, 1960; Duncan, 1966; Seeman, 1966).

The criteria defining "maturely organized" included only a few of the twenty hypothesized characteristics of maturity. They are so vague that it is dubious they had a *decisive* effect on the judgment of many judges. Numerous judges complained both orally to the assistants and wrote on their rating sheets that the criteria were too vague to be useful to them. I believe they did provide a "set," however, to consider more than just a narrow range of visible competences. Finally, judgments about the maturity of specific human beings are very complexly determined. From what we know of the judgment process, it is doubtful that deeply patterned cultural and personal values about qualities like individual "effectiveness" and "maturity," as one sees them manifested in day-to-day situations, will be overridden, though perhaps not unaffected, by the kinds of criteria we offered to the judges. I therefore do not believe the judges' judgments were so contaminated by the criteria to discredit the compelling network of findings the study produced. In fact, we discovered later from objective measures of the judges' perceptions of the mature and immature men, secured three to five months *after* they had made their original selections (and presumably had forgotten the criteria), that the judges describe the mature and immature men to differ on numerous traits not even contained in the initial selection criteria.

We probably do not entirely escape the tautological issue in research like this. But we begin to when we rely on a variety of independent measures for assessing how the judge-selected mature and immature groups may differ. *If* completely independent judges who know the men well and know nothing about the model of maturing and the criteria for selecting the men, and *if* participants who know little or nothing about the model of maturing themselves, and *if* a panoply of questionnaire, rating scales, performance measures, projective techniques, and other more objective procedures, all confirm our hypothesized differences between mature and immature men—differences not even remotely anticipated consciously by the selection judges—*then* we have an empirical basis for claiming that the issue of circularity is not as critical as theoretically it might seem.

Comparability of Cultural Groups

The model of maturing makes a very powerful assumption. It assumes that the *pattern* of personality differences between mature and immature persons of the same social class, educational or intellectual level, and culture is similar. This assumption has not been tested except for this study of cultural values. Until we know if the assumption is correct, ideally we must control for the presence of all factors other than cultural values that might confound their effects and our interpretation of the results.

This stance confronts us with two somewhat contradictory problems. On the one hand, we must guarantee that the cultural groups do not differ in educational, intellectual, and social class background. On the other, we must demonstrate that the groups differ in their cultural-religious values and "character." In other words, we have to face up to the issue of just how representatively "American," "Italian," and "Turkish" our groups are. Do our cultural groups mirror the values, expectations, and patterns of relationships we have earlier identified as possibly distinguishing the three cultures from each other?

Cultural groups' similarities. Ideally, the men should *not* differ too markedly in *parental background and socioeconomic status.* What did we discover? With few exceptions, the men's parents were still living with each other. One-third of the American but more than one-half of the men of the Italian and Turkish groups were first-born or only children. However, just as many mature and immature men were first-born or only children. The groups differed in the amount of their parental education. The median number of years of schooling for the Haverford (16), Pisa (16), Istanbul (15.5), and Ankara (15) fathers was similar; but the Sicilian fathers averaged only five years. With the exception of the American group, the men's mothers had had much less schooling than their fathers. The median number of years their mothers attended school was 16 for Haverford, 8 for Pisa, 5 for Sicily, 10 for Istanbul, and 8 for Ankara.

The men of all the groups came predominantly from the middle class, as each man judged his family's socioeconomic status. Twenty-nine percent of the American, 10 percent of the Pisan, zero percent of the Sicilian, 26 percent of the Istanbul, and 25 percent of the Ankaran men claimed their parents belonged to the upper class. Only four percent of the Haverford, three percent of the Pisa, 15 percent of the Sicilian, four percent of the Istanbul, and five percent of the Ankara men were from the lower classes. The Istanbul group was the most heterogeneous economically. Several men's fathers were exceptionally wealthy. The range of paternal occupations was much greater and more varied in the Italian and Turkish than in the American group. The European fathers were primarily businessmen and tradesmen, though the Sicilian group, composed of men from the provinces, had peasants and farmers in it.

The cultural groups were similar in the level of their *vocational aspirations*, for example, professional and business with considerable responsibility, but dissimilar in the types of vocations for which they were preparing. This was due to the compromises required in their selection, as well as to curricular differences between American and European universities. With the exception of the Sicilian and American men, almost half of each group planned to become engineers. The Sicilian men planned to enter medicine, science, and business. No one in the Turkish groups planned to enter medicine. Of all the groups, only the American had any number planning to enter teaching. One-fourth to one-third of every group planned to enter business, except for the Pisans, none of whom was interested in business as a career. Finally, in contrast to the Haverford group, no more than 18 percent of any group, and none in the Ankara group, were registered in arts and letters or the humanities.

With the exception, therefore, of the Sicilian group, the cultural groups were reasonably similar with respect to paternal education, socioeconomic status, and probably level of, though not type of, aspiration. The Sicilian men may have come from less culturally and economically advantaged and probably more rural areas.

Education and intelligence. We sought to control, though crudely, for educational level and quality by studying persons of similar academic attainment from similarly selective universities in the five cultural areas. But we were unable to select men to study in terms of roughly similar intellectual ability since no measures of such ability were available for the Italian and Turkish populations. So three different measures of intelligence were given to the Italian and Turkish groups: vocabulary, conceptual ability (Wechsler-Bellevue Similarities), and a nonverbal perceptual-motor test highly predictive of total IQ (Wechsler-Bellevue Digit-Symbol). Verbal and Quantitative SAT scores had been available on the Haverford men; unfortunately, it was not possible to give these tests to the other cultural groups. As might be expected, all of the cultural groups scored in the upper ranges of each test; no statistically significant differences were found between the Italians and Turks on the tests in common. For the purposes of the cultural comparisons, I propose that the cultural groups are roughly comparable in educational attainment and intellectual level.

Cultural groups' dissimilarities. We are examining the generality of a model of maturing in diverse cultures by studying small selected groups of those cultures. How representative are our groups of their culture? This question is ambiguous. Representative of what? The "what" depends upon our purpose. We are not studying the modal American, whoever he might possibly be. Our purpose is to assess if our groups reflect their culture's values and distinctive cultural qualities, some of which we have already impressionistically identified.

I will first examine the groups' religious identification and values, and then their "personality" differences. I do not mean to use our small groups to make surreptitious statements about the Italian "national character," an enduring concept that has proved to be extraordinarily resistant to empirical identification. I want to skirt that troublesome quagmire. The research does not provide the methodological bases for establishing such a "character." Rather, I summarize the statistically significant personality differences between the cultural groups in order to illuminate how their differences may affect the adequacy of the test of the model's hypotheses. In so doing, I am *not* trying to prove the groups are "representative of their culture," however that ambiguous statement may be defined. I am only trying to illuminate how they may reflect some of the broader distinctive cultural patterns described earlier.

Value differences among cultural groups. Because of time limitations, the comparison of the values of the cultural groups was based on a background questionnaire, the types of values assessed by the Study of Values (SV), and the religious items of the Minnesota Multiphasic Personality Inventory (MMPI).

The Study of Values (Allport, Vernon and Lindzey, 1960) measures a person's relative preferences for a theoretical, economic, political, social, aesthetic, and religious way of life. A previously published Italian version of the test was used. Except for some of the religious items, the Turkish team had no difficulty translating the SV. (Appendix B offers technical comments and information about the appropriateness of using each of the tests of the research with the cultural groups.)

To secure some clues about how the cultural groups differed, their scores on the SV (and all other tests used in the research) were compared. All my observations are limited to the statistically significant (two-tailed) differences found in such comparisons. The Turkish groups valued much more highly than did the Italians and Americans the use of power and entrepreneurial skills in the political arena and marketplace. The Pisans were significantly less interested than any other group, including their fellow Sicilians, in the use of power. Quite surprisingly, given its parental background and academic aspirations, the Haverford group valued the intellectual, scholarly pursuit of truth significantly less than the Turks and Italians.

What about differences in religious preferences, the value which has been used to select the cultures as different? All of the Turks were Muslims, all the Italians were Catholic, and all but two of the Americans were Protestants and Jews. In order of preference for and commitment to traditional religious beliefs and practices, the Pisa group led the others, followed by the Haverford, Sicilian, and the two Turkish groups. The Pisa group significantly valued the religious life more highly than every other European group, including the Sicilians.

To better understand the religious differences between the three cultures, the men's replies to the fifteen items of the SV and MMPI about religious beliefs and practices were tabulated. What was remarkable, and very unexpected, was the impressive similarity in the number of Americans and Turks, in contrast to the Italians, who adhered to religious beliefs and practices. Despite the differences between Protestant-Jewish and Moslem beliefs, and the difficulties in making equivalent translations of some of the items, the percentage of Americans and Turks differing from each other was no greater than 13. The Italians, on the other hand, deviated by that amount and more on ten of the fifteen items. The following items illustrate the similarity of the Americans and Turks and their differences with the Italians: "Christ performed miracles such as changing water into wine" (Turkish equivalent: "His Holiness has performed miracles like bringing water out of the desert"): 15%, 13%, and 72%. "I believe in a life hereafter": 46%, 35%, and 70%. "I pray several times every week": 23%, 27% and 48%; "I go to church almost every week": 8%, 4%, 67%.

The higher religious value preference of the American than the Turkish groups on the Study of Values, given their impressive similarity on the MMPI items, probably reflects the multidimensional nature of the SV's religious score. It consists of items that tap interest in philosophical-ethical concerns and meaning, items that are essentially unrelated to the other items of the SV that describe typical institutionalized religious practices, which is also the type of items measured by the MMPI (Heath, 1969).

Personality trait differences among cultural groups. Here I shall organize the mass of statistical findings about the principal personality differences (significant at two-tailed levels) found between the five cultural groups into four summary impressions. Since I am making only an exploratory foray into a highly complicated issue, and have not yet described in detail the basic test scores, I do not cite the test data on which the following very abbreviated impressions are based. I shall conclude with some reflections about how such possible differences may affect the adequacy of the test of the model's hypotheses.

The first impression was that the five cultural groups were more similar than they were dissimilar in personality organization. If we compare the two most discrepant cultural groups for whom the fullest test information was available, the American and the Pisan groups did not differ significantly on more than 60 percent of the principal personality scores used in the research. To illustrate more concretely how similar the cultural groups were on just one of the measures, I shall examine how the men described themselves on a 185-item Adjective Check List (ACL). The ACL consisted of traits cited by theorists and researchers as describing mature and immature persons. By checking those adjectives he believed best described him, each man sketched a picture of himself in terms of mature and immature types of traits (Heath, 1965, 67–68). We must be cautious when comparing the American and Pisan (the ACL was not given to the Sicilians) with the Turkish groups on this test, however. The Turkish language did not have precise equivalents for about 10 percent of the adjectives. The percentage of each group checking each adjective was compared to identify which group deviated most from the others. If a group deviated by more than 30 percentage points from the other groups on a trait, it was called deviant on that trait. The four groups did not deviate from each other on 90 percent of the 185 traits. Pisans deviated on only 11 and the Haverfordians on only 6 of the 185 traits. The men of the four cultural groups did not, for example, differ in describing themselves as adaptable, cheerful, conscientious, honest, sensitive, and sincere. They believed they were not authoritarian, cold, conforming, evasive, illogical, or unemotional. As one more example of the similarity of the groups, I will summarize the amount of dissimilarity among the groups in responding to the 566 items of the MMPI. Using a slightly more stringent and complex criterion of dissimilarity, the Pisans deviated on only 56, Sicilians on 46, Istanbul men on 18, Ankarans on 10, and Americans on 6 of the 566 items from the other groups.

The second impression was so compelling that I will not describe the supporting data in detail. The two groups from the same culture were much more similar to each other than either was to any of the other groups of the remaining two cultures. The men from Istanbul and Ankara, for example, did not differ in their ratings of their own maturity on any dimensions defining the model of maturing, the maturity of their values, sources of anxiety, and on most of the other test scores. I do not imply the groups were identical. They weren't. In contrast, for example, to the judgments of the close friends of the Ankarans, the friends of the Istanbul men called them more energetic, enthusiastic and self-centered. The Istanbul men were much more complicated. Yet, neither group differed as much from each other as each did from the American and the Italian groups. The same statement can be made about the Pisans and Sicilians.

The third impression was that the five cultural groups could be ordered on a continuum of decreasing psychological similarity, with the Americans and the Sicilians at the two extremes. The American and the two Turkish groups were more similar to each other than they were to the Italian groups. My impressionistic ordering of the psychological similarity of the groups, based on the statistically significant differences between the groups, was Haverford, Ankara, Istanbul, Pisa, and Sicily. To give a flavor of what this continuum may suggest, let us consider the American group in reference to how it differed significantly from the Turkish groups. The Americans maintained much more conscious control over their impulses. They were more intellectually efficient and able to use defenses more effectively, particularly for controlling aggressive impulses. They were cognitively efficient and realistic in their judgments about threatening information. On the other hand, the Americans quite paradoxically were more accessible to all forms of primary-process thinking which was consistently more fused with less socialized emotions. These differences became progressively more pronounced in comparison to the Italians, particularly the Sicilians, who seemed to have very little accessibility to primitive dreamlike images. In terms of their relations with others, the Americans were not as sensitive to or open with others; they were more suppressive of their affectionate impulses. They did not seem to be in as much conflict with authority. But their self-esteem was much lower than that of the Turks, particularly the men from Istanbul. What was intriguing was that the Turkish groups also differed significantly from the two Italian groups in very similar ways.

The fourth and last impression was that despite the similarities among the five cultural groups, each had its own distinctive "character," a character that could affect its power to confirm the predictions of the model of maturing. To help keep the five cultural groups in mind, I will sketch each very briefly and impressionistically. Some may quarrel with these comparative assessments, and point out that the meaning of psychological test scores may not be equivalent across several cultures, that linguistic inequivalences are present, and that noncomparable subjective anchoring points affect self-report types of data. Americans may have higher expectations of what "warmth in personal relationships" means; Italians do not even have an equivalent word for "warmth;" and Turks may equate "warmth" with friendly sociability. Yet, the contextual pattern gleaned from many different tests and judges shaped these impressions, not just the statistical findings of a particular test score.

The Haverford group described itself in terms very similar to what Turks and Italians told me about Americans. More than the other groups, it labeled itself as adventurous, aggressive, capable, changeable, curious, impatient, impulsive, and intense. This strongly self-assertive push into the world seems to emerge out of insecurity and uneasiness about its more tender and dependent qualities. Independent judges confirmed the thrust of these self-descriptions. The judges rated the men as more demanding, adventurous, and independent than the Italian or Turkish judges rated the men of their groups. The Haverford men also rated themselves least empathic, spontaneously warm, understanding, and other-centered. Again, the judges confirmed this assessment by identifying these men as the most cold, as well as self-rejecting, of all the cultural groups. My interpretation of these and other significant differences between the Americans and the other cultural groups is that the men, fearing more spontaneous but too close mutual or emotional relations with others, threw themselves aggressively and impulsively into action, perhaps to reassure themselves about their own competence and worth. Of interest is that this impression does not contradict the flavor of the cultural data secured from completely different American students, as reported in Appendix A.

The Ankarans saw themselves as the least pretentious, most solid, realistic, objective, and perhaps least culturally individualistic of the cultural groups. The judges rated the group as more other-centered, warm, placid, and clearest thinking, though least self-insightful, of any of the groups. On other tests, the Ankarans were the most self-doubting, anxious, and dependent. Actually, in contrast to the other groups, the Ankarans were distinguished by the absence of a distinctive type of "character."

The men from Istanbul were without doubt the most complicated and seemingly inconsistent persons of the study. The men rated themselves to be the most intellectual, demanding, flexible, imaginative, outspoken, and talkative (which they certainly were). They judged themselves to be very mature, particularly in the integration of their values and relations with other men. Their fantasies were more regressive and dominated by stronger impulses than were those of any other group, but they were also much less well controlled. Some vivid clues about the men's views of themselves came from their replies to MMPI items like: "I am an important person": 64% versus 21% (Ankara), 46% (Haverford), 25% (Pisa), and 8% (Sicily); "I certainly feel useless at times": 11% versus 50%, 23%, 57%, and 54% respectively; or "I have difficulty in starting to do things": 32% versus 54%, 46%, 82%, and 62%. My impression from these and other data was that the men's beliefs in their own importance was partially compensatory for conflicts about their own power and masculinity. More than the men of any other cultural group, they seemed to be estranged from the feminine aspects of themselves. They were the most anxious group about their own aggression, particularly toward maternal figures, and about being rejected and receiving love. Were the men in severe conflict about traditional Turkish authoritarian ideas of a male's sexual role with women? To maintain their own self-esteem, the men overemphasized their importance and ability, they also reassured themselves about their potency by persistent conscious preoccupation with heterosexuality, which emerged in the number of such images they projected onto the Rorschach blots.

The men of the Pisa group had very complicated interior lives and seemed almost tortured in their self-criticalness. They described themselves as apathetic, defensive, excitable, indecisive, rigid, scattered, and unfriendly, judgments that were strikingly and consistently confirmed by independent judges and their close friends. Although they were much less accessible to very primitive forms of primary process than the Americans and Turks, they scored consistently higher on moodiness, depression, and hypochondriasis. They were the most introspective group. With their fellow Italians, the Sicilians, they seem most estranged in their intimate relationships with others, as was poignantly revealed in their replies to the following MMPI items: "I frequently have to fight against showing that I am bashful": 89% (Pisa) and 81% (Sicily), versus 31% (Haverford), 46% (Ankara), and 29% (Istanbul); "I wish I were not so shy": 82% and 62%, versus 31%, 42%, and 14% respectively; "No one cares much what happens to you": 82% and 81%, versus 38%, 38%, and 50%. The tenor of these and other replies was one of pessimism, resignation, suspicion of others, feelings of being misunderstood, and lack of spontaneity in their relationships. The Pisans seemed to be struggling to fashion an inner coherence, a struggle that kept them from being preoccupied with affairs of the world. Again, this sketch is very similar to that of the Italians already given, as well as in Appendix A.

The men of the Sicilian group were puzzling. The judges rated them as more mature on the largest number of traits, including imagination, reflectiveness, realism, and fulfilling their potential. Yet, on tests measuring these traits, the Sicilians were impressively unreflective and unimaginative. Other evidence suggests that the judges' ratings were not very reliable. The Sicilian group seemed to be simpler, more fun loving, outwardly directed, and gregarious. More than the men of the other groups, they thought of themselves as good mixers and enjoyed being with others. Yet, as we have seen with the Pisans, their sociability may have been defensive, for they also gave the impression of distrusting too intimate relations with others. Only within the proverbially closeknit Italian family did the Sicilians and Pisans report a sense of belongingness and support. To the MMPI item, "My relatives are nearly all in sympathy with me," 85% of the Sicilians and 96% of the Pisans, but only 23% of the Americans, 25% of the Ankarans, and 21% of the Istanbul men agreed. For the item, "I have been quite independent and free from family rule," the corresponding figures were 39% and 21%, versus 69%, 79%, and 57%. The inner and outer lives of the Sicilians seemed to be discrepant and at odds with each other. Like the Pisans they thought of themselves as having difficulty taking "care of things" because of an inability to function 62% (Sicily) and 89% (Pisa), versus 31% (Haverford), 42% (Ankara), and 25% (Istanbul). The majority did not report themselves to be very happy. To "I am happy most of the time," only 42% of the Sicilians and 36% of the Pisans, but 81% of the Americans, 67% of the Ankarans, and 79% of the Istanbul men responded affirmatively. It was the most homogeneous group, and, given the small population from which it was selected, had fewer very immature persons in it.

The American and Turkish students seemed to be fighting the battle of autonomy from parental domination, control, and dependency. The Italians, particularly the Pisans, seemed to be preoccupied with the integration of their personal-familial with their social-outer lives. Barzini identified what turned out to be a persistent interpretive problem with the data of the Italian groups when he wrote,

> Most Italians still obey a double standard. There is one code valid within the family circle, with relatives . . . intimate friends and close associates, and there is another code regulating life outside. Within, they assiduously demonstrate all the qualities which are not usually attributed to them by superficial observers: they are relatively reliable, honest, truthful, just, obedient, generous, disciplined, brave, and capable of self-sacrifices. . . . the Italians' family loyalty is their true patriotism (1964, 194).

The Cultural Groups and the Model of Maturing

The five cultural groups are both similar and dissimilar. They are roughly similar in intellectual level, educational attainment, paternal (though not maternal) educational background, socioeconomic background (with the exception of the Sicilians), level of vocational aspiration, and in a large number of personality traits. The groups did not so differ on any of those factors that the differences threaten to obscure the interpretation of the relation of cultural values to maturing.

The groups did differ in their religious identification and in the pattern of some of their values. The American and Turkish groups were similar but the Italian groups were quite dissimilar in the degree of their religious commitment and frequency of religious participation. The fact that the groups differed in their religious identities and some of their values thus supported our hope of studying diverse cultures.

The American, Turkish, and Italian groups, however, did differ consistently in certain significant ways that may affect their ability to confirm some hypotheses of the model. The nature of these differences suggests that we probably cannot expect a clear unequivocal confirmation of the complete model of maturing by any one or all of the cultural groups. The Haverford men, for example, seem to be very self-assertive, controlled, achieving persons. But such focused goal achievement may be either compensatory for inadequate maturing, or distortive of interpersonal maturing. The men may not have adequately integrated their emotional needs with their concepts of themselves. The group may be limited in its allocentric and integrative maturing, particularly interpersonally.

My hunch is that the youthful Turks' conflict with authority, their struggle to control strong aggressive impulses, together with their openness to affectionate and sexual needs, even though they are in conflict about them, may confuse any generalized relationship between impulse expression and control. The cultural conflict between a Moslem and a Western identity, most acute in the Istanbul group, may adversely affect predicted relationships between self-esteem, which may be defensively compensatory, and other measures of maturity, particularly stability and autonomy.

Finally, the Pisan and Sicilian groups seemed to reflect Barzini's observations about the difficulty Italians generally have in integrating their private familial roles with their public social ones. *La bella figura* is a dominant cultural value, and may adversely affect the confirmation of the predictions about integration and its relation to other measures of maturity.

Summary

We have so far tentatively identified some of the principal ways in which the American, Turkish, and Italian cultures are both similar and dissimilar to each other. The three cultures are sufficiently diverse to provide a fair test of the generality of the model of maturing.

It was meaningful to ask nonpsychologists to identify mature persons in different cultures. The judges were able to reach agreement about who were the more mature and immature men of their institutions.

The cultural groups resembled each other in numerous ways, such as intellectual level and socio-economic background, that should not complicate our interpretation of the findings. But they did differ in seemingly culturally patterned ways and so created reservations about how clearly we can confirm the predictions of the model of maturing on all of the cultural groups. Insofar as the differences identified from the data are culturally patterned and affect both the mature and immature men similarly, the mature men may not have "freed" themselves of the immaturing effects of such values enough to be clearly distinguished from the immature men. Different cultural values and expectations create different problems in maturing. The challenge is, given cultures that selectively encourage and inhibit different patterns of maturing, can we still identify a core pattern common to the three cultures that confirms the principal hypotheses of the model of maturing?

CHAPTER 4

Procedures and Tests for Assessing the Model of Maturing

No replicated studies of a variety of samples of competent and mature persons exist. We have, therefore, no systematically accumulated knowledge about competence and maturity, and little certainty about what measures most vividly index them. Remarkably few standardized tests were available when this research was initiated that adequately indexed the hypotheses of the model of maturing. So the effort to map the broad terrain of cultural similarities in maturity was necessarily, and still remains, very exploratory.

Several methodological principles guided the exploration. First, the elusiveness of terms like *maturity* and *psychological health* required using a variety of holistic measures that might tap their complexity. Tests of adjustment like the MMPI and Rorschach that cast a net over a wide range of traits were used to tie the model of maturity to other concepts and methods. Such tests, I hoped, might also reveal aspects of maturity and immaturity not predicted by the model of maturing. Second, the person as a complex evolving system had to be studied at different levels of functioning from several perspectives. So I relied on independent judgments of judges, self-descriptions, standardized and specially designed questionnaires, measures of performance, and tests like the Rorschach that tapped less conscious but complex imaginative organizing processes. I also hoped that by using an intensive multifaceted assessment approach, I would avoid the criticisms that LeVine made of transcultural studies of personality, when he identified the too-restrictive use of inadequate personality tests and the failure to study individuals in depth as their critical limitations (1973). Third, exploratory research must first identify, no matter how crudely, the territory's boundaries and principal prominences before it begins to construct highly refined measures of any hills and valleys. To do otherwise is to risk designing highly reliable, psychometrically impeccable measures of prominences that upon investigation are not there. To complement, however, this predominantly exploratory stance, a systematic, focused experimental study was made of what I anticipated to be a critical attribute of a mature person, namely, the ability to maintain cognitive stability in the face of stress. The research can most accurately be viewed as a progressive distillation that is meant to filter out some statements about which attributes and methods most powerfully index competence and maturing in different cultures.

This chapter describes the training of the professional staffs, translation and experimental procedures, indices of general level of maturity and healthiness, and then the measures defining the specific components of the model. Reporting on the scope and complexity of the research, together with the use of specially designed tests for the study, poses a problem: the risk of surfeiting a reader with too much technical information and so obscuring the principal outlines of the research. So I shall briefly describe each test and the relation of its scores to the hypotheses of the model in this chapter, and relegate additional technical information about the translation, administration, and scoring problems that may have affected the reliability of the cultural groups' results to Appendix B. Appendix C defines and Appendix D collates the specific test scores used to index the hypotheses of the model.[1]

Procedures of the Study

Staff training procedures. A professional team was formed for each cultural area. It consisted of a psychologist on the faculty of the participating university who supervised the team, a psychologist to

[1] Technical information about the construction, reliability, and validity of the measures can be found in previous publications (Heath, 1965, 1968) and material deposited with NAPS.

be the experimenter, an assistant responsible for the selection of the men, and a secretary. No member of any team was aware of the model of maturing in detail; few knew of the model even in general terms.

To compare patterns of findings across five cultural areas required that the research procedures be replicated *precisely*. Each experimenter was trained to act in a standard way as defined by a detailed self-teaching manual describing the procedures step-by-step. With the exception of the Sicilian experimenter, who had less time, each had four months to master the procedures. Since a student's response to tests like the Rorschach may be influenced by the experimenter's attitude, emphasis was placed on developing a "clinical" attitude and rapport.

I supervised the training of each experimenter, relying heavily on role-playing techniques. Although I had learned Italian prior to the initiation of the research, skilled translators were used to communicate the more technical aspects of the research. The Turkish teams spoke English. When ready, the experimenters tested two students for practice. Tape recordings of the practice sessions were used to monitor mastery of test procedures. Finally, each experimenter administered the entire test procedure to me. After he began the actual testing program, I reviewed his first few protocols to assess his adherence to the standards of the research, and then rechecked the protocols on subsequent supervisory visits to each site. To check the uniformity of test administration, as well as to secure verbatim recordings of the imaginative material for subsequent analysis, parts of the procedure were tape recorded for each participant. Differences in test administration among the experimenters that might have unduly affected the results could thereby be determined—differences which did in fact occur.

Translation procedures. Much critical attention has been given in recent years to the methodological problems involved in creating test items that are linguistically equivalent across cultures (Brislin, Lonner, and Thorndike, 1973; Triandis, 1972a; Werner and Campbell, 1970). I used the preferred back-translation and a modified committee procedure (Brislin, Lonner, and Thorndike, 1973), teams of bilingually expert nationals, and informal pretesting procedures, as well as internal statistical checks of the tests' results to assess the psychological equivalency of the test scores. Because I was comparing mature and immature men *within* a culture rather than directly comparing groups *between* cultures, the problems of creating exactly equivalent test items, while severe for some tests used in the research, were not crippling. Idiosyncratic test items would presumably affect the mature and immature criterion groups within a culture similarly. Post-experimental interviews did not reveal any comments that the test items were inappropriate, ambiguous, or awkward. Nor did the local experimenters express any reservations about the translations. Appendix B reports the translation problems encountered with specific tests, as well as the steps taken to determine if the psychological meaning of a test was reasonably equivalent among the cultural groups. It was not unreasonable to expect such equivalence. Studies of the factorial similarity of translated American personality and attitudinal tests in cultures as diverse as Japan, Samoa, India, Finland, Switzerland, and others have demonstrated transcultural comparability in major though not necessarily minor factor patterns (Cattell, Schmidt, and Pawlik, 1973; Comrey, 1960; Cummings, Harnett, and Schmidt, 1972; Gordon, 1967).

During the first four months of the project, two bilingual teams of three persons each translated all of the instructions and materials into Italian and Turkish. No English was used at any time during the research. The translators were local Italians and Turks who were highly proficient in English. One member translated a test into Italian, for example; a different person, not familiar with the English text, then translated the translation back into English. The teams worked back and forth between the English and Italian translations until an English translation was produced similar to the original. At this point, a third highly fluent person from the culture then independently examined both the English and Italian editions for their equivalency. Numerous subtle changes had to be made in the Italian edition of some tests. For example, Italians do not have a word for "warmth," so suitable alternatives had to be created.

Due to the difficult structure of its language, the Turkish team encountered more imposing and time-consuming problems. The team was forced to alter the prescribed procedure. Two members of the team each independently translated a test into Turkish and then agreed on a common translation. To determine how the individually translated items were perceived by Turkish students, the translated tests were administered to groups of them. Then the tests were re-edited where necessary. The Istanbul supervisor, who had been trained as a clinical psychologist in America, then reviewed the English and Turkish translations for similarity of meaning. To check the final proposed translation, small groups of bilingual Turkish students interpreted the meaning of the test items. Other more formal ratings were used to test the meaning of translated items. The team had considerable difficulty translating tests such as the Adjective Check List in which single, rather than several, words carried the intended meaning. Words like "authoritarian," "deliberate," and "quick" can be translated by either of two words that give their positive or negative connotations. Or words like "impulsive," "bottled-up," "tender-minded," and words prefixed by "self-" have no precise single word equivalents; so, in consultation with me, phrases were substituted.

Once the materials had been translated, they were professionally printed, collated, and arranged in a coded folder for each participant.

After completing the test of a participant, some test protocols, like the Rorschach, were retranslated into idiomatic English for analysis. A different bilingual team of two to three translators worked on each culture's material. The translators were Americans this time who had lived in Italy or Turkey for many years, and who were highly proficient in Italian or Turkish. Each translator translated all of the protocols of only one test, thus ensuring consistency in the translations for the different tests. The Italian team worked directly from the verbatim notes of the experimenters and the tape recordings of the sessions. The Turkish protocols were typed first in Turkish and then translated from the typed copies. This more complicated procedure was required because of the nature of the Turkish language, and the very sensitive judgments required with respect to the connotations of the material. The Turkish translations were checked by the supervisor for accuracy.

Experimental procedure. The tests and experiments took eight hours and were given in five sessions to each individual of each group, except the Sicilians. The individual sessions were distributed over three to five weeks. The following overview briefly describes the tests, and identifies their purposes and the order of their presentation. The remainder of the chapter discusses each test in detail.

Test Session	Procedure	Estimated Minutes
1	Orientation to project and background questionnaire.	15
	Three tests of intellectual abilities.	20
	Adjective Check List (ACL): provided self-ratings about traits of maturity.	10
	Self-Image Questionnaire procedure (SIQ): private and social-self instructions were counterbalanced to provide data for measuring the dimensional maturity of the self-concept. Also the SIQ provided a general measure of self-and social-self-esteem.	15
	Study of Values (SV): provided data about value preferences of the men.	20
	Self-Image Questionnaire (SIQ): alternate instructions were given.	15
	Names of two adults and two friends secured: the two friends later completed the SIQ about the participant to assess accuracy of symbolizing the self-concept.	5

Total time 100 min.

2	Rorschach: provided general index of psychological healthiness and primary-process scores, measuring maturity of cognitive skills.	75
	Perceived Self Questionnaire (PSQ): provides comprehensive measure of maturity in terms of the model, as well as scores of dimensional hypotheses.	20
	Valuator Test: measures maturity of values.	5

Total time 100 min.

3	Minnesota Multiphasic Personality Inventory (MMPI): provided a general measure of maladjustment and specific scores indexing maturity of interpersonal relations.	45

Phrase Association Test (PT): a measure of amount of anxiety about different interpersonal types of information.   20

Total time 65 min.

4 Experimental study of cognitive stability: administration of three tests of cognitive skill whose content was the anxiety-arousing information of the PT. Two alternate forms of each skill test were systematically randomized and given across two sessions separated by at least three days to test for resiliency of the men in recovering their cognitive efficiency after their induced disorganization in this session. Order of skill test presentation and intertest sequences were matched for a mature-immature pair of men.

Total time 95 min.

5 Self-Image Questionnaire (SIQ): re-administered to test for stability and provide base-line for measuring autonomy of self-concept.   10
Experimental study of cognitive stability.   90
Phrase Association Test (PT): re-administered to secure stable anxiety threshold scores.   20
Test of autonomy of self-concept (SIQ)   10

Total time 130 min.

Discussion of reactions to tests with participants

Two friends and three or four of the student-faculty selection judges independently completed the SIQ about the participant three to five months following his participation in the research.

The Sicilian group received an abbreviated set of tests in three different sessions. Omitted were an intelligence test, the ACL, the cognitive skill procedure, and one of the PT test administrations. The group also took the Cultural Semantic Test and the Cultural Valuator Test (reported in Chapter 3 and Appendix A) following the completion of the formal test procedure.

The Haverford group's procedure was essentially similar, but it had not been given the PSQ and Valuator tests which had been developed as a consequence of the initial confirmation of the broad outlines of the model of maturing on three American groups.

Measures of General Personal Functioning

Social index of maturity. The groups studied had been selected on the basis of the number of judges who identified their members to be mature or immature. The men of each group were ordered from most to least mature in terms of the number of judges who had selected them. The mature person selected by the largest number of judges was assigned a rank of one; the least mature person selected by the largest number was assigned the last rank. The others were ordered accordingly. Such an ordinal scale is, of course, very crude. However, previous studies that used a similar ordering procedure demonstrated its usefulness in spite of its methodological faults. Given the compromises made in the selection of the Pisa, Sicily, and Ankara groups, and the different numbers of judges involved in selecting the Pisa and Ankara groups, the reliability of these ranks is very suspect indeed. How might we check their adequacy? Three to five months after their initial judgments, two to four of the faculty and student judges who were most intimately acquainted with a participant rated him on thirty trait scales descriptive of maturity. The ratings could be summed to provide an index of maturity.[1] These scores were converted into ranks to determine their relation to the social index of maturity. All of the correlations were significant— Haverford (.85), Ankara (.67), Istanbul (.83), Pisa (.62), and Sicily (.46)— indicating that the social index is a reasonably adequate predictor of behavioral traits associated with maturity for the cultural groups, with the questionable exception of the Sicilians.

Self-Image Questionnaire measures of esteem (SIQ). The SIQ consists

1 The judges did not know if the men had been selected as mature or immature; nor had they necessarily selected the person originally to be mature or immature.

of thirty bipolar scales, each of which has eight positions (see Fig. 4 – 1) that provide a measure of the degree to which the respondent agrees with the item. Each scale defines a trait selected to summarize the principal traits defining maturing listed in the Adjective Check List. For example:

Figure 4-1

Realistic	Unrealistic
Has good judgment and common sense; makes practical and appropriate comments and decisions.	Makes impractical, inappropriate suggestions that don't consider all aspects of a problem; others do not rely on his judgments.

| ☐ | ☒ | ☐ | ☐ | ☐ | ☐ | ☐ | ☐ |

The mature and immature ends of the scales were randomized to control for response biases. The person selects which side of the scale best describes him and then checks one of the four boxes. If he believes he is extremely realistic, he checks the far left box. In this example a person has checked himself as highly reliable. The test's theoretical rationale, structure, reliability and validity have been described elsewhere (Heath, 1965, 1968).

By assigning score values to each of the eight boxes in terms of their increasing maturity, and then summing up a person's scored ratings for the scales, a total score representing maturity in terms of the traits checked can be secured. For example, the person marking himself as highly realistic above received a score of +7.

Several different types of "maturity" scores can be secured. The private self-ratings of each person can be scored to secure an indirect index of his own judged maturity. To distinguish the SIQ's "maturity" scores from those of other measures, they are called "esteem" scores. The ratings a person makes when describing his social self, that is, completing the ratings as he believes others who know him well would rate him to be like, can be scored and summed similarly to give a social self-esteem score. Finally, the ratings independent judges made of each man on the SIQ scales can be scored and summed similarly to produce a judge esteem score. Unless explicitly specified, the SIQ judge esteem score is based on the independent ratings of two close friends of the men. The friends knew nothing about the research. Both the private and social self-esteem scores were significantly related to judge esteem scores for every cultural group except the Istanbul group (see Table B–1, Appendix B).

The esteem (or maturity) scores can be easily misinterpreted. They do *not* represent a single judgment by the participant or by judges of maturity. Persons completing the SIQ do not know it measures traits of "maturity." The scores are indirect and disguised, so they are not influenced by bias or deliberate efforts to appear "mature" as a single rating about one's maturity would be.

Rorschach index of psychological healthiness. The Rorschach is the most widely used clinical test for assessing psychological health. What a person sees and how he organizes what he sees in an ink blot reflects enduring traits and needs not readily symbolizable. The Rorschach was administered as prescribed by Klopfer, except that each man was given a maximum of three minutes to "associate" to each blot. A standardized inquiry was then conducted. To insure accurate and complete protocols, the procedure was recorded on tape, subsequently typed, and translated for scoring. Appendix B provides more details about the reliability of the Rorschachs of the cultural groups, and suggests that the Haverford, Pisa, and Ankara results are more reliable than the others.

The Rorschach elicts complex imaginative responses that provide rich information about a person that can be scored in several ways.[1] The test has been under attack for many years. A recent positive critique of its usefulness in crosscultural studies urged that it be incorporated within a multifaceted assessment battery to establish its concurrent validity for the cultural groups being studied (Abel, 1974), a recommendation I followed in this study. Certain ways of using the test have been more fruitful than others in studying maturing (1965, 1968). The test has provided, for example, useful information about which to make judgments of the "healthiness" of a person's personality. A distinguished diagnostician, Roy Schafer, had evaluated the Rorschachs of the Haverford men without any knowledge whatsoever of the study and of the men. He checked a standard line scale for the degree to which each man was a maturely organized person. Using his criteria of healthy organization, I similarly rated other Haverford groups participating in the earlier research. Our ratings significantly predicted the social index of maturity as well as other measures of maturity and adjustment (1965). I made similar clinical ratings of

1 Each protocol was scored for Klopfer categories. Appendix C describes scores used to index the dimensions of the model of maturing.

the psychological healthiness of the Italian and Turkish participants' Rorschachs. Appendix B, describes the rating procedure and its reliability in detail.[1]

Perceived Self Questionnaire measure of maturity (PSQ). A fifty-item questionnaire, PSQ, was developed to measure the basic components of the model. The maturity of interpersonal relationships was divided into two subcategories: male and female relationships. Each of the resultant twenty-five components of the model was indexed by two scales (sample items are given below). Its form was similar to that of the SIQ and is illustrated in Figure 4–2, which shows the item that indexes cognitive stability. A person checks one of the eight boxes as indicated.

Figure 4–2

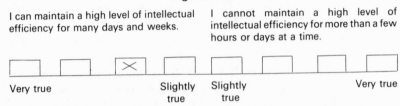

I can maintain a high level of intellectual efficiency for many days and weeks.   I cannot maintain a high level of intellectual efficiency for more than a few hours or days at a time.

Very true   Slightly true   Slightly true   Very true

Items indexing the same dimension and the mature-immature ends of the bipolar scales were randomized. The person is not told what the test measures.

For scoring, the end box of the scale indexing the most mature position was weighted eight, the next most mature position seven, and so on. The higher the score for the two items of each component of the model, the more maturely did the person rate himself. By summing the scores for each of the two items across the five dimensions defining the maturity of cognitive skills, for example, or for the ten items measuring symbolization, scores measuring the degree of maturing in terms of the basic hypotheses of the research were secured. The scores measuring dimensional and structural maturity were not completely independent, since, for example, the

1 Schafer's criteria can be categorized in terms of the model of maturing. *Symbolization*: presence of and quality of originally organized images; constrictedness of the record. *Allocentricism*: accuracy with which an image (including affectively organized images, *i.e.*, FC, CF, C) was accommodated to the blot; number of popular types of images organized around human activities. *Integration*: presence of skill impairment including the amount of inadequately integrated images. *Stability*: quality and rapidity of recovery after giving regressive images. *Autonomy*: amount and severity of morbid content. Presence of playful and humorous images index freed affect that results from maturing.

score measuring maturity of cognitive skills included scores for two of the items measuring symbolization. By summing the scores for all fifty items, one can secure a total score indexing maturity as defined by the model.

More extended discussion of the PSQ, its test form, slightly altered for the cultural groups, reliability and validity data can be found elsewhere (Heath, 1968). Appendix B provides additional validity data, and suggests that only the PSQ responses of the Istanbul group may not be as reliable as those of the other groups. Appendix C defines the principal PSQ measures of the model.·

Minnesota Multiphasic Personality Inventory index of psychological mal-adjustment (MMPI). The MMPI consists of 566 items describing different behaviors. Although its pervasive psychopathological emphasis has not made it very useful for research on healthy, competent persons, its basic scales can be averaged to yield a summary index of degree of psychological maladjustment.[1] Some other scales constructed using MMPI items, while not well validated, were useful for indexing specific, particularly interpersonal, hypotheses of the model of maturing. Appendix C describes these scores. Appendix B reports additional information about the cultural equivalence of the MMPI, and suggests the MMPI results of the Istanbul group may not be as reliable as those of the other cultural groups.

Tests of the Dimensions of Maturing

It is now time to describe how the maturity of a person's cognitive skills, values, self-concept, and interpersonal relations was actually measured. The specific tests used to determine how mature and immature men differed are the operational definitions of the model's hypotheses.

Measures of cognitive maturity. Cognitive maturity is defined by the degree to which intellective processes are symbolizable, allocentric, integrated, stable, and autonomous. Psychologists have long sought ways to measure individual differences in cognitive functioning, but their traditional measures of sheer intellectual or abstract conceptual ability predict to too narrow a domain of human

---

[1] Factorial studies identify a pervasive neuroticism factor underlying the separate MMPI scales. The total MMPI score gives an approximate index of such maladjustment (Mf and Si scales not included).

competence for our purposes, that is, primarily academic performance (Wallach, 1972). We needed to test how effectively a person cognitively dealt with a wider range of adaptive problems, problems that involved his values, self-concept, and interpersonal relationships.

The strategy for measuring the dimensions of the model was to rely on self-assessment methods and performance tests that directly measured, for example, the maturity of a person's cognitive skills.

The Perceived Self-Questionnaire was the one method that tapped a person's assessment of his maturity on all dimensions of the model. Examples of the mature pole of the PSQ's ten bipolar scales measuring cognitive maturity are

My thinking is usually consistent, precise, and takes into account the full complexity of a problem (integration).

My thinking usually remains efficient and clear when I encounter intellectual ideas that are personally disturbing (stability).

By summing how maturely a person rated his cognitive skills to be over the ten items, a score indexing cognitive maturity was obtained.

More compelling empirically would be measures of a person's actual cognitive effectiveness. Two principal approaches to this difficult problem were taken: use of Robert Holt's method for scoring primary process in the Rorschach (1960, 1968), and the development of an experimental procedure to assess how stably organized were the men's cognitive skills.

Rorschach primary process scores. In contrast to other tests of cognitive functioning, the Rorschach ink blots provide minimal constraints on cognition, and no *explicit* demands for secondary process or more logical conceptual thought. The person is told to say what he sees in the blots. He is *not* told to report what he is certain actually fits the structure of the blot, or what makes most logical sense to him. He does *not* have to accommodate his thought to a given external standard except as he defines for himself what the standard should be. A person thus defines for himself the interpretive task. Much of the difficulty encountered in reliably interpreting, not to mention validating, the maturity of a person's cognitive functions from his Rorschach comes from the ambiguity of the adaptive task.[1] The amorphous structure of the blots and the

1 Holt has commented, "It remains . . . [to be decided] to what extent different types of *S*s can and do modify the types of responses they give when the definition of the situation is

ambiguity of the instructions accentuate the production of images and ideas organized more around personal motives and memories than around reality-given information. However, the inkblots do have some organization. They are, for example, symmetrical, and consist of different sized gestalts. How a person accommodates to the structural properties of the blot, as well as how he organizes his own ideas and images are clues to the maturity of his thought.

It is characteristic of the primary process, as Freud discovered (1900), that it occurs outside of awareness, except under special conditions; expresses the most personal autocentric wishes; is coordinated or integrated by more primitive than conventional logical standards; is elusively shifting and unstable; and is primarily determined by earlier repressed memories and unresolved emotional conflicts. In other words, primary processes are the opposite of the symbolized, allocentric, integrated, stable, and autonomous secondary processes that describe more logical orderly thought. Although Holt's scores were not explicitly designed to measure the dimensions of maturing, they, and others derived from them, are the best approximations of immature and regressive cognitive processes that I know. Certainly, for example, his measure of formal thought disorganization indexes immature ways of integrating ideas with each other. It includes, for example, condensations like the fusion of two distinct images into an unrealistic one, and combinations of images in logically contradictorily ways. Or, a measure of the extent to which a person's thought is not autonomous, that is, pervaded by intensely unacceptable drives, can also be derived.

Those who know the Rorschach well know how subtle and complex these organizing processes are. Holt has created two sets of sophisticated scores that objectively measure 1) the degree to which a person's images and ideas have been organized by primary process, and 2) the adequacy with which primitive and anxiety arousing images are integrated with and controlled by defenses that make the idea more socially acceptable.[1]

---

modified from one that encourages the secondary process to one that encourages the primary. The research of Ackman (1960) shows that a direct encouragement of college students to be freely imaginative causes significant changes in certain types of scoring categories" (Unpubl. manual, 1968, ix).

[1] More detailed analyses of the theoretical rationale of Holt's scores, their relation to the dimensions that define maturing, discussions of the technical scores, evidence about their reliability, and extensive data about their validity can be found elsewhere (Heath, 1965).

But Holt warns us that the interpretation of excessive amounts of drive-organized images in fantasy is more complex than I have suggested (Holt, 1968). Compare these images given by two Istanbul men to the same area of the same blot:

Student A: "A thing like a black groove . . . stretched upwards. It doesn't remind me of a male organ or such. A nail driven into a pedestal." In the inquiry, he said, "White, erect. There's something there. It aroused the sensation of metal in me."

Student B: "The lower middle part again reminds me of female sex organ. Yes, this is all I can see here." (His voice trembles.) In the inquiry, he said, "Again, it reminds me of that. Again it would resemble many other things but there's nothing special about this."

The sexual images in each are scored by Holt as similar in intensity of aroused libido. Yet, Student B's response is more "mature," even though his voice trembled, indicating he may have been anxious about what he saw. He showed more intellectual control over his image, for it more accurately fit the blot than did the image of Student A. He also accepted his image without abortive efforts to deny the significance of what he had seen. Student A, on the other hand, apparently saw an erect male organ and tried to deny its presence by substituting a driven nail for it. But his substitute response did not successfully eliminate the preoccupation with the erect penis. In the inquiry he returned to speak of the nail as white, erect, and evoking a "sensation of metal" (hardness?) in him, words that fail to disguise adequately the libidinal feelings associated with seeing the erect "male organ."

The significance of an image organized by primary process must be understood in terms of how the individual marshalls his cognitive resources to cope with it. Several scores that measure the effectiveness of a person's defenses as well as his accuracy in accommodating his images to the blot have consistently predicted maturity in diverse American groups (Heath, 1965, 1968).

Holt's scores capture some of the systemic complexity of our ideas about cognitive maturity. But it should be clear even from this brief discussion that the assessment of the maturity of a person's thought is not a simple task to be precisely measured by factorially, and elegantly, pure, independent, unidimensional tests. Appendix B assesses the reliability of the primary process and control scores of the cultural groups; Appendix C describes the Holt scores that most saliently indexed cognitive maturing

Measures of cognitive stability. While Holt's scores measure cognitive maturing generally, their complexity precludes their precise and univocal identification with the specific dimensions defining cognitive maturity. The next four tests were specifically designed to test experimentally the hypothesis that mature men have more *stably* organized cognitive skills. In Chapter 1 I discussed the reasons for studying this component of the model in such depth, as well as the efficiency of certain cognitive skills rather than of others.

The stability of a person's cognitive skills can be tested by determining how well he thinks conceptually about, analyzes and synthesizes with, and makes realistic judgments about ideas that are personally threatening, that is, that have intensely disturbing emotional connotations for him. A mature person should be able to maintain secondary process thinking intact when reasoning with such emotionally intense ideas. If his thought were disrupted he should recover his cognitive efficiency more rapidly than an immature person would do. These two predictions defined the meaning of "stable cognitive skills," and were tested with the Haverford, Pisa, and Turkish groups. There was insufficient time to complete the skill tests with the Sicilians.[1]

The predictions were not easily tested. We had to control for two confounding variables. Sheer level of intellectual ability must be equated between the mature and immature men, else differences in reasoning with emotional ideas could be more parsimoniously explained by intellectual power alone. The intensity of the emotional ideas with which the men were to think must also be controlled. For if the immature men were found to be less stable cognitively, their inefficiency could be due to the greater anxiety associated with the ideas used, rather than to differences in skill in solving conflictual problems.

Since we have measures of intellectual ability for the men, we can control for its effects statistically if the mature and immature men differ intellectually.

How shall we determine if the emotional intensity of the ideas the men are to reason with is similar for the mature and immature groups? How shall we measure such intensity so we can control for

---

1 Extensive discussion of the tests, rationale, history, construction, reliabilities and validities can be found elsewhere (Heath, 1965).

its effects if they do differ? Psychoanalystic theorists have been preoccupied with those personal relationships that are most anxiety-arousing at different periods in development. Ideas about maternal and paternal rejection, hostility toward mother and father, and heterosexual and homosexual relations (hereafter called *threatening* information) were likely to be more anxiety-arousing than ideas about receiving affection, working cooperatively, or playfully relaxing (hereafter called *nonthreatening* information).

The Phrase Association Test (PT). I describe the PT briefly, since its rationale, structure, relation to the model of maturing, reliability and studies of its validity, including physiological correlates, have already been published (Heath, 1956, 1965; Mandler, Mandler, Kremen and Sholiton, 1961; Rosenwald, 1972). The experimenter recites thirty-six five word phrases, for instance, "He cursed the old lady," to each of which the person responds as rapidly as possible with the first phrase or sentence that comes to mind. Each threatening and nonthreatening theme is represented by four different phrases interspersed through the total list of phrases. The entire procedure was recorded on tape; the verbatim replies of the men were subsequently typed, translated, and scored by two independent judges.

The heart of the test is its scoring system, which can be adapted to assess the anxiety threshold for any type of information. A response to a phrase is scored for the amount of anxiety it arouses as indexed by twenty different scores. For example, a response that is *excessive in length, contradicting the meaning* of the phrase, and given in a *fragmented* way would be scored three—one point for each anxiety indicator. The total number of anxiety scores for the four phrases of each theme provide the anxiety-threshold measure for that information. Similarly, the sum of all the anxiety scores measures a person's general anxiety level to the test's disturbing information. The threatening information has consistently elicited significantly more anxiety scores than the nonthreatening information for every group, as well as for every person ever tested prior to the cultural studies. The Italian and Turkish groups also gave significantly more anxiety responses to the threatening than to the nonthreatening information, though in every group there were one to three persons who responded to the nonthreatening rather than to the threatening information with more anxiety. I conclude that the threatening content used in the skill tests was indeed of greater emotional intensity than the nonthreatening ideas. Appendix B discusses the reliability of the cultural groups' PT scores. The Istanbul and Sicilian groups' scores were least reliable. Appendix C defines the principal scores used in later analyses.

Thematic Concept Test (TCT). The TCT measured how well the mature and immature men conceptualized the threatening and nonthreatening information included in the PT. Explanation of the TCT, test examples, reliability coefficients and personality correlates have been published elsewhere (Heath, 1965). The TCT will be only briefly described here. Appendix B describes the reliability of the cultural groups' results, and Appendix C the specific scores measuring conceptual ability.

The TCT was modeled on Bruner's work on concept formation (1956). Sixty-four different instances of each type of information,[1] representing all combinations of three attributes describing the two people for each theme, were displayed on a board—for example, the sixty-four aggressive cards represented all combinations of adult (mother-father) and child (son-daughter), attacking or protecting, and holding or not holding a stick. As was true for the remaining skill tests, practice items were used to insure understanding of the task. When given an instance of a concept, the person identified its remaining three instances by selecting a similar card. He was told whether it was a correct instance or not. Each person had five minutes to discover the correct three instances. Conceptual efficiency was measured by combining time for solving the problem with number of errors made.

To test the prediction that mature persons would recover more rapidly from being cognitively disrupted than immature persons, the TCT, like the remaining two skill tests, was divided into two equivalent forms. One form was given in a systematically randomized way three to five days later in the next session. Rate of improvement between the first and the second administration was expected to be greater for the mature men. Each form consisted of six conceptual problems, one for each type of threatening and nonthreatening information. To compare conceptual efficiency with the different types of information, the number of attributes, difficulty of concept, order of concept as well as of test form presentation, and administration procedures were controlled for.

Thematic Analysis-Synthesis Test (TAS). The TAS test

---

1 Parental rejection and receiving affection themes were not included in skill tests because of lack of time. The sexual concept problems were replaced by aggressive problems due to local Italian objections.

measured the efficiency with which the men analyzed and synthesized the disturbing information used in the PT and TCT. Detailed information about the TAS similar to that for the other tests can be found elsewhere (Heath, 1965).

The TAS consisted of twenty-four scrambled sentences. Each of the threatening and nonthreatening themes was represented by four different sentences. Two minutes were allowed to rearrange physically the scrambled words to make a grammatically correct and sensible ten-word sentence. To complicate the analytic task, two additional words were added to the ten words of each sentence that could not be combined with the others to produce a correct solution. An example of a father-son aggressive sentence is:

death some was old on herd challenged the males leader by young

To compare analytic efficiency for the different themes required that the variables that make one sentence more difficult to solve than another be controlled. Sentence length, grammatical structure, word and sentence order, presentation order of the two forms, and differential numbers of alternative scorable sentences were all controlled.

A high analytic efficiency score could be secured by rapidly rearranging a sentence correctly. The answers were scored using a seven-point scale that took into account the number of words, grammatical structure, and meaningfulness of the solutions. Appendix B reports additional information about the reliability of the test and its scoring procedures; Appendix C defines the scores used in the test of the data.

Thematic Associative Judgment Test (TAJ). Although phrases like "reality testing" and "realistic and sound judgment" are widely used to describe persons, little research was available that provided either understanding about or models of the type of test to use to measure realistic judgment. Traditional psychophysical models of judgment were not appropriate for measuring the affective and meaning complexity involved in usual day-to-day interpersonal judgments. A test was needed to which a variety of alternative solutions could be given, and whose appropriateness to the information contained in the test could be evaluated objectively. Out of numerous exploratory studies emerged the TAJ. The relevant background, rationale, and technical information about the TAJ can be found elsewhere (Heath, 1965).

The TAJ consists of twelve large photographs portraying the different themes used in the PT and other skill tests. For example, one of the two pictures illustrating the heterosexual theme shows a half-nude man and a woman embracing in the middle of a field. The participant tells as many different but realistic stories as he can about the picture in five minutes. The stories were recorded for subsequent translation into English for scoring.

As with the other tests, the order of picture presentation and of the two forms was systematically randomized.

To measure objectively degree of realistic judgment from such imaginative responses required that the range and type of categories attributed to the pictures be identified and their *appropriateness* to the content of the picture be scored. It was possible to reliably identify the different categories of needs, occupational, and social roles given to each picture. Complex judging procedures using independent local judges helped to determine the degree of realistic appropriateness of each category to each action in each picture.

As with the other skill tests, it is possible to secure a total judgmental efficiency score, a judgmental score just to the threatening information, or similar scores for each type of information. It is also possible to secure measures from the TAJ of the frequency with which different interpersonal, occupational or role categories are used. The scoring system maps, in other words, the ideas readily available to awareness as well as the appropriateness with which they can be used to solve a problem. Appendix B assesses the reliability of the TAJ, and Appendix C describes the specific TAJ scores used to test the model's hypotheses.

Summary measure of Cognitive Stability. Our primary concern is not the individual cognitive skill tests, but the development of a summary score that enables us to test the general hypothesis that mature persons have more stable skills than do immature men. Our expectation that the three skill tests would be positive but minimally related was generally confirmed. Appendix B summarizes the nature of their relationships. The skill tests measure somewhat different aspects of stable cognitive functioning. A more reliable general index of cognitive stability for testing the general hypotheses was secured by converting each individual's test scores into standard scores following a procedure used with the Haverford men (Heath, 1965). Each test's total scale score was then added with that of the others to give a Total Cognitive Stability (also called

Cognitive Efficiency) score for each individual. Similar scores were obtained for measuring cognitive stability for threatening information and nonthreatening information, as well as for the first and second administrations of the tests. Appendix C defines the summary scores used to measure cognitive stability.

Measures of the maturity of values. A disproportionate amount of effort had been devoted to measuring the stability of cognitive functioning because of its centrality in theories of ego functioning. With the exception of the measures of the self-concept, much less energy and thought have gone toward developing as refined measures of the maturity of a person's values and interpersonal relationships. But research proceeds slowly. Furthermore, psychologists tended to ignore the topics, both theoretically and methodologically, until recently. Kohlberg's method of assessing the developmental maturity of values (1964), still being refined when the cultural study was initiated, while related to the model of maturing does not directly measure its dimensions. Contained within Holt's primary process scores, the MMPI, the Study of Values, and the PT are clues about the maturity of a youth's values. Appendix C describes those scores I believed relevant. But none of these measures was specifically designed to measure the predicted dimensional characteristics of more mature values.

The principal measures of the degree to which the values of the mature and immature men were symbolizable, allocentric, integrated, stable, and autonomous were self-report items. The PSQ contained ten items that measured the dimensions defining mature values. The mature poles of two of the scales were:

My values and beliefs are centred more on the lives and needs of others than on myself and my desires (allocentrism).

I find it easy to reflect on my motives and values and to understand the reasons for most of my behavior (symbolization).

To supplement the PSQ items, fifteen additional items were constructed, three for each of the five dimensions, and provisionally identified as the Valuator Test. Appendix B and Chapter 8 provide additional reliability and validity information about the test. The findings with the Sicilian and Istanbul groups are given special interpretation later. Appendix C identifies the scores used to measure the maturity of a person's values.

Measure of the maturity of the self-concept. Considerable research had been done to develop, test, and refine measures of the dimensional maturity of the self-concept. As with the approach to measuring cognitive maturity, we sought to measure the maturity of the self-concept not only by means of self-reports, but by procedures that would actually measure its dimensional maturity.

The PSQ, our comprehensive self-report measure of the model of maturing, contained ten items tapping the dimensionality of the self-concept. Two examples of the items are

My ideas about myself are reasonably stable and don't differ too much from what they were several months ago (stability).

What I think of myself is not easily influenced by what my friends and family tell me (autonomy).

The maturity of the men's self-concept was also directly measured by varying the instructions and administrative procedures of the Self-Image Questionnaire (SIQ). The procedures measuring the dimensionality of the self-concept are relatively free of the specific content of the SIQ's items. In this way, the effects of response sets, like defensively checking the socially desirable end of the scale, were reduced. The SIQ's rationale, development, reliability and validity data have been described elsewhere (Heath, 1965).

Symbolization of self-concept. The degree of symbolization of the self-concept was measured indirectly by testing the accuracy of a person's insight about himself. Accuracy was defined by the sum of the difference scores between a person's private self-ratings on each scale of the SIQ, and the average of the ratings several persons made about him on the same scale. The greater the difference between a man's ratings of himself and those of the judges, the more poorly symbolized was his self-concept. Each person named two faculty and two close friends whom he judged knew him better than anyone else did. Every nominated student judge completed independently the SIQ about the person who had named him. The judges did not know about the study.[1] (No nominated faculty were actually contacted.)

Allocentricism of self-concept. An allocentric self-concept means, among other things, that one believes he is a loving, other-centered person who is not so unique that he cannot identify with other human beings. The private and social self-esteem scores index this attitude in part. But since I wanted measures more independent of the content of the self-concept, a less self-manipulable measure was

1 The Haverford judges for each man were the four faculty and student selection judges who knew the man the best. Their ratings were not found to be too useful; hence, the change in the type of judge used for the remaining groups.

used. Increasing allocentricism also means the ability to take another person's viewpoint, even toward oneself. Presumably, a mature person, more aware of how others think of him, can predict more accurately than an immature person what they do think about him. Accordingly, the allocentricism of the self-concept was defined by the sum of the differences between a participant's estimate of others' ratings about him and their actual ratings of him. He completed the SIQ as he believed others would complete the scales about him (defined as his social self). The more discrepant was his prediction of their ratings from their actual ratings, the less allocentric was his self-concept defined to be.

Integration of self-concept. Again, there are several ways to define the integration of a person's self-concept. One might, for example, determine the difference between a person's ideal and his actual self. The index of the integration of the self-concept used was the difference between a person's private and social self. If a person believes others think differently of him than he does of himself, he is constantly faced by the dilemma of how to act. Should he just be himself? Or should he try to appear what he thinks others believe him to be like? By comparing a person's self-ratings on each SIQ scale with the comparable ones that he believes judges who know him well would assign, the discrepancy between the private and social selves could be determined. The greater the sum of the differences the less well integrated was the self-concept.

Stability of self-concept. Presumably a person who thinks of himself one way at one time and a different way at a second time does not have a very stable idea about himself. The stability of the self-concept was measured by the sum of the differences between private self-ratings when made in the first, and, three to five weeks later, in the last test session. A person who completed the SIQ scales very similarly both times received a low difference score and so had a very stable self-concept. Although highly rigid persons might be expected to get very low difference scores, thus leading to the interpretation that rigidity means a more mature self-concept, none of the extensive research with the SIQ has yet shown that low difference scores are significantly related to any measure of rigidity used in the various studies.

Autonomy of self-concept. The goal was to measure how readily a person's self-concept could be changed when he was confronted with information that was discrepant with what he believed about himself. The procedure testing the autonomy of the self-concept in the original American groups had proved to be invalid. A simpler and, putatively, more persuasive challenge to each man's concept of himself was then developed. Each man completed the SIQ for a second time about himself at the beginning of his last session. While he was preoccupied with other tests during that session, the experimenter prepared a Personality Form that *ostensibly* summarized the results of the faculty judges who the person was told had completed ratings about him, as well as of the results of the other tests taken the four preceding sessions. The summary was made by marking the boxes of the SIQ scales. (The format of the SIQ, including the paragraph definitions of each scale, was altered to disguise the fact he was rerating himself for a third time on the SIQ.) To challenge his concept, some of the private self-ratings he had just made were shifted, according to a prearranged system, in the opposite direction. At the conclusion of the session, each student received the Personality Form which gave his falsified position on each SIQ scale. The experimenter casually said, "I want to now check the accuracy of some of the tentative test and judge results. I will be able to understand the total pattern of the results better if you will give me your frank reactions to these tentative results." Each man studied where he had been placed on each scale, and then marked on a second similar form the position where he thought he really should be. The experimenter indicated the faculty judges and test ratings might not be very valid, thus giving the participant "permission" to disagree with the authority of the tests and judges if he wished to. When the student completed his ratings, he was told the results were probably not correct. Each person was encouraged to express his feelings about the entire program. No man questioned the deception. Each was later informed the ratings were not correct.

Autonomy of the self-concept was measured by the sum of the differences between the private self-ratings made at the beginning and end of the session. It was assumed that the greater the discrepancy between the two private self-ratings, the more the last ratings had been influenced by the intervening challenge to the man's ideas about himself.

How did the cultural groups compare in the intra-scale patterns of their results? Table B–2 in Appendix B reports the pattern of SIQ dimensional correlates. Comparison of the intercorrelations for the symbolization and allocentric scores, based on ratings of the selection judges, with those based on close friends, shows the friends' ratings to be much more consistent. This result supports the hunch that it was the use of selection judges rather than close friends with the Haverford group that had contributed to its unreliable results.

The expectation that the dimensions of maturing would be positively intercorrelated among the groups was confirmed, though the lack of independence of some scores spuriously inflates the number of high positive correlates reported in Table B-2. But certainly it can be said for the three cultures that persons who have more accurate ideas about themselves also can more accurately predict what others think of them, and tend to have more stable and autonomous self-concepts as well; also, persons who have more stable self-concepts have more integrated and allocentric self-images. The other hypothesized relationships tend to be supported also. The SIQ dimensional scores seem to have similar meanings for the cultural groups.

Measures of the maturity of interpersonal relations. Resources were too limited to develop the measures necessary to test fairly and in depth the model's hypotheses about interpersonal maturing. The one test specifically designed to measure the dimensional hypotheses was the PSQ. Two parallel scales of ten items each were constructed. One included items measuring male-male and the other male-female relationships. Since the content of both was similar, I list two PSQ items for only mature male-female relationships.

I could resist the influence of a woman I love if it went against my values (autonomy).

The interests of a girl I like frequently become my interests (allocentricism).

As with other PSQ scores, the more maturely a person rated himself in the dimensional maturity of his relationships, the higher was his score.

Contained in the richness of the diverse tests used in the study were other indices about the quality of the men's personal relationships that could be interpreted as measuring the dimensions of maturing. MMPI scores for tolerance and social responsibility measure allocentric personal qualities; Rorschach scores like FC% measure the ability of a person to integrate his emotional reactions in socially accommodating ways. The Phrase Association Test, by measuring the amount of anxiety that a person has about different relationships, may index immature stabilization and autonomy. Finally, the SIQ does provide independent judge ratings of numerous traits that describe the dimensional maturity of the men's personal relations. Appendix C lists the specific scores used to define further the maturity of personal relationships. But it is a major gap in the research to have no observational or experimental measures of how the men actually functioned in their relations with other men and women.

Critique

Was the program adequate for determining if different cultures defined maturity similarly?

A number of factors reduce the probability of discovering similarities in cultural definitions of maturity. Differences in the style and skill of the experimenters, lack of linguistic as well as psychological "equivalence" among a few of the tests, too limited tests of some of the components of the model of maturing, differences in the reliability of the data of the cultural groups, and probably unknown differences in the attitudes and test-taking behavior of the cultural groups—these and undoubtedly other sources of errror warn that it will not be easy to demonstrate that the model of maturing has some transcultural generality.

Yet, despite these potential sources of error, the accumulative evidence demonstrates a remarkable similarity in the test-taking behavior of the five groups. This is not to deny there are not differences, and important ones, between the groups. The American, Ankara, and Pisa groups produced much more consistent and reliable intratest patterns than did the Istanbul and Sicilian groups. We have stumbled upon a number of clues, reported in Appendix B, that may help interpret the latter groups' results. While the differences between the Sicily and Pisa groups conceivably could be explained primarily in terms of uncontrolled differences among the experimenters, we cannot so readily explain the differences between the Ankara and Istanbul groups. True, the Turkish experimenter learned with the Istanbul group and increased his skill and self-confidence. However, there probably are other differences intrinsic to the predictably unpredictable Istanbul group that also may account for its deviant character.

The chapter provokes one final and certainly unexpected, but reassuring, observation. The patterns of the intratest findings to date suggest that we may well find greater intercultural similarities among the more reliable groups in personality organization than we will discover similarities among the groups from the same culture. If so, such a finding would be, at the least, ironical. The principal sources of dissimilarity may not be the allegedly powerful effects of different cultural values, but the typical methodological problems that always complicate personality research.

CHAPTER 5

Cultural Similarities and Differences in Maturity

. . . you will be doing us a favor to broaden the concept of national differences, and especially SIMILARITIES. As Cantril shows, "strivings" are not so different among nations. Wertheimer used to insist that "justice" is a universal (although it may differ in aspects); and no people approves cruelty to children (although they may define cruelty differently).

So wrote Gordon Allport when the research was in its initial stages.

Is the concept of maturity a universal, though it may vary in some aspects from culture to culture? This chapter asks these questions: Do American, Italian, and Turkish judges use similar traits to distinguish mature from immature men? Do mature and immature men in the three cultures describe themselves similarly? Do the mature men of these cultures differ similarly from the immature men in their accomplishments and strivings? And finally, is socially judged maturity related in the three cultures to the comprehensive measures of maladjustment (MMPI), esteem (SIQ), maturity (PSQ), and psychological healthiness (Rorschach)?

Similarities Among Mature and Immature Men

Judge traits of mature and immature men. Did the judges who selected the groups of mature and immature men agree about a core set of traits that define maturity? If the mature and immature men of the five cultures do not differ from each other at least in a core group of traits, then the research is immediately in deep trouble. How can we reasonably expect to ferret out the predicted underlying dimensional differences if the groups cannot be distinguished consistently on more obvious surface types of traits? Recall that four selection judges for each of the five cultural groups had rated the men they knew best on the thirty scales of the SIQ three to five months following the initial selection procedure. Also, two of each man's close friends, ignorant of the purpose of the study, had also completed the SIQ about him.

Given the discouraging difficulties encountered in selecting the men, I had not expected the judges of the five cultural groups to agree so remarkably well about the traits that did in *fact* discriminate the mature from the immature men. The selection judges of the five groups rated the mature men to be significantly[1] more mature than the immature men in 65 percent of their total number (150) of SIQ ratings. The immature men were rated to be more mature on only three percent of the traits by the selection judges. For example, the Pisan and Turkish *immature* men were rated to be more adventurous, a trait found to be characteristic of the American *mature* men. That few significant differences (only 26 percent) were obtained between the Sicilian mature and immature men was not unexpected. They had been drawn from a very small population, and were not as homogeneously extreme as were the mature and immature men of the other cultural groups. The selection judges of *all* five cultural groups agreed in describing mature persons to be understanding of others and insightful about themselves, realistic, and to have strong convictions. The mature men of *four* cultural groups were consistently rated to differ significantly from the immature men on 57 percent of the thirty SIQ scales. In addition to the traits just mentioned, the following traits described the mature person: accepting of self, anticipates consequences, calm, clear-thinking, decisive, fulfilling potential,

---

1 All findings reported in the book are significant at least at a .05 two-tailed *p* level, unless stated otherwise.

objective, ordered, other-centered, predictable, purposeful, reflective, and unshakable. Clearly, there is a core set of traits that reliably distinguish a mature from an immature person in the three cultures. Of interest are those traits on which there was minimal agreement. Mental health experts and personality theorists may be as surprised as I was to discover that Italian and Turkish mature men were not more energetic and warmer in their personal relationships than immature men.

Although there was much more similarity than dissimilarity in the patterns of traits separating mature from immature men among the three cultures, each culture did differ distinctively on some traits it attributed to mature persons. A mature Italian does not have to be imaginative, open, aspiring, enthusiastic or flexible; but mature Americans and Turks probably do. And mature Americans must be more energetic, adventurous, and warm in their personal relationships, and probably do not have to be as gentle as mature Italians and Turks must be.

If the data were firmer, more reliable, and extensive, these differences might help us better understand cultural prejudices. To an European, for example, the restlessly energetic, friendly, intrepidly intrusive American tourist may not be the representative of virtue he may think himself to be.

It is a temptation to overinterpret the suggestive hints in our too-limited data. We must heed those critics who are muttering, and rightly so, that the judges are more biased than I have indicated. They were scarcely naive about the study and its purposes. Agreed. After all, they had selected the men, though their SIQ ratings were not necessarily made on the men they individually had selected to be mature or immature. Actually, none of the traits about which the selection judges agreed had been given them as preliminary criteria of maturity in the selection procedure. The independent SIQ ratings of the close friends of the men were used to check the findings of the selection judges. The use of several friends who knew a man well of course introduces another bias. Friends may be predisposed to rate other friends more favorably. So it is not unexpected that the immature men are not rated to differ as consistently from the mature men among the cultural groups—most obviously, again, for the Sicilian men. The mature men of the four non-American groups were rated to be significantly more mature on 37 percent of the total number of ratings (45 percent if the Sicilian group is excluded), among which were the following traits: anticipates consequences, calm, objective, ordered, purposeful, realistic, and reflective. The immature men were rated more mature on only one trait (three percent), again on adventurousness.

Both the selection judges *and* the friends agreed that the mature men differed significantly from the immature men on seven core traits. Mature persons are more able to anticipate consequences, are more reflective, calm, objective, ordered, purposeful, and realistic. There is little doubt we do have contrasting groups that differ on traits typically identified with effectively functioning persons.

Self-judged traits of mature and immature men. Both the selection judges and close friends of the mature and immature men consistently agreed the groups differed as we had expected. What did the mature and immature men think of themselves?

All of the men, except the Sicilians, completed the Adjective Check List in the first few minutes of the study. I compared the self-impressions the mature and immature men of the three cultures brought with them to the study. Neither group described itself in terms that contradicted the judgments of the selection judges and friends of the men. The mature men checked adjectives like "adaptable," "clear thinking," and "planful," that describe maturing. Understandably fewer of the immature men described themselves by terms connoting immaturity: "bottled-up" and "erratic" (American); "talkative" (Turks); "earthy and impatient" (Italians). If we had accepted a .10 two-tailed p level, the immature men would have also called themselves "suspicious," "hard to convince," and "distractible."

Fascinating to me was the cast of the self-descriptions of the three cultures. They seem to reflect some of the culturally patterned differences we have been noting. The mature Americans rated themselves to be significantly more adaptable, conscientious, independent, and self-driving—positive expressions of traits stereotypical of the American character. The mature Turk described himself as intellectual, planful, resourceful, scheduled, and well-coordinated. The self-portrait of the mature Italian was quite different. It was strongly cast in terms of "inner" qualities expressive of tranquillity, harmony, and integration: calmness, peacefulness, mildness, deliberateness, deep interests, and introspectiveness. He also called himself cautious, clear thinking, commonsensical, independent, and tactful. Barzini talks of the flambuoyant, talkative, mercurial emotionality that the "typical" Italian shows the world—traits that apparently Italian judges do not identify with maturity or that do not differentiate mature from immature Italians. It is as if the Italians were saying, "We value our inward lives more highly than the traits we show in our outward lives."

The men's ratings of themselves on the SIQ also confirmed that, in contrast to the immature men, the mature men consistently described themselves to be more mature on a variety of traits. Of the total number of different ratings that the men of the five cultural groups made about themselves, the mature men placed themselves closer to the mature pole of the SIQ traits than did the immature men in 67 percent of their ratings; the immature men rated themselves higher on such traits than did the mature men only nine percent of the time. The mature men actually rated themselves significantly more mature than did the immature men 18 percent of the time. The immature men rated themselves to be significantly more mature only one percent of the time, *i.e.*, more adventurous.

Table 5–1 summarizes·how the more mature men's private and social selves differed from those of the immature men's. It reports those traits on which the mature men of five, and then of four cultural groups consistently rated themselves more favorably than did the immature men. Since the men rated their private selves at two different times, only those traits are listed on which the men rated themselves as more mature *both* times. It is quite clear that a mature, but not an immature, person thinks of himself as predictable, ordered, calm, able to anticipate consequences, and clear thinking. His energies are not bound up in anxieties and worries, but are channeled into strong convictions and the fulfillment of his potentials. The pattern of trait differences between the mature and immature men's private selves is intriguing. Its salient traits are those that facilitate adaptation to reality concerns, almost to the exclusion of traits associated with affective or interpersonal aspects of life.

If we turn now to the differences in the social selves of the men, we find even more consistent differences between the mature and immature men. The mature men described themselves to be more mature than did the immature men in 80 percent of the total number of their ratings. The immature men rated themselves to be more mature on the SIQ trait scales in only eight percent of their ratings. Twenty-three percent of the mature men's ratings actually differed significantly from the immature men's ratings. The data are thus overwhelmingly consistent. The mature men correctly

Table 5–1
Private and Social SIQ Self-Ratings
of Mature Men that Differed from Immature Men

Agreement Among Mature Men all Five Groups	Agreement Among Mature Men for Four Groups

PRIVATE SELF-RATINGS

predictable (3)[1]	ordered (3)
— — —	— — —
anticipates consequences (1)	calm (2)
fulfilling potential (1)	clear thinking (2)
strong convictions (1)	— — —
	energetic (1)
	over-controls impulses (1)
	purposeful (1)
	reflective (1)
	unshakabale (1)
	— — —
	realistic

SOCIAL SELF-RATINGS

purposeful (4)	high aspirations (3)
— — —	ordered (3)
anticipates consequences (3)	— — —
— — —	accepting of self (1)
flexible (2)	calm (1)
objective (2)	energetic (1)
over-controls impulses (2)	strong convictions (1)
predictable (2)	trustful (1)
realistic (2)	— — —
reflective (2)	imaginative
— — —	independent
clear thinking (1)	other-centered
fulfilling potential (1)	
gentle (1)	
— — —	
unshakable	

1 Number in parenthesis refers to number of groups for which mature men differed significantly (two-tailed) at .05 *p* level from immature men on trait listed. Traits listed in order of agreement to highlight the principal trait differences.

believed that others thought they were very mature; the immature men realized that others judged them unfavorably on many important personality traits.

What is extraordinary about the social-self differences between the mature and immature men is the amount of agreement between what the men believe others think of them and what others actually do think of them. The men accurately, in one sense, predicted fourteen of the seventeen traits that the selection judges actually identified as those that the mature and immature men differed on. The mature men failed to predict that persons like the selection judges would rate them to differ from the immature men in being more decisive, insightful about themselves, and understanding of others.

What general conclusions can we abstract from these results? First, regardless of how we examine the information about the men, the consensually-selected mature men of the three cultures are consistently higher than the immature men on most of the traits commonly associated with maturity. This generalization does not hold as well for the Sicilian mature and immature men who were neither judged by others, nor rated by themselves, to differ very noticeably from each other. Of the total number of statistically significant differences found between the five cultural groups' mature and immature men, the Sicilians accounted for only seven percent. The Haverford differences accounted for 25 percent, Pisa for 24 percent, and Istanbul and Ankara 22 percent each of the total number of mature and immature group differences.

Second, a core pattern of traits consistently differentiates the mature from the immature men. These core traits can be identified in several diverse ways: ratings by the selection judges that are generally confirmed by ratings of close friends who knew the men more intimately; by the men's own private self-ratings; or from the beliefs that the men have about what others think of them. Any core set of traits defining a mature American, Italian and Turk probably would have to include at least these traits:

anticipates consequences   purposeful
calm (not worrying or anxious) realistic
clear thinking   reflective
fulfilling potential   strong convictions
ordered   unshakable
predictable

Third, traits describing the maturity of the men's interpersonal relationships, and possibly temperamentally related traits, such as enthusiasm, energy level, and aggressiveness, do not discriminate as consistently between mature and immature men.

And fourth, each culture has its own unique and limited set of behavioral traits it identifies with maturity or competence. For example, the Americans seem to relate maturity to energy level as it is manifested in enthusiasm, drive and aspiration level, and adventurousness. The Italians certainly do not—if our groups are typical of mature and immature Italians.

Accomplishments, problems, and hopes of mature and immature men. Previous research has indicated that mature and immature persons may view their past accomplishments, current problems, and future hopes differently (Heath, 1965). Each Italian and Turk had answered questions about his past, present, and future while completing a short biographical sheet at the beginning of the study.

The question, "What have you accomplished in your life of which you are most proud?" uncovered striking differences between the cultures more than it did differences between the mature and immature men. Sixty-three percent of the Italian mature men and 73 percent of its immature men cited some personal quality, frequently a moral or religious virtue, as the accomplishment of which they were most proud. Qualities like honesty, altruism, being "very human," or having a "serious desire for the good," and reaching "balance and sexual control" marked the accomplishments of the mature men. While many of the Italian immature men cited similar accomplishments, like "my youth and frankness towards others," "character," "religious agnosticism," "my life," and "my ideals," their descriptions had a noticeably different flavor to them. Forty-one percent of their accomplishments, in contrast to only 15 percent of those of the mature men, related to having been given something for which they had not had to assert their will, drive, or use their talents. For example, they were proud "of having been born male," "of my religion," of their families, particularly their fathers, of "my intelligence." Only one immature Italian cited an accomplishment that had taken unusual exertion of his will, and even then he cited no specific accomplishment actually achieved: "I am proud of having been able to get ahead by my own will-power, ignoring others' wills and overcoming the relative obstacles." And in very sharp contrast to American and Turkish men, none of whom gave this type of response, 24 percent of the mature and 33 percent of the immature Italian males said they were most proud of their families, or of having lived up to their expectations and having secured their esteem. Only 24 percent of the mature, and seven percent of the immature, men described achieving something in the world of work, like having done well in school, receiving awards, or assumed some major responsibility.

The impression was inescapable that the Italian men highly valued the creation of a less visible but more perfect moral character, a harmonious sense of "being," of "being an altriust and very human." Certainly, few of the men mentioned striving, asserting their wills, or enthusiastic involvement in externalized rather than self-oriented types of experiences. The immature Italians accentuated these trends, and turned even further away from the externalization of themselves in action and achievements in the outside world to emphasize the blessings they had received from their parents and Church.

As day is to night, or night is to day, depending upon one's point of view, so were the Turks to the Italians. Only 15 percent of the mature and only one immature man gave any reply even remotely similar in tone to the personal, moral, or "harmonious being" kind of accomplishment that so typified the Italian mature and immature men. And again, in sharp contrast to the Italians, not one Turk cited as a personal accomplishment his family status or the passive receipt of some blessing. The character of their personal accomplishments emphasized striving: "I consider the distance I've gone from my starting point to where I stand now (which is not much) as the greatest accomplishment in my life. I had started from the extreme in which all the opportunities for personal development had been rejected by an excessive pride." "I've lived my own life." "I have become a person. I have gained personality. This is what I am proud of."

The overwhelming thrust of the Turks was to have accomplished some change in the external reality of their lives. Sixty-two percent of the mature and 65 percent of the immature men cited very specific achievements in contrast to the more generalized and vague ones cited by the Italians: being an honor student, winning a national Turkish tennis championship, founding the school's newspaper, becoming successful in the field of art photography. The Turkish empasis was on what they had done, and how they had asserted and extended themselves beyond just the requirements of the immediate situation. Forty percent of the mature, but only 23 percent of the immature Turks had achieved some distinction, so they said, in activities *not* connected with their formal education, the sole type of achievement mentioned by the Italians. Perhaps because their measure of success was some visible, concrete effect they had had on the world, rather than the more elusive, subtle personality perfection the Italians emphasized, 19 percent of the mature and 27 percent of the immature Turks felt there was nothing they had done about which they were yet proud.

If the Italians were like night, say, and the Turks day, then Americans were like twilight, for they shared some features of both. Not having comparable information from the Haverford group used in this book, I used the replies of another Haverford group of ten mature and ten immature men who had been selected and studied similarly. The mature men were more like the Turks in emphasizing visible, concrete, externalized achievements such as singular academic distinctions, elective student government positions, or, as one man said, having learned the name of everyone in the college. The immature men, on the other hand, were superficially similar to the Italians. The cast of their achievements was the mastery of some willful and capricious part of their own personalities, like "pulling myself out of the complete slumber I was in in high school," or "becoming aware of things in life of which I had never dreamed when I was little," or modestly being proud of accomplishing "little things." But, in contrast to the Italians, the flavor of the immature men was more negative, as if they were in conflict and were pained about not being able to control and master themselves. "It bothers me that I can't make myself do these things," or "I went to my grandfather's funeral against my parents' wishes," scarcely an Italian-like act of self-assertion. The immature Haverford men had internalized the idea of competence, of achieving some visible effect on the environment; unable to control their energies sufficiently to achieve that effect, they consequently felt vaguely restless and discontented with themselves. The Italians' preoccupation with their internal lives and personal development did not seem to spring as clearly from the motive to make some noticeable impact on the external world; rather, they valued perfecting the art of being, of fulfilling themselves as a person whether it manifested itself in external signs of competence or not. Maturity seems to mean in Italy perfecting one's "being," while in Turkey and America it means creating an effect in the world.

The second question, "What do you consider to be your most important current problem, preoccupation, or conflict that you have yet to solve?" did not elicit noticeable differences among the cultural groups. Two-thirds of both the Italian and Turkish mature as well as immature men were preoccupied by specific reality-oriented problems, like their academic work, vocational plans, and to a lesser extent, sexual and women problems. The Haverford mature men responded similarly.

The remaining men's most salient problems involved their character and internal adjustment. These problems were most typical of the Italians and the Haverford immature men. A mature Italian youth identified, "Certain fears that at times obscurely make me give up certain plans, and can poison my relations with those I love." Another said his primary current problem was, "What in life is reality?" One immature youth said, "Inner peace—a balance between day-to-day life and religious problems." The Haverford immature men were more preoccupied with shadowy and elusive questions like, "What is true?" and personal failings like "fear of failure" and "finding security within myself."

The question, "What would you like to be like or have accomplished ten years from now?" did not draw out clearcut cultural or mature and immature group differences. More Turks than Italians (93 percent of the mature and 73 percent of the immature Turks, versus 74 percent of the mature and 66 percent of the immature Italians) wanted to have a good job in their field of interest, be married, and have a family. Although the Haverford group had responded similarly, almost all of its mature in contrast to none of its immature men had stressed in addition the importance of excellence, achieving distinction, continued growth: "I want to be damn good at some profession," "to grow intellectually . . . my mind, I hope, will still be growing." Only 15 to 20 percent of both the mature and immature Italians and Turks aspired to distinction: "a top official in Turkish government," "a millionaire," "a brilliant professional," "to have made important scientific discoveries," and this very distinctive goal of an immature Sicilian, "To be considered an exemplary person and at the same time to be looked upon as a phenomenon, with a bit of a dose of anticonformism."

The men of the cultural groups seem on the whole to be struggling with the human problems common to most young adults, and to share typical middleclass hopes and values. Most seek contentment and happiness, "tranquility" in the words of several Italians. Only a comparative few hoped to serve their countries, to create some distinctive place for themselves in the world, to live an idiosyncratic adventurous life. Throughout their descriptions ran the themes of responsibility, competence, financial security, and a happy family life. As Cantril found also, the strivings of most people seem to be quite similar, regardless of the culture from which they come (1962, 1965).

Social judgments of maturity and comprehensive personality measures. Our entry into the study of maturity was by way of the effectiveness or competence with which the men functioned in the colleges in which they were identified. With the exception of the ACL and SIQ measures of the men's private self-concepts, our measures of their "maturity" to this point have been based on the ratings of others, or on the perception of the judgments of others by the men themselves. Our focus has been largely on manifest, observable traits and on more conscious descriptive methods of assessing the men. The core group of traits identified to separate mature from immature men could just as plausibly be considered to define competent and not-so-competent men. It is now time to turn our search inward, so to speak, to the internal dynamics and less visible personality organization of the men. Is there a close relationship between the effectiveness of a man's adaptation and his seeming "maturity," as observed by others, and the maturity of his internal life, his organismic integrity, as indexed by the comprehensive measures of psychological adjustment, health, and maturity?

Table 5–2 reports the relationships between the judgments of the selection judges (Social Index of Maturity), as well as the ratings of the men's close friends (SIQ Judge Esteem), and the comprehensive measures of maturity used in the study. To facilitate the interpretation of the findings obtained with the ranked Social Index of Maturity, the scores of the comprehensive tests of maturity (with the exception of the MMPI score for maladjustment) have been so ranked that a low rank indexes greater maturity. The table gives us an overview of the similarities in psychological functioning among the cultural groups; these similarities will be worked out in detail in subsequent chapters.

There are several salient, even remarkable aspects about Table 5–2. First, every correlation is in the predicted direction except for two. Second, 65 percent of the predicted relationships are statistically significant at least at a one-tailed .05 level, the criterion used in this study to test specifically hypothesized relationships. Third, the SIQ Judge Esteem ratings of the close friends tend to be more consistently predictive than the judgments of the selection judges about the maturity of the men (68 percent of the former's and 56 percent of the latter's correlations are significant). Fourth, there is a striking congruence or consistency among the five cultural

Table 5–2
Relation of Judge Judgments of Maturity and Measures of General Personality Functioning

Social Index of Maturity[1]	SIQ Esteem Scores			MMPI Psychol. Maladj.	PSQ Maturi- ty	Rorschach Psych. Health
	Judge[2]	Social	Private			
Haverford	.85**[3]	.71**	.44*	−.41*	(.56**)[4]	.45*
Ankara	.55*	.65**	.26	.13	.21	.21
Istanbul	.41*	.47**	.26	−.26	.21	.34*
Pisa	.75**	.42*	.22	−.11	.19	.35*
Sicily	.70**	.49**	.39*	−.39*	.39*	−.11
SIQ Esteem Judge[2]						
Haverford		.52**	.38*	−.41*[5]	(.42*)[4]	.35*
Ankara		.64**	.60**	−.38*	.33	.20
Istanbul		.47**	.17	−.10	.10	.28
Pisa		.42*	.46**	−.05	.32*	.55**
Sicily		.49**	.51**	−.56**	.43*	.03

1 Rank order correlations (*rho*) used *only* for Social Index of Maturity. Scores of all tests, except MMPI maladjustment score, so ranked that a low rank means greater maturity.

2 Correlations (Pearson *r*) based on ratings of those four selection judges who knew each man best for Haverford group only; all other groups' ratings based on close friends' SIQ judgments.

3 * significant at least one-tailed .05 *p* level; ** at least one-tailed .01 *p* level.

4 Haverford PSQ scores are retrospective ratings made by nineteen men of group ten years later (see p. 127).

5 High MMPI Total score means greater psychological maladjustment. High scores for all other comprehensive measures of maturity mean greater maturity, though for this table high maturity scores are ranked low.

groups between the judgments of maturity made by the selection judges, the ratings of traits descriptive of maturity by independent judges (SIQ Judge Esteem), and the predictions by the mature and immature men themselves of how other persons would perceive them (SIQ Social Esteem). And fifth, the consistency of the *pattern* (though not necessarily of all the component correlates) of the results strongly supports the basic thesis of the study that the three cultures have very similar concepts of maturity.

Table 5–2 clinches the findings reported earlier that different types of judges using different types of assessment procedures can agree about who is and who is not mature. The Social Index of Maturity for each cultural group was significantly related to the SIQ Judge Esteem scores. To appreciate the full significance of this finding, we must recall two facts about these measures: First, the selection judges knew of the study's general purpose, so that their idiosyncratic biases could readily affect their choices. The close friends of the men, more knowledgeable about them than the selection judges, knew nothing about the purpose of the study. And second, in identifying persons as most mature and most immature, the selection judges made holistic and scarcely precise types of judgments about the maturity of the men which we combined in a very crude way to give us the Social Index. The close friends, on the other hand, rated specific SIQ trait scales of the men but did not know that their ratings could be summed to yield a reasonably precise measure of the concept of maturity. The fact that two different types of judges with different understandings of the study independently traveling different assessment routes converged so consistently to identify the level of the maturity of the men thus has an important implication. While particularistic and cultural biases about the meaning of "mature organization" undoubtedly influenced the holistic judgments of the selection judges, the likelihood such values affected the specific behavioral trait ratings of the friends is very much less. That the accuracy of the judgments of the selection judges was so amply and consistently confirmed in every cultural group by such different procedures confirms our assumption that more than just idiosyncratic and cultural biases define who is and who is not mature.

The very powerfully consistent relationships between the SIQ Social Esteem of the men and the judgments of the selection judges, as well as of their close friends, brings a third confirming perspective to the pattern of results. To validate the judgments of both the selection judges and the men's friends by the mature and immature men's judgments of what they considered other persons to think of them is fascinating. What it suggests is that even the immature men in the five cultural areas accurately understood how the "social other" viewed them, even when the "social other" judged them not very favorably on a variety of traits. The consistency of the pattern between three different perspectives on "maturity," using different methods of assessing it, is our first hard evidence that the concept of maturity may be transculturally similar. These results, it seems to me, can most simply be understood in terms of the three cultures sharing similar objective criteria based to a large extent on the adaptive criteria defining maturely effective persons. Judgments of maturity based on evaluations of competence predict to specific trait ratings not themselves formally or experimentally associated with the concept of competence or maturity.

The pattern of the judge and "social other" ratings is also striking when examined in the context of the men's SIQ Private self-ratings. The men's SIQ Social ratings and the independent judges' ratings powerfully converge. But there is much less powerful congruence between the SIQ private ratings and the judges' ratings. If the SIQ self-ratings are adequate indices of esteem-maturity (recall they are based on traits commonly attributed to mature and psychologically sound persons), and the judges' ratings, primarily based on the observed effectiveness of the men, are adequate indices of competence, then the data suggest that socially defined competence, while related, is *not* equivalent to psychological concepts such as maturity and psychological healthiness. Both concepts are needed; we blur important distinctions if we fail to clearly distinguish between them.

As we leave the social perspectives to move into more personal, perhaps "deeper," more complex, and defended levels of the personality, there is some diminution in the predictive efficacy of the social judgments of maturity. A man's self-esteem still predicts the judgments of other persons of his maturity, but less consistently so; particularly, as could be expected, when the other persons (like the selection judges) do not know him as well as his close friends do. With the exception only of the Istanbul men, the men's private self-esteem successfully predicted their friends' judgments of their maturity. That the men's private selves did not coincide as consistently as their social selves did with the judges' ratings suggests that the men's private self-concepts are not simply reflected appraisals of what other people think of them. The individual has his own inner autonomous stance toward himself that modifies the internalized impact of the social others' perceptions of him.

A puzzling question is why the Istanbul men failed to view themselves in the same way as their friends viewed them. The Istanbul men's private and social selves are strongly related *(p <* .005), indicating the Istanbul men think of themselves as they *believe* others think of them. As Table 5–2 shows, however, although their social selves accurately predict how both the selection judges and their friends described their maturity, their private descriptions of themselves do not significantly agree with the outside world's view of them. Since the independent judges' assessments are validated by nonself-report types of measures like the clinical Rorschach ratings, I can only conclude that the Istanbul men had a rather special, if not unrealistic, perhaps defensive, and (based on other hunches) exalted view of themselves.

When we compare the judges' ratings of maturity with the MMPI score of maladjustment and the PSQ score of maturity, we encounter the first of a series of minor and occasionally major disappointments, as well as interpretive challenges. Just how are we to draw a generalization out of the MMPI correlates of Table 5–2, when only 50 percent of them are significant, particularly when one of the less reliable group's correlations, the Sicilian, were significant, but one of the more reliable group's, the Pisan, were not. Istanbul's findings were not unexpected, since we know it responded to the MMPI deviantly. What is of interest is that at least one group from each of the three cultures confirms that increased psychological maladjustment is inversely related to maturity when rated by knowledgeable friends. This is probably not a bad batting average, given the difficulty that psychologists have in replicating results even on persons from the same culture.

Of greater theoretical interest is the relationship of the Social Index of Maturity and the SIQ Judge Esteem scores to the PSQ Maturity score. The PSQ score is the only comprehensive measure of the dimensions defining the model of maturing that we have. Unfortunately, the test was not available for the Haverford group, since it had been developed after the initial studies had confirmed the potential utility of such a measure. A longitudinal follow-up study of the Haverford group ten years later made it possible to secure a methodologically very feeble clue about the PSQ, however. The men completed the test as they recalled what they were like at the time of their college graduation—the year most of the men had participated in the original study.[1] Table 5–2 includes these flawed ratings in parentheses to remind us of their suspect nature. The general results indicate that PSQ-defined maturity significantly predicted the judges' ratings of maturity, particularly of judges who know the men well, for the Italian, and, *mirabile dictu*, the Haverford groups. That the correlation of the Ankara men approaches significance ($p = .06$) enables us to conclude that the model of maturing, as measured by the PSQ Maturity score, *may* apply across the three cultures.

The most surprising pattern of findings reported in Table 5–2 was that the independent judges' ratings of maturity predicted the clinically evaluated healthiness (Rorschach) of at least one group from each of the three cultures. This general finding confirms that

1 Other studies using retrospective PSQ ratings have shown that they can be very consistently and significantly predictive of other measures of adjustment secured *at the time being retrospectively rated*. One possible explanation for such singular findings is that the reliability of PSQ type ratings may be higher than might be expected because of reduced defensiveness about what one was like earlier in one's life (Heath 1968, Appendix B).

the Rorschach test can discriminate the psychological healthiness of men in several different cultures a result not heretofore obtained so consistently in cross national studies (Lindzey, 1961).[1] The bare statistics of Table 5–2 just do not reveal the richness of the inner lives of the men, and the complexity of the relation of their psychological health to their consensually judged maturity. The closeness, yet complicatedness, of this relation was much more intuitively compelling to me than is captured by objective ratings and correlations. So I take a frankly impressionistic, and probably too dogmatic, approach as I examine each cultural group in detail for clues about the relation of social judgments of maturity and clinical evaluations of healthiness.

My first salient impression was that differences between the three cultures in types of imagery, modes of control, and sources of persistent conflict were much more dramatic and identifiable than were similar differences between groups from the same cultures. That is, the Sicilians and Pisans were more similar to each other than either was to the other cultural groups. The impression that each man shared a Turkish or an Italian "character" was very powerful—in spite of all the research that has never satisfactorily identified such differences in national "character" *objectively*. And that may be at the heart of the problem of such studies.

This leads to my next impression, which confirmed similar ones from previous intensive analyses of American Rorschachs. A holistic method of analysis is the only way I know to take account of the complex systemic organization of a person and of cultural differences in its patterning. The clinical evaluations predicted socially judged maturity not *because* the evaluations were based on the presence or absence of specific signs, scores, types of images, or modes of control that consistently differentiated the mature from the immature men. The traditional method of validating the Rorschach by comparing the frequency with which certain scores or

1 I was "surprised" about the results for the many reasons indicated in Appendix B. Another reason was that correlations are attenuated when there is very limited variability in small samples. For example, on a Rorschach line scale of thirty points one-half of the Pisa group was evaluated to be between a range of only six points. It is unreasonable to expect complex judgments like those required for Rorschachs to distinguish reliably within such a narrow range; yet, the remarkable result was that 50 percent of the Pisa evaluated ranks deviated from the judges' ranks by no more than five rank positions. And we must recall that the Social Index of Maturity is not very precise either. Sixty percent of the Istanbul, 54 percent of the Ankara, and 50 percent of the Haverford groups' Rorschach and selection judge ranks also deviated from each other by no more than five ranks. The evaluations just did not discriminate between the Sicilians, as Table 5–2 clearly shows.

images is given in comparison groups is an extraordinary weak and inappropriate approach. The mature and immature men, for example, did not differ in the frequency with which they responded to the Rorschach in the ways clinical lore suggested that they might, that is, by rejecting a card, or giving images of human beings. The significance of an image about a human being or an atomic explosion depends on a host of other factors—the number and pattern of other images in which it is embedded, their accuracy, the defensive adequacy with which they are controlled, the effect their emergence into awareness has upon subsequent images, and so on. Only trained clinical judgments can, at this stage in the history of personality assessment, take into account the multiplicity of factors that influence the "meaning" of a particular Rorschach score or sign.

A third very powerful, but complicating, impression was the confirmation of the theoretical necessity of distinguishing between competence and maturity. This necessity became very real to me when evaluating the Rorschachs. I frequently had to resist the temptation to predict *how the judges might rate the men*. I noted in 23 percent of my evaluations that the judges might well disagree with my ratings. To illustrate some interpretive dilemmas I quote a few excerpts:

Very debatable how mature he is; effective control, high intelligence, differentiated thought, but obsessed by sex and conflict about own role. Too much sexual confusion and latent uncontrolled sadism. Could well appear socially to be a mature person, and in Turkish culture his potential impulsivity could be acceptable.

Or, *is a boring intellectual with little warmth. High achiever. How rate him?*

Or, *his obsessional control could make him productive; his excessive sensitivity and passivity could keep him out of trouble. So he could be obliging socially; and given the value on that type of behavior, he could be judged to be socially mature.*

And, *is a very well organized person, but lacks integration of his emotionality with intellect; too deliberate, too self-controlled, too self-critical, too perfectionistic. Obsessive-compulsive whom judges might rate as excellently organized.*

If "outside" judges identified maturity primarily with productive achievement, self-control, intelligence, social sensitivity and adaptability, and the efficient organization of energy and time, then we cannot necessarily expect an isomorphic relation between their ratings and clinically evaluated maturity. From the "inside" of the men, such traits might mask or defensively channel emotional impulsivity, obsessional defenses, repressed conflicts, and other motives not accepted or well integrated into the men's more public social selves.

I compared the Rorschachs of the socially judged mature and immature men to understand them better as well as to discover clues about why the clinical ratings were not more predictive of the judges' ratings for some of the men.

I had correctly identified twelve of the fourteen immature men of the Pisa group to be immature from their Rorschachs, but only ten of the judged mature men to be mature. In my comments for three of the four incorrectly judged mature men I noted that the Italian judges would probably call them mature, despite their immaturity as rated from their Rorschachs. The men's productivity and social adaptability did not seem to be integrative of their emotional needs. More generally, the mature Pisans were more productive, made more precise differentiations, and had healthier, more direct, and spontaneous relationships with other persons than did the immature men. The immature men tended to relate to other persons in formalistic, stylized, and inhibited ways, were less acceptant of their heterosexual impulses, and were potentially more predisposed to explode impulsively under stress.

The Sicilians caused me the greatest difficulty. I misassigned eight mature and eight immature men, although my notes indicate that the Sicilian judges probably would rate six of the eight Rorschach-evaluated immature men as mature persons. Three factors may account for this disastrous finding that seemingly healthy Sicilians are socially judged to be immature and vice versa. I cannot get out of the dilemma by pleading my judgments were unreliable. When I discovered the magnitude of the disaster, I reviewed the ratings again, and although I knew by this time who had been judged mature and immature by the judges, I could find no reasons to justify changing my ratings.

The first factor explaining this could have been that the socially judged immature men were just not very immature in terms of my experience with the Rorschach or of its traditional norms. I would like to argue that because the Sicilian group was quite homogeneous, having been drawn from a very small population, it did not contain many immature persons. And I noted earlier that the mature and immature men were not distinguished on many SIQ traits by the judges. But how can I make this argument persuasively when Table 5-2 shows that the Sicilian group more consistently confirmed the hypotheses presented in this chapter than most of the other more heterogeneous groups? So the second factor offers a more appealing explanation: the administration of the Rorschachs deviated so markedly from that of the other groups that the protocols themselves were probably unreliable. But there is a third possible factor that may be peculiar to the Sicilian culture: its socially judged mature men differed from the selected mature men of the other groups very strikingly. Although seemingly as intellectually striving and achieving, the amount they produced was just not commensurate with their striving. They were quite sociable and affable, but their affability seemed to cover a strong schizoid tendency. The Rorschach, according to all traditional clinical lore, suggested they were unable to establish genuinely intimate, spontaneous emotional relationships with another person, particularly with a woman. They were quite wary; they frequently resorted to evasiveness, vagueness and intellectual pretentiousness, and resisted abandoning the suppression of their imagination. This behavior could very well have been a reaction to the authoritarian style of the experimenter to which these mature men were not going to submit! If it was not that, could it be that the men were selected as mature exemplars because of their self-sufficient autonomy, reflecting the Sicilian value on *machismo*, which, when integrated with an affable gregariousness protects them from becoming too dependent in an intimate personal relationship? Their autonomy may not be well integrated with allocentricism in other words. I shall return to this hypothesis in Chapter 8.

Of the socially judged mature Istanbul men, I identified four of the fourteen to be immature, though my notes questioned my judgment about three of them. They were rated immature because the intensity of their primary process imagery was such as possibly to interfere with their functioning. The socially judged mature and immature men were very similar to each other in terms of their Rorschach images. More than any other group, the Istanbul men, both mature and immature, expressed themselves in intensely vivid and passionate terms. The mature men were just as sexually preoccupied and aggressively predisposed as the immature men, though the latter were much more emotionally explosive. In contrast to the Italians, the Turks, both mature and immature, were strongly oriented toward other persons. They expressed their feelings openly, were very sensitive to and needful of affection, and gave many images of persons in close physical, affectionate and sensuous contact, having sexual relations, shaking hands, leaning on one another, standing shoulder to shoulder, and "drawing close to one another."

It was possible to examine in detail the relation of the Rorschach clinical ratings to the social judgments of maturity because the Turkish supervisor knew sixteen of the Istanbul men. Her judgments about the men had not been solicited or used in their selection. We had wanted to test "pure" Turkish judgments of maturity; her American training as a clinical psychologist might have biased her ideas about maturity. Several years following the study, she analyzed the maturity of the men she knew independently of any knowledge of the men's ranked maturity. She correctly identified the maturity status of thirteen of the sixteen men. To illustrate the complexity of the relation between competence and maturity, I describe two of the men about whom there was disagreement. The man ranked by the judges to be the most mature person of the Istanbul group was identified by her to be immature. His earlier suicidal inclinations and hallucinatory-like experiences, unknown to the college community, had led a psychiatrist to diagnose him as an acting-out psychopathic character. However, the supervisor rejected the diagnosis as too severe. He was selected by the judges to be most mature because of his persuasive and charismatic impact in nonacademic activities. Despite his history of maladjustment, however, my completely independent evaluation of his Rorschach had ranked him fourth in maturity.

The youth whom the judges ranked third in maturity was known by the supervisor to have suffered several depressions, together with withdrawal and other schizoid symptoms. His best friend was a schizophrenic. The judges apparently rated him mature because they interpreted his intuitive, feminine sensitivity as a sign of artistic genius. The Rorschach clinical rating placed him near the midpoint of the group. (Reanalysis of some of the Istanbul data omitting the disputed men accentuated the magnitude of many of the results, but did not alter their pattern.)

Comparing the Rorchach and the selection judges' ranks of the men showed that discrepancies in judgment about only two men markedly reduced the magnitude of the results. For example, the man rated most mature on the Rorschach was rated by the judges to be the most immature man of the Istanbul group. The man rated to be next most mature on the Rorschach was ranked by the judges also as very immature. What had gone wrong? The supervisor had described this second person this way in her analysis:

> His friends do not like him . . . they cannot tolerate him because he talks so much. A real obsessive compulsive. But believe me, he talks very well . . . an excellent intelligence plus a full determination to make the most of it plus full determination to show everyone that he is the brightest of all. Has no tact in dealing with the mediocracy of the general public . . . but also has a beautiful sense of humor. He is a peculiar character that you do not meet often. The brainy obnoxious type.

Fragments of my blind analysis of him supported her observations:

> Highly intelligent, productive and sensitive person . . . imaginative, even creative streak in him, but problem may be with social adaptation. Is strongly drawn to other people but in intellectualizing and aggressive ways. Has image of self as an aggressive predator. May protect himself by playing a role . . . humorizes and rationalizes fear and hostility, particularly toward authority. Has deep empathic qualities, good judgment, but he may be very introversive, perhaps too much so for the Turkish culture.

If a culture values social competence very highly, then such an obnoxious person, despite his impressive strengths, may be, as this man was, judged by others quite harshly.

Because of reasonable doubts about the reliability of the judgments of these two men's maturity, I reanalyzed the Istanbul data omitting them. The Rorschach clinical ratings were more predictive of the selection judges' rankings ($rho = .52, p < .01$) and now significantly so for the SIQ Judge ratings as well ($r = .38$, p < .05$).

The Rorschach clinical ratings of the Ankara group agreed much less well with the social judgments of maturity. Table 5–2 shows that the social judgments did not predict well to most of the comprehensive measures of maturity. I do not consider its Social Index of Maturity to be very reliable. Its selection procedure was the most irregular; its and the Istanbul group's Index were the least predictive of the ratings of close friends. I identified six judged-immature men to be mature, and five of the judged-mature men to be immature. No better than chance. I could discover few consistent differences between the socially judged mature and immature men in their imagery, conflicts,' and motivational patterns on the Rorschach. The mature men were much more productive and achieving, and tended to be less anxious and tense persons. My impression was that the mature men were less dependent and child like in their female relationships.

Examination of the Ankara data revealed that the low statistical relationships reported in Table 5–2 were due almost entirely to four men who accounted for more than half of the discrepant variance in the ratings. The man the selection judges ranked second in maturity would have received a Rorschach rank of seven (indicated by an erased check mark on the Rorschach line scale) if I had not changed him to a position that ranked sixteenth. My notes said he was a "very well organized person who had an excellent integrative and original view of the world," as well as a lot of "vigorous assertive energy that is well integrated with sensitivity for others." But I rated him immature because of a very focused problem with women. I hypothesized he feared impotency which he compensated for by overly-strong sadistic behavior toward women. I agreed with the judges in hindsight about the second man. They rated him mature, but I rated him immature. I overestimated the pathological implications of his very sadistic imagery, and underevaluated his ability to control its expression. The third person I had rated as most mature was rated as eighteenth in maturity by both selection judges and his friends. His Rorschach was very similar to that of the Istanbul man who was the "brainy obnoxious type." A fourth person whom I rated very mature and the judges immature was in a major transitional growth phase, according to my interpretation. He seemed to be emerging from being a markedly passive and dependent to a more assertive and autonomous person. I probably overestimated the degree to which such a change had then appeared in his behavior. Eliminating the four men about whom there was greatest disagreement would have, of course, greatly increased the magnitude of the relation between the judges and my clinical evaluations, and easily have made them significant statistically.

Similar types of problems characterized the Haverford group, as

I have discussed elsewhere (1965). Roy Schafer, who made the clinical evaluations, correctly identified ten of the immature and six of the mature men. As with the other groups, social judgments of maturity inferred primarily from observable competences were not always very reflective of the men's internal state. For example, one of the socially judged mature men had an ulcer; another had tics, a psychiatric history, and subsequent episodic hospitalizations.

I have gone into such detail about the clinical evaluations not to rationalize away some of their apparent failures, but to indicate by a few fragments the complexity of the men and of the problems that dogged this research. The dominant thrust of the study is objectively analytic, dryly reductionistic, and impersonally statistical. We risk distorting our understanding of competence and maturity if we fail to appreciate subjectively the living contextuality and personally idiosyncratic nature of a human being.

My fourth and concluding impression of my experience with the Rorschachs is more tentative. I could not discover highly visible, consistent differences between the judged mature and immature men in their imaginal preoccupations, conflicts, or dynamics. In fact, my evaluations seemed to have gone awry when I rated the presence of such specific motivational conflicts as fear of impotency or sadism as indicative of immaturity. Yet, the clinical evaluations of healthiness were moderately predictive for at least one group in each culture. What made the difference, if specific motivational differences did not? One clue comes from the core group of traits that distinguished the mature from the immature men. They reflect primarily adaptive attitudes and skills such as clarity of thinking, purposefulness, realism, orderedness, and so on. Maturity may have less to do with the presence or absence of specific types of conflicts; it may have much more to do with the attitudes and skills (ego) that mediate adaptation.

Some Concluding Reflections

Social judgments of maturity (or competence) are influenced by many factors: 1) The values of the culture that prize some personality attributes more than others; for instance, the Americans seem to prefer the assertion of one's will in doing, the Italians the creation of a harmonious sense of being; 2) Observed competence in responding to the demands of the local setting, particularly competence in producing and in being socially adaptable; and 3) An intuited sense of a person's psychological healthiness and maturity. These probable components are not independent of each other, but reflect the factorially complex nature of social judgments.

Despite, or perhaps more accurately, because of their complexity, the judgments of the judges, particularly those who knew the men well, predicted the adjustment, maturity, and healthiness of representatives from three different cultures. The judgments of the judges did not predict to just one type of measure; they predicted to indirect self-reports, formal objective psychological tests, and more subjective imaginative responses. Findings are more convincing when they result from the convergence of a variety of different measures.

Although each culture emphasizes and values some personality attributes differently from other cultures, the Italian, Turkish, and American cultures do use some similar criteria to define a maturely organized person. The odds are high that an Italian, Turkish, or American youth selected by persons of his own culture to be mature would be similarly judged mature by judges of the other cultures if they had the same opportunity to know him well.

CHAPTER 6

Social Judgments and the Model of Maturing

That judges of five cultural areas agree about who is and who is not a competent and mature person is a reassuring first step in our effort to confirm a transcultural model of maturing. Such agreement does not, however, confirm *the* principal and more specific argument, that increasing maturity is related to the increasing symbolization, allocentricism, integration, stability, and autonomy of one's cognitive skills, self-concept, values, and personal relationships. We have had some glimpses that the hypothesis may be valid. We discovered that the more, in contrast to the less, mature men of each culture were more reflective and better able to anticipate consequences (symbolization); realistic and clearer thinkers (allocentricism); ordered and fulfilling of their potentials (integration); predictable, and had a firmer sense of direction and greater inner equanimity (stability); and were more unshakable, perhaps due to their stronger convictions (autonomy). Another welcome glimpse came from the Perceived Self Questionnaire (PSQ), the one test that comprehensively measured the model of maturing. It generally predicted the judges' ratings of maturing in the five cultural areas.

An Overview of the Validity of the Model of Maturing

To test transculturally the validity of the model of maturing was not a simple task. Furthermore, the complex, technical, and frequently novel measures indexing the model's hypotheses produced an almost unmanageable amount of data for each of the five cultural groups. To report these results in their technical detail risks obscuring the principal findings of the study, and, more important, also risks satiating even the most diligent reader. Instead, I have ordered and simplified the results in a way that, hopefully, highlights their principal patterns. I will be unapologetically interpretive and evaluative. The skeptical reader should first refer to Appendix C, where I define the principal scores of each dimension and their rationale, and then to Appendix D, where I collate the results of the test indices for the five cultural groups.[1]

Tables 6–1 and 6–2 each provide a different overview of the results of the tests of the model of maturing reported in Appendix D.[2] Table 6–1 reports the status of the total 531 predicted findings for the cultural groups. Table 6–2 reports the percentage of findings that confirmed or were consistent with the hypotheses of the model of maturing.

Table 6–1 contains some surprises, given the evaluations previously reported in Chapters 3 and 4 of the reliability of the groups and their findings. The Haverford and Pisa groups provided the most persuasive support of the hypotheses, and the Ankara group the least. That the Italian and Turkish groups were less confirming than the American group was not unexpected, given the typical shrinkage in cross validation studies, and the other methodological problems we encountered. The more homogeneous Sicilian group unexpectedly consistently supported more than two-thirds of the hypotheses. If the assessments made in Chapters 3 and 4

---

1 Some readers will quarrel with my use of certain technical scores of tests like the MMPI and Rorschach as indices of a particular dimension of maturing. The specific "meaning" of many of psychology's traditional personality scores is ambiguous, reflecting, in part, the atheoretical nature of the tests themselves. Few of their scores univocally defined the dimensions of the model. Actually, it is not the fate of a particular test score that is decisive; rather it is the convergent validation or consistency of the patterns based on diverse, possibly equivocal, test scores that is compelling (Campbell and Fiske, 1959). Appendices C and D illustrate how traditional measures of personality might be more profitably ordered theoretically in exploratory research like ours to illumine such patterns.

2 One-tailed p levels were used to assess the significance of a finding. "Consistent" refers to the number of differences between the mature and immature men that were in the predicted direction though they were not significant statistically. Some of the results in Appendix D are not independent of each other, *i.e.*, some tests' scores are based in part on similar items. So Tables 1 and 2 should not be interpreted too literarlly; they only crudely summarize the central weight of a complex pattern of findings.

Table 6–1
Status of Predictions for
Socially Judged Mature and Immature Groups

# of Predictions	Haverford 82	Ankara 116	Istanbul 116	Pisa 116	Sicily 100
% Significantly Confirmed	40	9	9	28	10
% Consistent	37	50	64	46	61
% Total	77	59	73	74	71

are correct, then the more psychologically dissimilar American and Italian groups, rather than similar American and Turkish groups, supported the hypotheses most consistently. While it is reassuring that the model of maturity may hold across diverse cultures, the pattern of findings raises interpretive embarrassments about what I had judged to be the more similar-to-American Turkish groups. I had not expected the Istanbul, but I had expected the methodologically more reliable Ankara group to be more supportive. The Ankaran social judgments of who was and who was not mature may be even less reliable than I had anticipated; as I shall report in Chapter 7, when the maturity of its men was defined by psychological tests, the group was more confirming of our hypotheses.

The principal pattern of the findings in Table 6–2 is quite clear: the indices used to define the model of maturing do distinguish the mature from the immature men. Seventy percent of the total number of the hypothesized differences were in the predicted direction, 18 percent at conventional levels of statistical significance. That only 8 percent of the indices measured, however, the dimension of integration warns us that its findings may not be as substantially based as those of the other dimensions. A second

Table 6–2
Summary of Status of Predictions
About Model of Maturing

# Predictions	PERSONALITY				DIMENSIONS OF MATURING					
	CgSK 174	Self 120	Values 89	Pers 147	Symb 95	Alloc 129	Integ 44	Stab 144	Aut 118	530
% Significantly Confirmed	19	30	10	12	21	23	20	17	10	Total % 18
% Consistent	58	48	57	45	53	50	57	53	52	52
% Total	77	78	67	57	74	73	77	70	62	70

salient pattern is that the hypotheses about the dimensional maturity of the men's cognitive skills, and, particularly, self-concepts were more powerfully confirmed than were the hypotheses about the maturity of their values and personal relationships. This pattern may well reflect the fact that the focused methods for assessing both cognitive skill stability and the self-concept were much more sophisticated and reliable than the methods for assessing the maturity of the men's values and relationships. The third obvious pattern is that the model's hypotheses about the differential autonomy of the mature and immature men were not as convincingly confirmed as were the other dimensions. Again, my hunch is that the reason probably is the inadequacy of our methods, due in part to lack of clarity about the meaning of autonomy in the three cultures, an issue I return to in Chapter 8.

Such is the very rough scaffolding of the results. What can we now say about the specific hypotheses of the model?

Validation of the Model of Maturing

Symbolization. Are mature persons better able to symbolize their experience and accurately understand themselves; and are they more aware of their own values as well as of their relationships with other persons than are immature persons? Our answer to this most general phrasing of the question, based on the differences between the mature and immature men on the PSQ's dimensional score of symbolization, is, "Probably yes." The Pisan mature men were significantly more developed in symbolization than the immature men $(p < .05)$. Its findings were supported, though not significantly, by the Ankarans and Sicilians, but not by the Istanbul men.

More illuminating are the specific findings (see Table D–1, Appendix D). With respect to the differential ability of the mature and immature men to reflect upon their thought and to recall with facility a wide range of different memories and images, the evidence is suggestive but not decisive. We have seen that the judges of every cultural group described the mature men to be more reflective and better able to anticipate consequences than the immature men. The mature and immature men themselves agreed with this assessment of the judges. But I had difficulty consistently confirming the hypothesis using more objective tests. The mature men of every cultural group tended to describe themselves as better able to symbolize their experience on the PSQ. The other tests provided some support for the hypothesis. More than the immature men, the mature men produced greater numbers of images as well as more differentiated ones in response to the Rorschach. Except for the Istanbul men, they also created more imaginative stories to the TAJ, and allowed regressive, less socialized ideas more readily into their consciousness without suffering impairment in their logical control of such themes. And finally, there is the suggestion that they can shift their perspective more readily to be more introspective. These affirmative statements sound very definite; they should not be read that way. The data support the hypothesis, but not very strongly.

With only a twinge of equivocation, we can assert that mature men in the five cultural areas know themselves more accurately than do their immature counterparts. This conclusion stands regardless of whether the accuracy of the men's awareness of themselves is measured by the independent SIQ assessments of their close friends, or by more distant observers like the selection judges. Only the friends' judgments of the Sicilian mature and immature men did not agree with the men's judgments of themselves. As I have already reported in Chapter 5, the judges of every cultural group identified the mature men to be significantly more self-understanding than the immature men. The consistency with which the mature men in every culture were more self-insightful is very impressive, given the numerous factors, like defensive efforts to protect one's self-esteem, that limit the reliability of private self-ratings as well as the judgments of independent judges. Accuracy of self-insight, as philosophers since Socrates and psychologists since James and Freud have insisted, is a cardinal attribute of maturity, at least for Protestant–Jewish, Catholic, and Moslem cultures.

The mature men tended to differ from the immature men on our inadequate measures of their ability to symbolize their values and personal relations. They were more preoccupied about people, and the judges agreed they were more understanding of others.

Summarizing, the hypothesis that mature in contrast to immature persons: 1) have a more differentiated and reflective inner life was confirmed;[1] 2) are more self-insightful was very

---

1 The criteria defining degree of confirmation are described on p. 163. They cannot be as precisely applied in this chapter since I evaluate data from a variety of scores in the summary judgment.

strongly confirmed; 3) are more aware of their values was neither confirmed nor disconfirmed; and 4) are more able to symbolize their relationships with others was only minimally supported. No subhypothesis about the symbolization dimension of the model was disconfirmed.

Allocentricism. The model of maturing assumed that because mature persons can take the perspective of other persons more readily than immature persons can, they will be more logical, objective, and realistic in their thought; have more allocentric self-concepts and caring, social values; and be more socially adaptable, tolerant, and respectful in their relationships with other persons. Again, with the exception of the deviant Istanbul group, the most general measure of the men's allocentricism, the PSQ score, qualifiedly supported the hypothesis. The Sicilian mature men were significantly ($p < .05$) more allocentric than the immature men—a finding supported by the remaining groups except the Istanbul men. But it is the details of the subhypotheses that are more illuminating (see Table D–2, Appendix D).

Although the judges of the five cultures had consistently agreed that the mature men were more realistic and objective in their thought than the immature men, a judgment the men themselves predicted would be made about them, the test results only hinted that such might be the case. The mature men were consistently, though not significantly, more reality-oriented and accurate in their responses to the Rorschach; the evidence was only suggestive that the thinking of the mature men was less distorted by highly personal wishes and fears.

We can proclaim as loudly as we just did about the men's self-insight that mature men from the three cultures have more allocentric self-concepts. Very consistently, the mature men of every cultural group predicted more accurately than did the immature men what the "social other" thought about them. They were able to take the point of view of someone else and then view themselves from that perspective. This finding holds whether the men are predicting what their close friends or a vaguely defined "group of faculty and students" think about them. Certainly a hallmark of maturity is the ability to take an objective, reality-oriented stance toward one's self.

Another meaning of an allocentric self-concept is that a person takes a humane, accepting view of himself. He thinks of himself as a good human being, because he understands and accepts his own humanness. Another very powerfully supported finding, the one most consistently confirmed by the research for every cultural group, was that the mature men believed that other persons thought they were valued and mature persons. They believed that others would rate them highly on traits typical of more mature persons. And they tended to take this same positive acceptant attitude toward themselves as well.

With respect to the values of the mature in contrast to those of the immature men, the evidence generally supports the hypothesis. The values of the mature men were more other-centered and concerned about the welfare of others. The mature men of every cultural group agreed more strongly (significantly so for the Sicilians) than the immature men did with statements like, "My values and beliefs are centered more on the lives of others than on myself and my desires."

The status of the hypothesis about the allocentricism of the men's personal relationships remains ambiguous. Mature persons may well be more socially responsible as well as sensitive to the nuances, particularly affectional, of their personal relationships. They seem to be less guarded and suspicious than the immature men. Perhaps confirming our hunches that intimate and warm personal relationships are not critical to being mature, at least in the Turkish and Italian cultures, the mature men were not consistently or notably less aloof or detached from other persons than the immature men.

We can summarize the status of the allocentric hypothesis this way. The hypothesis that in contrast to the immature men the mature men: 1) think more logically, objectively, and clearly was only minimally confirmed; 2) have more allocentric self-concepts, are able to take another persons' perspective that results in a more objective concept of themselves, have greater self-esteem, and believe that others think highly of them was very strongly confirmed; 3) have more other-centered values was only supported, but not firmly confirmed; and 4) have more allocentric personal relationships was minimally confirmed. None of the allocentric subhypotheses were disconfirmed.

Integration. Do the mature men have more integrated cognitive skills, self-concepts, values, and personal relationships? Relying again on the PSQ summary measure of integration, we can say that the mature men consistently described themselves as generally more integrated than did the immature men, though the differences were significant only for the Pisans $(p < .025)$. If we had used the judgments of the men's friends of the Ankara group rather than those of the selection judges to form the mature and immature groups, the conclusion would have been more firmly supported.

As Table 6–2 indicates, the dimension of integration was not specified by many indices. I relied on Holt's Rorschach scores that measured different types of failures in thinking integratively. But as Table D-3, Appendix D, shows, only the American mature men had significantly fewer illogical, bizarre, and disorganized modes of thought than the immature men. The Italian and Turkish mature and immature men only tended to differ in the integrative quality of their thought. In contrast to the Americans, the Italian and Turkish students just did not give as many responses to the ink blots that revealed disorganized thinking. Consequently, the range of scores indexing poor integration of thought was considerably restricted for all of the Italian and Turkish groups, reducing the possibility of finding significant differences between the mature and immature men. The PSQ measure of cognitive integration, however, showed that the mature Italian and Turkish men consistently reported their thinking to be better integrated, more consistent, precise, and sensitive to the complexity of a problem than the immature men reported their own thought to be. The judges of the three cultures, as well as the men themselves, identified the mature men to be more ordered.

The evidence is much clearer about the integration of the men's self-concepts. With only a few exceptions, the mature men had much more integrated self-concepts, as measured by three different test scores, than did the immature men. How they rated themselves on the SIQ coincided with what they believed other persons thought of them. The mature men had no difficulty affirming that, "I really am what I believe other people think me to be." The consequence of the mature men's more consistent self-concepts was, as the judges told us in Chapter 5, that they were more ordered, predictable, and less erratic than the immature men.

The psychological tests provided only the barest hint that the mature men had also worked out for themselves more consistent values. No statement can be made about the integrative quality of the men's personal relations generally. The mature men tended to assent to statements like, "I am almost completely myself when with a close male friend; there is little I hide from him," but they admitted more difficulty in their relations with women than did the immature men. My other studies have suggested that the PSQ items measuring the maturity of such relationships may elicit great defensive activity that complicates the validation of the items (1968).

What can we conclude? I think we must conclude that the integrative hypotheses defining maturing have not been substantiated very well. The hypothesis that maturity is associated: 1) with more logical, consistent, and ordered thought was minimally confirmed; 2) with more integrative self-concepts was strongly confirmed; 3) with more integrative values and 4) mutuality relationships with others was neither confirmed nor disconfirmed. The judges agreed, as did the men themselves, that the mature men were more predictable and fulfilling of their potential than were the immature men. These traits may be the consequence of successfully "getting one's self together."

Stabilization. I predicted that the cognitive skills, self-concept, values, and personal relations of the mature rather than of the immature men would be more stably organized. Generally, this was the case, when comparing the men in terms of the PSQ dimensional score for stability. Only the mature Sicilians, supported by the other groups except the Ankarans, were significantly ($p < .025$) more stably organized than the immature men. Much of the research effort was devoted to developing procedures to test the cognitive stability of the men. Before abstracting out the basic patterns of the results from this complicated experimental procedure, let us examine how the mature and immature men differed in the stability of their self-concept, values, and personal relationships (see Table D–4, Appendix D).

Congruent with the self-concept results to date, it was the SIQ measure of the stability of the self-concept that provided the most consistent support of the stabilization hypothesis. We can again affirm, though not quite as vigorously as we did for the other dimensional properties of the self-concept, that mature men in the five cultural areas had more stable concepts of themselves. This more stable self-concept cannot be attributed to greater rigidity; the mature and immature men did not differ significantly on scores indexing rigidity. The SIQ results are also supported by a different method of assessing the stability of the self-concept. The mature men generally described themselves on the PSQ as more stable in their concepts of themselves than the immature men did. The four Italian and Turkish mature groups consistently agreed that, "My ideas about myself are quite stable; I think I am the same person now that I was several months ago." The immature men said that they were more changeable.

The mature men tended to have (significantly so only for the Sicilians) more stable values. On the PSQ, they reported that their "beliefs and values are rather stable and don't differ too much from what they were like many months ago." The immature men disagreed with this type of item.

Each man had been administered the Phrase Association Test (PT) which assessed his anxiety thresholds for different types of interpersonal information. It was possible to test directly just how stable his values (emotional reactions) and interpersonal relationships might be. I have shown in other research that a person who is easily disorganized and upset by various types of interpersonal information is in conflict about such relationships (1956, 1965). The presence of anxiety and conflict in a relationship implies that a person has not yet resolved his feelings about that relationship, and so may find his reactions to be erratic and unstable. I expected, therefore, that the anxiety thresholds for different feelings in different relationships would be lower for the immature than for the mature men; that is, the immature men should be prone to be more anxious when confronted with potentially disturbing interpersonal information.

Generally, the Haverford, Istanbul, and Pisa mature men tended to have higher anxiety thresholds about their interpersonal relationships. Only the mature men of Pisa were significantly less anxious than the immature men, particularly about their aggressive feelings toward their parents and about heterosexual relationships.[1]

The PT data also demonstrate the similarity of personality dynamics among the five cultures. Confirming studies of other American groups, from 80 to 100 percent of the men of every cultural group responded with more anxiety to the *a priori* defined threatening than to the nonthreatening information. With only a few exceptions, the mature and immature groups as groups were much less anxious about the defined nonthreatening information, like receiving affection, working cooperatively, and relaxing with others, than they were about the more threatening themes, like rejection, aggression, and sexual relationships. All of the cultural mature and immature subgroups, except the Istanbul immature

1 The PT data for the cultural groups can be secured from NAPS.

men, were least anxious about being deserted by their families. And as has been found for numerous American male groups, the homosexual information produced the greatest number of anxiety responses in every mature and immature group except the immature men of Pisa and Istanbul.

We must conclude, however, that we have not convincingly shown that mature persons are less susceptible to anxiety and disruption when their values and interpersonal relationships are first threatened. While this result is disappointing from one viewpoint, it is a welcome finding from another. For we have just demonstrated that with the exception of the Pisans, the anxiety thresholds of the mature and immature men did not differ significantly with respect to the information used in the tests to assess the stability of their cognitive functioning.

We have now demonstrated that mature men have more stable self-concepts than do immature men in three cultures. They are neither more nor less tense or anxious persons; they have similar thresholds for experiencing anxiety in different personal relationships. It probably is not the presence of conflict, within moderate limits, or the potentiality for becoming anxious and disorganized that distinguishes immature from mature persons. I reached a similar conclusion in Chapter 5, after noting the difficulty of identifying mature from immature men in terms of signs of anxiety and conflict on the Rorschach. The critical issue is, more likely, how well can a person marshall his resources to respond adaptively to a situation that may trigger anxiety? or, if he does become anxious, how well can he cope with its consequences?

It was just this question we studied when we examined how mature and immature men used their cognitive resources to adapt to potentially disruptive information. Are the cognitive skills of mature men more stably organized and resilient than those of immature men, irrespective of their cultural background? Remember that this hypothesis tests a central insight of Freud that a mature person can more effectively deal "with the connecting paths between ideas, without being led astray by the *intensities* of those ideas" (1900, 602). Mature persons should be able to maintain their secondary processes better under stress; they have stronger egos.

If we confirm the hypothesis, we must be assured that its confirmation is not caused by the mature and immature men differing in their anxiety thresholds for the emotional ideas with which they reasoned, or in their intellectual level. The PT data have just told us that the emotional intensity of the content of the cognitive tasks was similar for all of the mature and immature groups except the Pisans. If we discover that the Haverford, Ankara, and Istanbul mature men are more cognitively efficient, we cannot therefore claim their greater efficiency was caused by being less anxious about the content of the tasks. With respect to intelligence, we must distinguish between its effective use, which presumably depends on a person's maturity, and its level. The mature in contrast to the immature men of every cultural group scored higher, though significantly so only for the Haverford group, on intellectual efficiency. We have reliable academic grades for only the Haverford and the Istanbul groups. Their mature men had significantly higher grades. So we have some hints suggesting that the mature men may more effectively use their intellectual resources with nondisturbing types of information. But we must control for sheer intellectual level. The Haverford mature and immature men did not differ in their quantitative and verbal abilities. The Italian and Turkish mature and immature men also did not generally differ on three widely used measures of general intelligence. Only the mature Ankarans performed significantly better than the immature men on the Digit Symbol test, one of the best predictors of the Wechsler-Bellevue total IQ score.

I must now clarify the hypotheses that we tested about cognitive stability. The principal hypothesis was that the mature men are more cognitively stable or efficient than the immature men when they must reason with disturbing information, that is, threatening and less threatening themes. (I define "nondisturbing" information to be the typical nonemotional content of most intelligence tests.) The second hypothesis was that the mature men will improve in cognitive efficiency more rapidly than will the immature men.[1] Recall that each man's scores for the conceptual (TCT), analytic (TAS), and judgmental (TAJ) tests were combined using standard scores to form one summary score indexing cognitive stability.[2]

With respect to the first hypothesis, the mature men were more cognitively stable than the immature men of every cultural group.

1 These hypotheses greatly simplify the complex subhypotheses that guided the initial studies of cognitive stability on several Haverford groups. I am content not to test the more complex hypotheses because the use of standard scores eliminated significant differences between the threatening and nonthreatening information. Results with the Haverford groups suggested that the hypotheses were too precise for the quality of data secured (see 1965, Appendix D, for the technical details).

2 The specific Cognitive Stability as well as the TCT, TAS, and TAJ test results are available from NAPS.

However, only the Haverford ($F = 6.97, p < .025$) and the Pisa ($F = 9.8, p < .01$) mature men were significantly more efficient in solving disturbing problems.[1] To highlight more sharply the differences between the mature and immature men, average Cognitive Stability scores were secured for all the mature and all the immature men irrespective of their cultural areas. (Their scores can be combined because they were scaled using the same transformational base.) The mature men taken together responded more efficiently to both the threatening and nonthreatening information in both the first and the second test sessions than the immature men.

The hypotheses that mature men will be more cognitively resilient and improve more rapidly over time than immature men was informally supported by all of the groups except the Ankara men. It was the failure of the immature men to improve much to the nonthreatening information that contributed most to the overall advantage of the mature men. Excluding the Ankara group for the moment, the mature men improved almost three times as much as did the immature men from the first to the second test session.

Such are the general results. What were the results for the specific groups? Although the Haverford mature men generally were cognitively more efficient, they were significantly better than the immature men on only the test of analytic skill efficiency ($p < .001$). The mature men resisted the potential disorganizing effect of the threatening information more successfully than did the immature men in both test sessions. Interestingly, the mature men improved more to the nonthreatening than threatening information, while the immature men showed no improvement whatsoever to the nonthreatening information. Since the mature and immature men did not differ in their anxiety thresholds or intelligence, we can accept the results as supporting the two hypotheses about cognitive stability.

The mature men of the Pisa group were significantly more cognitively stable than the immature men as well. They were more efficient in solving analytic ($p < .05$) and judgmental ($p < .025$) problems. The mature men tended to improve more than the

---

1 I report results based on the same methods of analysis used with the Haverford group reported elsewhere (1965). The results described are drawn primarily from analyses of variance of each cultural group's data. The study of cognitive stability had also been replicated on a randomly selected second Haverford sample that did *not* consist of selected mature and immature men. Its results were similar, but did not reach acceptable levels of significance.

immature men, but not impressively so. Why were the mature Pisa men so consistently more efficient than the immature men in solving both threatening and nonthreatening analytic and judgmental problems, as well as nonthreatening conceptual problems ($p < .005$)? Their greater cognitive efficiency was not due to higher intelligence, since the mature and immature men did not differ significantly on any of the three measures of intelligence. Moreover, intelligence as we measured it was not related in any way to judgmental efficiency on the TAJ test, which the mature men did very well on. Was their better performance due to the fact that the immature men had significantly lower anxiety thresholds for the information contained in the cognitive tests? A closer analysis of the immature men's PT anxiety thresholds revealed that: 1) They were significantly more upset by the threatening than by the nonthreatening information ($p < .05$); 2) They were significantly more upset than the mature men in response to both the threatening ($p < .025$) and the nonthreatening ($p < .05$) information in their *first* encounter with the PT; and 3) They did *not* differ significantly from the mature men in their anxiety thresholds for either the threatening or nonthreatening information by the time of their second PT. *But* the immature men were *initially* no more efficient in solving problems containing nonthreatening than threatening information, even though the PT had shown that they differed in their anxiety thresholds for the two types of information. Therefore, differences in anxiety about the information among the mature and immature men in their first encounter with it did not seem to be critical, since no difference in cognitive efficiency occurred for the varied information. This conclusion is buttressed by the fact that the immature men failed to improve in their efficiency over time with the nonthreatening problems, but they did improve in their cognitive efficiency with the threatening problems. The failure to improve their efficiency to the nonthreatening information resulted in their lower total Cognitive Stability score, as well as their lower mean improvement score. These observations lead to the conclusion that the immature Pisans' initial lower anxiety thresholds probably do not account for their significantly poorer cognitive efficiency.

As a group the Istanbul men were more efficient with the nonthreatening than the threatening problems ($F = 5.53, p < .05$), and improved significantly from the first to the second test session ($F = 5.92, p < .05$). Although the Istanbul mature men initially were no more cognitively efficient than the immature men with either threatening or nonthreatening information, they improved markedly, though not significantly, in their efficiency for solving the nonthreatening problems. The immature men showed no improvement whatsoever to the nonthreatening problems. This pattern of cognitive improvement was identical to that of the Haverford men. Can we account for this support of the hypothesis in terms of differential intellectual or anxiety factors? The type of intellectual skill measured by the Digit Symbol test did contribute significantly to the cognitive skill efficiency of the Istanbul men. But since it was the immature rather than the mature group which scored better (though not significantly so) on the Digit Symbol test, we cannot reasonably account for the greater cognitive efficiency of the mature men in terms of possibly lower intelligence. If the mature men's tendency to have higher anxiety thresholds for the threatening information was the cause, then they should have been *more* rather than less efficient than the immature men in the first test session. Actually, the immature men showed significantly better judgment on the first day of the TAJ test than the mature men ($p < .01$), but by the second test day, the mature men had recouped their forces and routed the immature men by significantly outperforming them ($p < .005$). So I conclude that neither intelligence nor anxiety accounts for the findings. The mature men were just more stably organized, at least in terms of their resiliency in handling stress.

Finally, the Ankara group. The mature men were consistently, though not significantly, more efficient generally than the immature men with both the threatening and nonthreatening information during both test sessions. It was the one cultural group, however, that improved most, and significantly so ($F = 19.91$, $p < .01$). But it was the one group in which the immature men improved, though not significantly, more than the mature men. Their greater improvement was due, in part, to their greater disorganization in the first test session to the nonthreatening information. No other cultural group's immature men did as poorly initially. The consequence was that the immature men recovered from a lower base level, and so could make a more dramatic improvement.

Recall that the Ankara group was the one sample for which we had the most difficulty securing reliable selection judges. Since the men's close friends, presumably more reliable judges, had described them on the SIQ items indexing maturity, it was possible to reform the Ankara men by dichotomizing them into mature and immature groups on the basis of their SIQ Friend Judge Esteem score. The results were more reassuring. The reformed groups differed as predicted in their cognitive stability $(F = 9.16, p < .01)$. The mature men were significantly more efficient with the threatening $(p < .05)$ and nonthreatening $(p < .05)$ information with some of the skills $(F = 4.92, p < .05)$, like analytic and synthetic thinking $(p < .01)$ than the immature men. Furthermore, the mature men were more resilient $(F = 14.34, p < .001)$, improving more from the first to the second session than the immature men did.

Although the Ankara results confirm the hypotheses about cognitive stability when we use the judgments of the men's close friends for defining maturity, I conclude that the Ankara findings are only supportive, since the selection judge-defined groups did not differ significantly as had originally been predicted. We cannot account for the trend of the Ankara results to support the hypotheses by differences in anxiety thresholds of the mature and immature men. Because it was the mature and not the immature men who tended, but not significantly so, to be more anxious about the disturbing information, we obviously cannot account for their better efficiency in terms of greater anxiety, according to the line of reasoning we have been following.

On the other hand, the greater cognitive stability of the Ankaran mature men may possibly have been due to their better intellectual ability on the Digit Symbol test, which positively and occasionally significantly predicted our summary score of Cognitive Stability. A covariance analysis to control for intellectual ability was not justified, since the mature and immature groups had not been randomly selected, an important condition required by the analysis. Although the correlation between cognitive stability and the social judges' judgments of maturity was not significant, I partialled out the effect of intelligence to secure an approximate glimpse of its effect. Intellectual ability did account for some of the relationship, thus suggesting that the mature and immature Ankarans may not have differed in the stability of their cognitive processes.

How shall we evaluate this experimental study of cognitive stability in four different cultural groups? I consider the similarity in the pattern of the results to be quite remarkable, particularly given the difficulties that I (and probably many other personality psychologists) have had in replicating results on groups from the same institutional locale; the lack of linguistic comparability of the Thematic Analysis-Synthesis Test among the three cultures; the omission of the sexual information in the Thematic Concept Test for the Italian and Turkish groups; the use of different normative weights to assess the degree of realism of the men's stories to the Thematic Judgment Test (see Appendix B for a discussion of these limitations); and the differences among the experimenters.

What shall we conclude about the stabilization hypotheses? The hypothesis that mature rather than immature men have 1) more stably organized skills was confirmed; 2) more stable self-concepts was confirmed; 3) have more stable values remains unconfirmed; and 4) have more stable personal relationships remains unconfirmed. With the exception that the anxiety thresholds, presumably indirect indices of unstable values, of the mature and immature men did not consistently differ, no evidence emerged from the study that disconfirmed the stabilization hypotheses.

Autonomy. Are mature persons more autonomous than immature persons? My answer will be, "I don't know." Most of the results were ambiguous, due primarily to inadequate as well as too few validated measures of autonomy. An intratest analysis of the PSQ, reported in Appendix B, warned us that its measure of autonomy was probably not very reliable. The warning was correct. The mature men of Ankara and Pisa reported themselves on the PSQ to be less autonomous, though not significantly so, than the immature men reported themselves to be.

Let us turn to the specific subhypotheses (see Table D-5, Appendix D). To test the autonomy of the men's cognitive skills I had relied on Holt's measures of primary process that indexed the extent to which a person's thought was dominated by less conscious dreamlike images and primitive unconscious modes of coordinating them. The evidence from the basic scores was equivocal, possibly because maturity may not involve screening out of consciousness or repressing intense socially unacceptable daydreams as much as it involves the ability to control their emergence in a way that does not lead to being overwhelmed by such fantasies. Quite suggestively, the Holt scores measuring the effectiveness with which a person assimilates into awareness, with good control, oral, aggressive, and, particularly, sexual wishes and impulses very consistently, and occasionally significantly, separated the mature from the immature men as predicted. The mature men were judged by the judges, confirmed by the men's own self-ratings, to be unshakable and controlled; but these meager hints certainly do not permit us to conclude that we have convincingly confirmed the hypothesis about the autonomy of the men's cognitive skills.

Complete comparative data about the autonomy of the men's self-concepts were not available. The failure of an earlier experimental method of assessing the autonomy of the self-concept with American groups spurred the use of alternative measures for the Italian and Turkish groups. After the sterling results the SIQ has provided to date, it is a disappointment to have to conclude that the mature men only tended to have more autonomous concepts of themselves. I go even that far because of other data not reported in Table D–5, Appendix D. If the mature and immature groups are reformed on the basis of their close friends' SIQ judgments of their maturity, then the mature Ankarans are significantly more autonomous than the immature Ankarans in their self-concepts; and all of the other cultural groups support this finding. There are also hints from the MMPI that the mature men do not think of themselves as being dominated or driven by aggressive impulses, and, from the PSQ, that they are not easily influenced by the ideas that their parents and friends have about them.

The data are even more silent about the autonomy of the men's values. The judges, again confirmed by the men themselves, rated the mature but not the immature men to be purposeful persons of strong convictions. The mature Sicilians, supported by their Turkish counterparts, had more autonomous values as measured by the Valuator Test. Nothing more can be said, however.

Finally, of the several scores indexing more autonomous personal relationships, only an MMPI score measuring uncontrolled, irresponsible, impulse-driven behavior characterized the immature in contrast to the mature men.

Our final concluding summary can be very brief. The hypothesis that maturing is accompanied by increasingly autonomous 1) cognitive skills, 2) self-concepts, and 3) values are minimally supported but not confirmed; and 4) interpersonal relationships remains moot. Despite these fragments of supporting bits and pieces, I must conclude that the autonomy hypothesis has been neither confirmed nor disconfirmed. It remains a reasonable hypothesis; it is just darn hard to test.

Toward an Evaluation of the Model of Maturing

Table 6–3 summarizes my evaluation of the hypotheses of the model of maturing when tested using socially-defined mature and immature groups. About one-third of the dimensional hypotheses were confirmed; one-third weakly confirmed; and one-third neither confirmed nor disconfirmed. No evidence permits us to reject any of the twenty basic hypotheses. No consistent patterns of disconfirming results held for several cultural groups.

Table 6–3
Degree of Confirmation of the Model of Maturing

Very Strongly Confirmed	Strongly Confirmed	Confirmed	Weakly Confirmed	Neither Confirmed Nor Disconfirmed
Symb Self-con	Integ Self-con	Symb Cgsk	Symb Per Rel	Symb Values
Alloc Self-con		Stab CgSk	Alloc CgSk	Integ Values
		Stab Self-con	Alloc Values	Integ Per Rel
			Alloc Per Rel	Stab Values
			Integ CgSk	Stab Per Rel
			Aut CgSk	Aut Per Rel
			Aut Self-con	
			Aut Values	

How shall we interpret the confirming findings? It is probable that mature in contrast to less mature Americans, Italians, and Turks have more accurate, symbolized, integrated, and stable self-concepts, as well as more symbolized and stable cognitive skills. But do these findings mean we have identified the common core traits that define the essence of maturing? Have we found *the* keys by which to separate mature from immature persons in the future? The implications of these questions make me uncomfortable. Certainly we can agree with the self-theorists that a person's concept of himself is an important clue for predicting his behavior. And we can agree with the ego psychologists that the stability of a person's cognitive skills (an aspect of ego strength) contributes to his adaptation. What makes me uncomfortable is that the dominance of the results by the self-concept and cognitive skill findings may distort our understanding of the core pattern of traits necessary to define maturing. Other traits may be just as important for assessing a person's maturity. My doubts are twofold. The first doubt is methodological. The confirmed hypotheses were just those for which we had developed highly focused and reliable measures to test them. The unsupported hypotheses were those to which we had devoted the least amount of effort and methodological concern. If as much care had been given to securing behavioral measures of the dimensional maturity of the men's personal relationships or of their autonomy, would we have confirmed the hypotheses as consistently and so established a more complete pattern of core traits as keys to selecting mature and immature persons in the future? The second doubt concerns the adequacy of social judgments as the primary or sole criterion against which to validate the model of maturing. I shall discuss this and its related issues in the next two chapters.

CHAPTER 7

Psychological Tests and the Model of Maturing

A recurring daydream I had during the frustrating months spent finding judges to select the mature and immature men to study may clarify what this chapter is about. An image of a portable shiny black box, labeled MD for "maturity detector," kept pressing into my awareness, particularly when I was walking the streets of Ankara. The MD, like a psychological geiger counter, emitted clicks, the frequency of which identified the maturity of each person I passed on the street. Like Don Quixote, I had an impossible dream: to identify the components necessary to make a maturity detector that could be used by any psychologist in any city at any time. Although I have already identified some possible components of the MD, I do not know if they are sufficient or if other components are required. Even if we had precisely tooled measures of the remaining components of the model of maturing, we still have only the judgments of judges of the men's maturity against which to test the validity of our measures.

Because no maturity detector was available by which to test the model of maturing, we had no choice but to begin with the judgments of local judges. They were practical and economical to secure. How else could the 1156 qualified men of five cultural areas have been as readily surveyed to identify the sixty-five most mature men and sixty-five most immature men of that population? Social judgments can also take into account the multidimensionality and complexity of the concept that more objective and focused psychological tests cannot. Furthermore, the original American research had demonstrated that social judgments could be a useful and potentially valid preliminary screening method (Heath, 1965, Ch. 13).

But social judgments are complexly determined, as I pointed out. They are influenced by individual and cultural values, by the observed competence to adapt to the demands of the institution in which the person is being judged, and by a person's inferred psychological healthiness and maturity. Such social judgments might not always agree very well with the readings of a maturity detector, particularly one that filtered out idiosyncratic cultural or individual judgmental biases. And unlike a psychological geiger counter, social judgments may not penetrate very deeply into the interior of the person being screened to gauge whether his manifest competence is defensive and nonintegrative. Faculty judges may be impressed by the demonstrated competency of a person adjusting to their competitive academic demands, as occurred in the selection of the Haverford mature men. Student judges may be swayed by the charismatic power of certain types of student leaders, as may have occurred in the selection of some of the Istanbul mature men. Yet, competency in the classroom may reflect a compulsively neurotic control that leaves some persons empty of vitality, and charismatic power may manifest a paranoidal power complex. The Italian *la bella figura* complex may mask a schism between the persona and the personal unconscious. American entrepreneurship may contain elements of deep guilt about repressed tenderness. Turkish self-controlled gentleness may be protective against sadistic passions.

Now, social judgments do not have to be as unreliable as these examples suggest. We can and did enhance their reliability and discriminating power by using numerous diverse judges to view persons from several different perspectives. One hundred and fifteen faculty, student, and other adults served as judges in the research. Like a magnifying glass that concentrates the sun's rays to burn a hole in a piece of paper, so diverse judgments, when combined, may provide a focused, in-depth reading of a person's maturity. As I have shown above, social judgments, when carefully secured, are useful in identifying some core components of a possible maturity detector.

Can we discover other, or more powerful ways to identify who is and who is not mature? Judgments based on visible socially evaluated competences need to be anchored to a comprehensive view of a person's interior life. The earlier research on American groups suggested that supplementing social judgments by psychological tests might purify the groups of some persons whose judged effectiveness was channeling or producing psychopathology. Is this suggestion supported by the Italian and Turkish studies?

Here I will explore two questions: first, which of the several tests of general personality functioning more powerfully predicts maturity across the five cultural areas? and second, if mature and immature criterion groups had been selected by the different tests rather than by judges, which hypotheses of the model of maturing might have been validated among the five cultural areas?

Comparison of Principal Tests of Personality Functioning

After reviewing how the tests of maladjustment, maturity, esteem, and psychological healthiness were related among themselves, we will examine the validity correlates of the different measures in more detail. Table 7-1, which describes the patterns of relationships between the comprehensive measures of maturity, when combined with Table 5-2, which describes the relation of the tests to the social judgments of maturity, provides the most general overview of the principal results of the study.

Table 7-1 is both provocative and disconcerting. Provocative because of the extraordinary consistency among the five groups in the patterns of some of their test relationships; disconcerting because, in contrast, the Rorschach clinical ratings of healthy personality organization were so unpredictive of the more verbal types of tests. Certainly, one of the exceptionally clear findings is that increasing self-esteem, measured by the private SIQ ratings, is strongly and unequivocally related to the esteem that one believes that others have of oneself. To state this finding more concretely, men who rate themselves as less mature on a variety of traits believe others also rate them similarly.

How shall we interpret this finding now verified at very high confidence levels in five cultural areas? A critic might charge that Table 7-1 merely shows that the men are verbally consistent in their responses to the SIQ. The results say nothing about how the men actually behave. Or he might claim that the men were asked to do the impossible—summarize how some mythical "social other"

Table 7–1
Intercorrelations of Comprehensive
Measures of Maturity for the Cultural Groups

Groups	MEASURES OF MATURITY			
	SIQ Social	*PSQ Total*	*MMPI Total*	*Rorschach Clin Rtg*
SIQ Private¹				
Haverford	83****	(34)²	−38*	56****
Ankara	71****	76****	−60****	34
Istanbul	76****	64****	00	11
Pisa	74****	71****	−53****	25
Sicily	66****	70****	−66****	−31
SIQ Social¹				
Haverford		(46)**²	−52****	63****
Ankara		63****	−36*	26
Istanbul		63****	−25	05
Pisa		58****	−30	23
Sicily		63****	−48****	−12
PSQ Total¹				
Haverford			(−48)**	(31)
Ankara			−66****	12
Istanbul			−19	−02
Pisa			−33*	35*
Sicily			−71****	06
MMPI Total¹				
Haverford				−41*
Ankara				−02
Istanbul				−20
Pisa				00
Sicily				10

**** .005; **** .01; ** .025; * .05.

1 High SIQ Private, Social, PSQ Total, and Rorschach scores and low MMPI Total score indicate greater maturity.

2 Haverford-group's retrospective PSQ ratings included in parentheses to indicate their questionable reliability.

would rate them on thirty traits— so that what the men did, as any reasonable person would do, was to ascribe to others what they thought about themselves. The results of Table 5–2 provide the data to refute both these criticisms. They ground, so to speak, the men's subjective ratings to the objective ratings of independent judges. The men accurately described their own behavior as observed by both the selection judges and their close friends. Furthermore, and this is the clincher, the men's predictions of the ratings of the other judges were highly accurate. So the men were doing more than just being verbally consistent or indiscriminately projecting their own concepts onto some blank screen. They were describing some real forms and shapes.

One of the most dramatically persuasive results of the study was the consistency with which the MMPI, PSQ, and SIQ measures covaried. Psychological adjustment, maturity as defined by our model, and private and social self-esteem very powerfully predict each other. The different routes to maturity used in the study have converged. The image of the seven blind philosophers comes to mind. Each claimed that the part of the elephant he was touching was the *real* elephant. Each test measures a portion of the same common reality. But again a critic might say the multiple routes used to target in on the elephantine concept of maturity are not very different. All that the pattern shows is that Americans, Italians, and Turks answer similar questions similarly. The argument is too simplistic. Each test differs from the other. The MMPI differs from the PSQ and SIQ in form, content, and mode of scoring. And no person knew or fathomed how the test scores on which Table 7–1 are based were secured.[1]

A more economical and plausible explanation of the striking consistency among the tests is that the men were consistently making an evaluative judgment about themselves. Persons who think poorly of themselves and who are self-rejecting will slant any question negatively; conversely, those who think highly of themselves and are self-accepting will slant their answers positively. This argument is not fully convincing. Most of the items of the three tests deal with very specific behavioral traits. What percentage of the variance of the responses of the men to each of the 646 items that make up the three tests can be attributed to a self-rejecting or self-accepting attitude is an empirical question. I doubt that the total variance due to such a common factor would be so great as to account for the magnitude of the findings of Table 7–1.

If only the Rorschach's clinical ratings of psychological healthiness had covaried more powerfully with the other measures of maturity! The Rorschach is not as consciously manipulable as are the other tests; it is radically different in its structure and the demands it makes upon a person; and it was analyzed in a way diametrically opposed to the way the more objective MMPI, for example, was scored. If it had consistently covaried with the other

---

1 For a trenchant defense of the strategy of using convergent but diverse procedures to validate a construct, see Campbell and Fiske, 1959.

tests, then the criticisms could have been dismissed out of hand. If we ignore the Sicilians at this point because of the unreliability of their Rorschach clinical ratings, we can make these assertions about the results of the Rorschach. The clinical ratings of psychological healthiness did not predict psychological adjustment as measured by the MMPI (except for the Americans), and minimally predicted the men's self-esteem (the Ankara finding is significant at the .06 level), social self-esteem, and PSQ-defined maturity.

The Istanbul group maintained its idiosyncratic stance. Given the consistent confirming patterns for the other cultural groups, including its fellow Ankaran group, the Istanbul group's MMPI measure of adjustment failed to predict significantly to any other measure of maturity, or, as Table 5–2 reminds us, significantly to the judgments of the selection judges and of the men's close friends. Combining these facts with the group's quite deviant intra-correlational pattern of MMPI scores, the conclusion seems inescapable that its MMPI is unreliable. Some unknown artifactual, attitudinal set, or other personality factor has so reduced the test's reliability that its results should not be very heavily weighted in our subsequent interpretations. Our clues about the deviant character of the Istanbul group increase, but no clear answer has yet emerged to make it understandable.

The following conclusions seem to be warranted by Table 7–1. Regardless of the differences among the three cultures' values and expectations:

1 high self-esteem is associated very strongly with good personal adjustment, knowledge that others judge one to possess traits of mature persons, greater maturity, and, possibly, with healthy personality organization.

2 psychological maladjustment is very strongly related to poor self-esteem, beliefs that others think one is immature, and self-ratings of the dimensional immaturity of one's self-concept, cognitive skills, values, and personal relationships.

3 maturity when defined by increasing ability to symbolize experience, allocentricism, integration, stability and autonomy is strongly associated with high self-esteem, beliefs that others think similarly of one's self, good personal adjustment and possibly healthy personality organization.

4 the consistency of the relation of healthy personality organization to other measures of maturity across the three cultures remains unclear. There may be some minimal to moderate relation-

ship between psychological healthiness and self- and social-esteem, as well as maturity.

5 the validity of the model of maturity as well as its theoretical rationale received additional though indirect confirming support.

Such is the general framework of the psychological test results. It is now time to complete the structure by examining what type of comprehensive measure of maturity more powerfully predicts the various indices used to define the components of the model of maturing. To simplify the reportorial task of summarizing the findings of the tests, I restrict the analysis to the MMPI, PSQ, and Rorschach clinical ratings, the three most distinctively different measures of general effectiveness. The MMPI, empirically generated, has been the most widely researched psychometric measure of personal adjustment in America. Just how powerfully discriminating is it in different cultures? The PSQ is an exploratory self-rating procedure which, in contrast to the MMPI, was generated on the basis of a theoretical rationale. Its correlates indirectly provide more information about the status of the model of maturing. The Rorschach clinical ratings of healthiness reflect the more holistic approach of psychodynamically oriented clinicians. Because the SIQ private and social self-esteem measures correlated so highly with the PSQ Total score, their results, which were very similar to those of the PSQ, are not reported.

To highlight the principal validity patterns of each test, I will simplify the massive amount of data from the five cultural areas by using the following convention. The correlates of each test are assessed in terms of the degree to which the results of each cultural group supported each other, at least at a one-tailed .05 p level when the directionality of the results had been predicted.

Very strongly confirmed[1]: the results of at least four of five cultural groups are significant and remaining group (if its data are available) is supportive.

Strongly confirmed: at least three of the cultural groups are significant and remaining groups are supportive.

Confirmed: at least two of the cultural groups are significant and at least two others are supportive.

Weakly confirmed: at least one group is significant and at least two others are supportive.

---

1 I continue to use these categories summarizing gradations of confirmation to enable me to compare later the results of social judgments and psychological tests, though technically the categories refer to consistency, not strength, of relationship.

Consistent: at least four of the five groups are in the predicted direction.

Obviously, some discretion must be involved in making such judgments. Incomplete data, limited reliability of some of the test indicators, some differences in the cultural groups' procedures, and other factors moderated some of the judgments.

The validity correlates of the MMPI. In interpreting the validity correlates of the MMPI Total maladjustment score (and the other test scores as well), we must keep in mind that they are based on small non-random groups preselected by judges to be mature or immature. We could expect that we thereby have maximized the opportunity to obtain consistent validity correlates, since each group would contain more extreme members of its population. However, Table 5–2 indicated the MMPI Total maladjustment score did not consistently predict the judges' assessment of maturity. The following summary, therefore, probably does *not* overstate the power of the MMPI Total score to predict to a range of other indicators of maturity or healthiness. Obviously, the summary provides only hints and clues, not definite results, of what might be discovered about the MMPI if it had been used to select more extreme criterion groups from larger cultural populations.

The more well-adjusted in contrast to the poorly-adjusted, person, as defined by the MMPI Total score, is more likely to

Trait
Very Strongly Confirmed
Be mature, have high positive self-esteem, and a stable and integrated concept of himself (PSQ Tot[1]; SIQ Priv, Stab, Integ).

Strongly Confirmed
Be mature in his intellectual skills, values, and relations with males as well as more stable and allocentric (PSQ CgSk, Val, Rel M, Stab, Alloc).

Have more mature values, particularly more autonomous ones (Val Tot, Aut).

Believe others rate him very maturely, which in fact his close friends do; have a more allocentric concept of himself (SIQ Soc, Friend Judg, Alloc Sel).

1 See Appendix C for description of the test score abbreviations

Confirmed

Be mature in his concept of himself, as well as be more integrated and autonomous (PSQ Self-con, Integ, Aut).

Have more stable and integrated values, though he does not prefer a more aesthetic way of life (Val Stab, Integ; SV Aes).

Have a more accurate concept of himself as verified by his close friends (SIQ Symb Friend).

Be selected by other judges as mature (Sel Judg).

Weakly Confirmed

Be mature in his relations with women as well as more able to symbolize his experience (PSQ Rel F, Symb).

Have more allocentric and symbolizable values (Val Alloc, Symb).

Be more cognitively efficient when first encountering disturbing information, particularly in his judgment about both threatening and nonthreatening information (Cg Eff Tl; TAJ Tot, Th, Nt).

Be less dominated by primitive unsocialized thoughts and images; maintain logical and consistent thinking (Ror Con%, Form%, Ll%).

Be more imaginative (TAJ No. St).

The validity correlates of the PSQ. Similar analyses were made of the PSQ Total maturity score as well as of the PSQ's component dimensional scores. The fact the PSQ's allocentric, integration, and stability scores were highly related to its Total maturity score means that their validity correlates will be similar. While the patterns of the validity correlates of the symbolization and autonomy dimensions were similar, they were not as powerfully confirmed by as many cultural groups.

The more mature a person is, as defined by the PSQ Total score, the more likely will he

Trait
Very Strongly Confirmed

Be well-adjusted, assertively dominant, tolerant, and independent, and less impulsive, anxious, distant and aloof in his relations with others (MMPI Tot, Do, To, Dy, Im, At, Sc).

Have a healthy esteem for himself, judge others to value him positively, and have a more stable and integrated self-concept (SIQ Priv, Soc, Stab, Integ).

Have mature values that are well-integrated and autonomous (Val Tot, Integ, Aut).

Strongly Confirmed

Be socially responsible, intellectually efficient and well-adjusted as well as neither inconsistent nor obsessionally self-doubting (MMPI Rer, Ie, Tot, F, Pt).

Be more imaginative about a wider range of different types of personal relationships (TAJ No. Int).

Have values that are readily symbolizable, allocentric, and stable (Val Symb, Alloc, Stab).

Confirmed

Be able to bounce back flexibly if disrupted by stress; be reflectively controlled and give the impression of being socially adjusted; be relatively free of moods that could plummet him into depressions or escalate him into highs; be free of suspicions of others (MMPI Es, Rgm, K, Sr, D, Ma, Pa).

Be judged by friends and others to be mature, and be able to predict accurately what others think of him (SIQ Friend, Judge, Alloc).

Be more imaginative in mastering disturbing information (TAJ No. St).

Weakly Confirmed

Not be preoccupied by his bodily health, or aloof from social groups; not socially irresponsible in how he satisfies his needs, or uncontrolledly emotional (MMPI Hs, Si, Pd, Hy).

Have a more accurate and autonomous self-concept (SIQ Symb, Aut).

Make more realistic judgments about personally disturbing information (TAJ Tot, Th, T1, T2).

Have better control of aggressive impulses (Ror Agg DE).

Be theoretically inclined and interested in symbolizing ideas, but aesthetically disinclined; distrust relying on his feelings when making judgments (SV Theo, Aes).

This summary of the validity of the PSQ is intriguing and disturbing. Why was such a consistent pattern woven between the PSQ and tests like the MMPI, Valuator Test, and the SIQ, but no pattern woven with the Rorschach, PT, and cognitive skill tests? The MMPI, Valuator, and SIQ tests differ in a significant way from the other tests, since their scores are ultimately derived from direct verbal statements about the self. True, the SIQ dimensional measures do *not* directly reflect the content of verbal reports; they measure, though, the degree of consistency between different types of statements. The PSQ did not predict to the more performance type of tasks, except for the Haverford group, the one group for which I had been the experimenter. Since the Rorschach, PT, and cognitive tests were the only tests in which the nature of the personal relationship between the examiner and testee intruded into the procedure, and which required considerable testing skill, could a major uncontrolled variable moderating the intercultural consistency in the results be examiner characteristics? No definite answer can be given, since replicate groups from the same cultural area tested by different experimenters were not available. But such a research program with students who are not as testwise or sophisticated about the role of "experimenter-subject" may be more easily affected by the experimenter's manner and style. Appendix B reported some informal evidence supporting this hunch.

The chapter is considering the comparative validity of psychological tests and social judgments of maturity. Certainly, the PSQ and social judgments predict to different patterns of behavior. The PSQ is much more consistently and powerfully related to other self-report measures like the MMPI and Valuator Test than are the social judgments. Both the judges and the PSQ seldom consistently predicted any Rorschach or PT score. The social judgments more consistently predicted every dimension of the self-concept as well as a greater range of psychological measures. The PSQ did not predict cognitive efficiency; the social judgments did but not very powerfully.

How shall we assess the PSQ? Its unusually consistent and statistically significant relations with the MMPI may mean that the validity network that has been forged by countless studies of the MMPI for the past several decades may apply in some as yet unknown way to the PSQ. The PSQ's strengths are that it has a theoretical rationale, is economical, students enjoy taking it, and it validly predicts a variety of personality traits of maturity in several diverse cultures. Its weaknesses are those of an exploratory method not yet subject to rigorous psychometric procedures. Now that the test has been shown to predict a variety of other tests and judgments, more sustained psychometric studies are in order.

The validity correlates of Rorschach clinical ratings. The Rorschach ratings of the psychological healthiness of the men are the last of the different types of methods I shall examine.

The healthier a person is psychologically, as defined by Rorschach clinical ratings, the more likely will he

Trait
Strongly Confirmed
Be identified as mature by others (Sel Judg).

Confirmed
Be rated mature on traits typical of mature persons and have a stable sense of identity (SIQ Friend Judg, Stab).

Be more cognitively efficient in mastering nonthreatening information and, more specifically, conceptual types of disturbing information after he has had an opportunity to adapt to it (CgEff Nt; TCT T2).

Master whatever anxiety oral, aggressive, and sexual thoughts or wishes may arouse in his relationships (PT Tot, Th, Nt, Oral, Agg, Sex).

Weakly Confirmed
Be mature, particularly in his relations with women, as well as more able to symbolize his experience, take different perspectives, and be more stably organized (PSQ Tot, Rel F, Symb, Alloc, Stab).

Be more stably organized in his values (Val Stab).

Have a more integrated, allocentric, accurate, and autonomous concept of himself as well as a belief of himself as mature, and a belief that others think similarly of him (SIQ Integ, Alloc, Symb, Aut, Priv, Soc).

Be more intellectually efficient and socially responsible, but less inconsistent, rigid, depressed, impulsively antisocial, anxious, and dependent (MMPI Ie, Rer, F, Rgm, D, Pd, At, Dy).

Master both threatening and nonthreatening types of information, as well as be more cognitively efficient with all types of information whether he has had the opportunity to adapt to it or not; be able to analyze and synthesize, conceptualize, and make realistic judgments about all types of disturbing information (All CgEff scores; TAS, TCT, TAJ).

At first glance, these very meager consistent findings suggest that the Rorschach clinical ratings are relatively useless in differentiating mature from immature persons. Before making such a conclusion, and returning to the question of what type of procedure might be most useful for selecting mature and immature persons in the future, let us re-examine the data of the five cultural groups from the point of view of the second question posed above— how confirming or disconfirming were the tests of adjustment, maturity, and healthiness of the hypotheses of the model of maturing? We will reorganize the same results now in terms of the theoretical predictions of the study.

A Summary Evaluation of Model of Maturing

To compare the power of the MMPI, PSQ, and Rorschach clinical ratings with that of the social judgments to confirm the model of maturing, we followed the strategy used in Chapter 6. Adjusted and maladjusted, mature and immature, and psychologically healthy and unhealthy groups were formed in terms of their MMPI, PSQ, and Rorschach scores respectively. That is, the men in each cultural group who had, for example, the highest and the men who had the lowest MMPI scores were identified as the maladjusted and the adjusted MMPI groups. The MMPI-defined adjusted and maladjusted men were then compared in terms of the model's hypothesized differences between them. But to reform the extreme groups meant we had to use the one hundred and thirty men the judges had already elected rather than the 1156 men of the total population, since not all of the latter had been given the three psychological tests. Consequently, the MMPI-, PSQ-, and Rorschach-defined groups do not represent the most extreme contrasting groups we might have secured from the population. The cards are stacked, so to speak, *against the psychological tests*. As a consequence, they are unlikely to be as discriminating as social judgments. If we had been able to select the extreme MMPI groups, for example, from the entire population, then we would have been able to make a fairer test of the MMPI's comparable power to confirm the model's hypotheses.

Rather than describe the technical details about each reformed test-defined group and its pattern of differences, as was done in Chapters 5 and 6 for the socially judged mature and immature groups, I shall only summarize the principal conclusions.[1]

Tables 7–2 and 7–3 summarize the degree to which each hypothesis of the study was confirmed by the MMPI-defined adjusted and maladjusted, PSQ-defined mature and immature, and Rorschach-defined healthy and unhealthy groups. The judgments about the "degree of confirmation" of the model's hypotheses for each test were made similarly to those made for Table 6–3. The judgments are more complexly and therefore more subjectively based than those reported earlier in this chapter. The criteria defining each "degree of confirmation" were designed to assess the validity of individual test scores. The judgments on which Tables 7–2 and 7–3 are based rely on the several test scores used to index a specific hypothesis as given in Appendices C and D, as well as on the established ACL and SIQ trait differences found between the criterion groups. To establish some checks to these judgments, the degree of confirmation of the more reliable and principal indices of an hypothesis set a rough upper limit to the judgment. For example, it was *very strongly confirmed* that the MMPI Total maladjustment score was correlated with instability and nonintegration of the self-concept as measured by the SIQ. Yet, Table 7–2 indicates that the hypothesis that MMPI-defined adjusted men would have more stable and integrated self-concepts was only *strongly confirmed*. The mature and immature men did not differ as significantly on other measures of the stability and integration of their self-concepts to provide the consistent support judged necessary to indicate *very strong confirmation* of the hypothesis. Furthermore, greater weight was placed on findings from those indices that were based on independent observations or the actual performance of the men than on only self-report types of data; for example, the SIQ measure of accuracy of self-insight was weighted more heavily than was the PSQ self-report score for symbolization of self-concept. Table 7–2 thus takes a generally conservative stance in assessing the degree of the confirmation of a hypothesis.

I will return to Table 7–2 after I discuss Table 7–3, which assesses the status of the hypotheses based on the social judgments of maturity, described in detail in Chapter 6, and on the psychological tests. The degree to which the combined psychological tests

1 The data describing the criterion groups and their patterns of differences, organized similarly as in Appendix D, as well as an interpretive evaluative summary, reported similarly to that of Chapter 6, for the MMPI-, PSQ-, and Rorschach-defined groups can be secured from NAPS. The material also includes trait differences found between the groups as determined from separate analyses of the ACL and SIQ traits.

Table 7-2
Comparative Summary of Degree of Confirmation
of Predictions of Model of Maturing for Each Test

Degree of Confirmation	TYPE OF PSYCHOLOGICAL TEST		
	MMPI	PSQ	Rorschach
Very Strongly Confirmed		Stab Self-con	
Strongly Confirmed	Alloc Self-con Integ Self-con Stab Self-con	Alloc Per Rel Integ Self-con Integ Values Aut Values	
Confirmed	Stab Values Aut Values	Symb Cg Sk Symb Per Rel Symb Values Alloc Self-con Alloc Values Stab Values Aut Self-con Aut Per Rel	Stab Self-con Stab Values
Weakly Confirmed	Symb Cg Sk Symb Self-con Symb Values Integ Values Integ Per Rel Stab Cg Sk Aut Per Rel	Symb Self-con Alloc Cg Sk Stab Cg Sk	Symb Cg Sk Symb Values Alloc Cg Sk Alloc Self-con Alloc Values Alloc Per Rel Integ Self-con Stab Cg Sk Stab Per Rel Aut Cg Sk Aut Values Aut Per Rel
Neither Confirmed nor Disconfirmed	Symb Per Rel Alloc Cg Sk Alloc Values Alloc Per Rel Integ Cg Sk Stab Per Rel Aut Cg Sk Aut Self-con	Integ Cg Sk Integ Per Rel Stab Per Rel Aut Cg Sk	Symb Self-con Symb Per Rel Integ Cg Sk Integ Values Integ Per Rel Aut Self-con

confirmed each hypothesis was determined by the central weight of the three tests' findings. The Combined Evaluation indicates the extent to which the study confirmed the hypotheses of the model. Generally, I assigned the degree of confirmation to the hypothesis that either the social judges or the psychological tests had confirmed most strongly. With only a few exceptions—symbolization and

Table 7–3
Social Judgment and Psychological Test Confirmation
of the Model of Maturity

EVALUATION OF MODEL BY

Degree of Confirmation	Social Judgment	Psychological Tests	Combined Evaluation
Very Strongly Confirmed	Symb Self-con Alloc Self-con		Symb Self-con Alloc Self-con
Strongly Confirmed	Integ Self-con	Integ Self-con Stab Self-con	Integ Self-con Stab Self-con
Confirmed	Symb Cg Sk Stab Cg Sk Stab Self-con	Symb Values Alloc Self-con Stab Values Aut Values	Symb Cg Sk Stab Cg Sk Stab Values Aut Values
Weakly Confirmed	Symb Per Rel Alloc Cg Sk Alloc Values Alloc Per Rel Integ Cg Sk Aut Cg Sk Aut Self-con Aut Values	Symb Cg Sk Symb Self-con Symb Per Rel Alloc Cg Sk Alloc Values Alloc Per Rel Integ Values Stab Cg Sk Aut Self-con Aut Per Rel	Symb Values Symb Per Rel Alloc Cg Sk Alloc Values Alloc Per Rel Integ Cg Sk Integ Values Aut Cg Sk Aut Self-con Aut Per Rel
Neither Confirmed nor Disconfirmed	Symb Values Integ Values Integ Per Rel Stab Values Stab Per Rel Aut Per Rel	Integ Cg Sk Integ Per Rel Stab Per Rel Aut Cg Sk	Integ Per Rel Stab Per Rel

allocentricism of self-concept, and stability of values—the social judges' or psychological tests' evaluation did not differ by more than one degree of confirmation of each hypothesis.

How shall we answer the question about the validity of the model of maturing using different ways of selecting the groups of "mature" and "immature" men? The psychological tests *confirmed* about the same number of hypotheses that the social judges confirmed. The tests *weakly confirmed* more of the hypotheses. The social judgments and the psychological tests together *confirmed* 40 percent of the model's hypotheses (20 percent of them *strongly* so), *weakly confirmed* 50 percent, and *neither confirmed not disconfirmed* 10 percent. The failure to confirm that the mature person has more integrated and stable personal relationships does not mean the hypotheses were disconfirmed. The number of findings markedly contradicting the hypotheses using either social judgments or the psychological tests was surprisingly small, less than three percent. Furthermore, no consistent pattern of disconfirming results occurred among the five groups. The model of maturing has been grounded on a substantial foundation of replicated evidence.

Tables 7–2 and 7–3 also tell us something about a maturity detector, a more technical topic discussed in the next chapter.

The question about the comparative power of the social judgments and type of psychological test indices of maturity is not as easily answered. That each test confirmed, even though weakly, to be sure, different patterns of hypotheses only confirms the assumption that the complexity of personality organization requires a multifaceted assessment if it is to be faithfully described. Because our measures of maturity are so exploratory, it is too premature to consider too precise statistical weighting procedures like multiple regression analyses. More critically, just what criterion would we predict to? The research shows that no single procedure, whether social judgments or a psychological test, adequately assesses the multi dimensional quality of a person's maturity.

Let us review some data. Table 7–4 summarizes how well the social judgments and the psychological tests predicted the model's hypotheses.[1] A warning is necessary. The table's percentages should not be interpreted too precisely. The percentage of significantly confirmed findings was affected by a host of artifacts. To cite just one, let us say that the research had a total of one hundred different indices, plus the twenty-six MMPI scores and the eleven PSQ scores. The MMPI scores are not independent of each other; nor are the PSQ's scores. We now know the scores of both tests covary with each other quite highly. An MMPI-defined group can differ on one hundred and eleven scores; the PSQ-defined groups on one hundred and twenty-six scores. If the MMPI groups differed significantly on only all eleven PSQ scores, their percentage of confirmed scores should be ten percent, as we have constructed the table. But the comparable figure for the PSQ-defined groups would be 20.6 percent. Other factors make precise comparisons of Table 7–4 results suspect. Generally, however, the four different procedures supported roughly two-thirds of the predictions.

1 The data on which this table are based can be found in Table 6-2, and in the comparable tables available from NAPS.

Table 7–4
Comparative Status of the Predicted Differences
Between Different Definitions of Maturity

Predictions	Social Judg	MMPI	PSQ	Rorschach
% Significantly Confirmed	18	10	21	11
% Consistent	52	52	45	60
% Total	70	62	66	71

Every procedure produced significant findings better than we would expect by chance, though the PSQ and the selection judges predicted more significant findings than the MMPI and Rorschach. The table confirms the multiform nature of personality organization. The research could have begun with any one or combination of the four procedures and would have confirmed some of the model's hypotheses, as Tables 7–2 and 7–3 demonstrate. The PSQ and the social judgments of maturity seem to be the more powerful procedures. Table 7–4 suggests that the Rorschach is more supportive than either the MMPI or PSQ, but this is deceptive. The Rorschach clinical rating failed to confirm any hypothesis for more than two of the five cultural groups. In this sense, the MMPI was more powerfully predictive, even though it did not confirm the largest number of hypotheses. The PSQ was as confirming as it was because it was designed to measure explicitly the hypotheses of the model. Since each potential selection procedure is being held up to the model of maturity, whose validity I am assuming for purposes of discussion, then the PSQ should be more powerfully predictive than the atheoretical MMPI and the diffuse Rorschach.

So how might we most economically and validly select more or less "pure" mature and immature groups in the future? My choice would be to still rely on social judgments, but clarify the criteria offered the judges and check their judgments by the PSQ or possibly the SIQ self-esteem procedures. Clinical psychologists, long under the thumb of the psychoanalytic assumption that self-ratings are only self-deceptive, defended id derivatives, historically have generally distrusted conscious reports. The research on maturity consistently has demonstrated that even highly disorganized and immature men still can make some realistic judgments. As Allport long ago wisely insisted, "If you want to know something about a man and his personality, ask him." I think Allport was correct, provided we ask him in the *right way*.

CHAPTER 8

Transcultural Measures of Maturity for the Future

W e have identified mature and immature persons by the judgments of observers and personality tests. Social judgments of maturity are determined to some unknown degree, probably predominantly, by the observable effectiveness of a person's adaptation. Psychological measures of maturity also reflect to some unknown degree, though probably considerably, a person's view of himself, and certainly, in the case of the Rorschach, his interior imaginal or dynamic life. As the data in Chapter 5 told us, the perspectives of social observers and of psychological tests about mature and immature persons are similar but not identical. Those in Chapter 6 suggest that social judgments of maturity predict some components of the model of maturing but not others, and those in Chapter 7 show that three different personality tests also predict similar but not identical components. A combined exterior and interior view of a person identified a larger number of components of the model than either view did separately.

Now let us look at where we have been and where we are going from the perspective of the model of maturing. Chapter 5 reassured us that the concept of maturity might be one of Wertheimer's and Allport's universals. Chapter 6 affirmed that maturity could be specified in ways that made sense in at least three diverse cultures. Chapter 7, focusing on the concept from different psychological perspectives, confirmed that the map we have followed has generally oriented us correctly. We have used social judgments and psychological tests as bench marks of maturity, though we have claimed that they may not be very valid. We have followed a map drawn from fragments of notes and observations of previous explorers. We have shifted back and forth between our approximate bench marks and map readings of where we might be. Gradually we have learned that certain bench marks are misplaced, that our map is occasionally vague, and that new, more discriminating tools are needed. But we have made progress. Certain prominences of the terrain, now more fixed, can serve as more reliable reference points for future explorers.

What have we learned about maturity? If we walked the streets at least in America, Italy, and Turkey, and met a person who had an accurate, allocentric, stable, and integrated concept of himself, who responded to provoking and disturbing questions reflectively without losing his control, or who recovered quickly if he did, and who had some stable and strong convictions, he most likely would be a more mature American, Italian, or Turk. These probably would be some of the core components of a maturity detector.

But we are not yet ready to put together a maturity detector to try out on the streets of Hong Kong and Jakarta. Quality control studies of its components are necessary. We also do not know how they fit together inside our black box. What guidance does the research provide to researchers who may wish to examine in the future the transcultural meaning of psychological health and maturing? In this chapter I will assess the validity of three of the novel instruments used to measure the more promising components, and reflect about their factorial structure. I will then return to the troublesome issue of how the expectations and values of a particular culture may alter the meaning of the results that a maturity detector might provide. My entry into this complicated issue will be an interpretive analysis of the unexpected and disconfirming findings of the Istanbul and the Sicilian groups. I will search for principles that may assist in the future to understand more accurately the relation of maturing to cultural values.

Table 7–3 identified at least eight probable components of a transcultural model of maturing: cognitive skill (symbolization and stabilization), and four self-concept (symbolization, allocentricism, integration, and stability) and two value (stability and autonomy) candidates. I will examine here only those tests specially designed to measure some of the components: the Cognitive Stability, SIQ stability and integration, and Valuator Total scores. Each differs methodologically. The Cognitive Stability score measures actual problem-solving efficiency; the SIQ procedures measure directly the dimensions of the self-concept; the Valuator Test is a more familiar self-rating scale.[1] Each measures ideas that are of theoretical significance. Cognitive stability is, I believe, close to the heart of what theorists mean by ego strength. Stability and integration of the self-concept approximate Erikson's rather diffuse concept of identity (1963). And the Valuator Test takes a theoretical approach toward the meaning of maturity of values different from that taken by Kohlberg, for example (1968). I will examine the SIQ measures of stability and integration, rather than of symbolization and allocentricism, because, as Tables 7-2 and 7-3 show, they were more consistently related to both the social judgments *and* the psychological tests of maturity. The validity of the Valuator Test Total score will be discussed because it is more reliable than its component scores.

Focused Tests of Maturity

Stability of cognitive skills. Ego psychologists have emphasized the centrality of man's rational, logical thought processes for adaptation. Clinical assessments of a person's psychological health rely heavily on a close scrutiny of his intellectual processes. The diagnostician is sensitive to lapses in his ability to recall memories, disruptions in his ability to think logically, failures in forming and integrating concepts, erratically stabilized cognitive skills, and disruptive intrusions of emotionally inappropriate ideas into the content of his thought. Other evidence has demonstrated that intelligence is an important determinant of adaptation, one reason that Wechsler defines intelligence in adaptational terms (1958). But just sheer level or amount of intelligence does not ensure mature adaptation. A longitudinal study of the maturing of adults suggests that adolescent scholastic aptitude as well as other measures of academic intelligence do not predict several hundred measures of the adaptation and competence of men in their early thirties. In fact, scholastic aptitude was *inversely* related in this group to many measures of their adult psychological maturity, as well as of their

1 I do not examine the validity of the PSQ subscales whose patterns of results are very similar to the already reported pattern for the PSQ Total score. The Valuator Test represents self-report types of scales in this chapter.

judged interpersonal competence. Psychological maturity as I have defined it was much more predictive of their adult adaptation (Heath, 1976a, c; 1977a). Many intelligent persons are tragically inept in managing their lives. What is critical, as Freud saw, is how a person uses intellectual processes to solve the emotional and social problems of his existence. It is this use of intelligence for resolving the ordinary affairs and dilemmas of one's life, not just for meeting scholastic demands, that the measures of cognitive stability sought to tap. The research has confirmed that equally as intelligent but mature, in contrast to immature, persons are better able to conceptualize, analyze, synthesize, and make realistic judgments about personally disturbing kinds of information.

Now what do we know about the personality characteristics of persons who vary in their cognitive efficiency (or ego strength) as measured by the scaled score summarizing analytic, conceptual and judgmental efficiency. My generalizations are based primarily on correlational analyses for each cultural group between the measures of cognitive efficiency and the other measures of their personality.

Are cognitively efficient or stable persons more intelligent? No general answer can be given for the intellectual levels that we studied. The answer is "No," for the Haverford men, and "Erratically so," for the other cultural groups. For the Pisans, vocabulary, and for the Ankarans, the Wechsler Digit-Symbol test facilitated cognitive efficiency, depending upon the amount of prior experience with the cognitive tasks or type of information with which they were dealing. The contribution that intellectual skill made to the results that I report was eliminated by statistically partialling it out of the findings. We cannot thereby explain the consistent personality traits associated with increasing cognitive efficiency in terms of sheer intellectual level.

Do more cognitively efficient or stable persons have higher anxiety thresholds for the interpersonal information we tested? The answer is "Yes" for the Americans, and, strictly speaking, "No" for the Italians and Turks. It was strongly confirmed only for the Haverford men that increasing cognitive efficiency varied directly with higher anxiety thresholds. Only the Pisans confirmed the finding and only the Ankarans supported it. Not unexpectedly the Istanbul men did not support anything. Their intrascore PT pattern just made no sense whatsoever, as Appendix B describes. Moreover, when the contribution of intellectual level to cognitive efficiency was controlled, most of the Pisan relationships between anxiety and cognitive efficiency no longer were statistically significant.

Do the personality traits associated with cognitive efficiency vary depending upon the type of information with which one must think, as well as the amount of practice one has in thinking about such information? The answer is "Yes." Thinking efficiently about personal rather than impersonal types of ideas calls out different resources. This is a reason why traditional intelligence tests frequently do not predict a wider range of competences than just academic ones (McClelland, 1973). Rehearsal and practice facilitate the stabilization of habits and skills; as problems are mastered more efficiently and economically, the contribution of motivational and personality traits to performance changes. To make clear that generalizations about the personality traits associated with cognitive efficiency must be qualified, I indicate in parentheses when summarizing a finding if it holds for the general measure of cognitive stability (Tot), the first (T1) or second (T2) session, or the threatening (Th) or nonthreatening (Nt) information. To simplify the presentation, I report the conclusion *only* for the time or type of information which was most strongly confirmed. Classification of the finding by the degree of confirmation allows a reader to assess the extent to which the summary is capitalizing on a chance finding.[1] I also summarize the patterns of SIQ traits related to general cognitive efficiency (total score).

Persons who can increasingly maintain the stability of their cognitive processes when thinking about disturbing information

Trait
Strongly Confirmed

Are rated by faculty and students to be more mature (Tot) on specific traits characteristic of maturity, particularly in fulfilling

1 The criteria defining the degree of confirmation were based on the number of the five cultural groups supporting the finding (p. 163). Since only four cultural groups participated in the studies of cognitive stability, the assessment of the personality traits associated with cognitive stability *underestimates* the potential degree of confirmation, particularly of those results involving procedures like the PT which seemed to be unreliable for the Istanbul group. By reporting the relationships only for the cognitive score which most strongly confirmed them, the listing also understates the number of significant (though not independent) findings associated with the different Cognitive Stability scores. For example, the finding that the cognitively stable person was rated by others to be more mature on the SIQ was *confirmed* for all of the other Cognitive Stability scores (Th, Nt, T1, and T2) even though this fact is not reported in the table.

their potential, thinking clearly, decisiveness, and independence (SIQ Judg, Trait differences).

Have more allocentric self-concepts (T2) (SIQ Alloc Judg).

Confirmed

Are less aloof, emotionally isolated from others (T1), compulsively self-doubting (T1), and repressed (Nt) (MMPI Sc, Pt, R).

Are not as disorganized in their thinking; have greater imaginal resources, and are more resilient (T2) and accurate in their judgments (Tot, T1, Th); use their defenses more effectively to master disturbing ideas (T2), and can cognitively regress adaptively (T2) (Ror Form 1%, M%, FAcc%, Mean DE, DD × DE%).

Are judged more mature (Tot, T2, Th, Nt) (Sel Judg).

Describe themselves more accurately (T1, Th, Nt) (SIQ Symb, Sel Judg).

Are rated by friends to be self-driving, and by other judges to have high aspirations and be unshakable (SIQ trait differences).

Weakly Confirmed

Are less maladjusted (T1, Th) and erratically inconsistent (Tot, T2, Th), possibly because they are less moody (Tot, T1, Th, Nt) and anxious (T1, Th), and have better reflective (Th) control over their impulses (Nt) (MMPI Tot, F, D, At, K, Pd).

Are also less dependent (Tot, T1, Th), socially introversive (T1, Th), and guarded in their relationships (T1); are not rigid (Tot, Th), intellectually inefficient (Tot, T1, Th); give the impression that they are socially mature (Tot, T1, Th) and are more tolerant (Tot) (MMPI Dy, Si, Pa, Rgm, Ie, Sr, To).

Are rated by friends to be clear thinkers, predictable and decisive; and by independent judges to anticipate consequences, to be imaginative, reflective, self-insightful, understanding of others, objective, self-acceptant, enthusiastic, and to have strong convictions (Tot) (SIQ trait differences).

Have more stable (Tot, T1, T2, Th, Nt) and integrated (Tot, T2, Th) self-concepts (SIQ Stab, Integ).

Are not as troubled by as regressed types of disturbing images and dreamlike forms of thought (T2); are more imaginally productive (T2), and so can put ideas into reflective perspective (T2, Th); are commonsensical (Th) and socially accommodative (T1) (Ror L1%, No. R, FK%, No. P, FC%).

Have higher anxiety thresholds for disturbing information generally (Tot, T1, T2, Th, Nt) (PT scores).

The synopsis of the personality traits associated with cognitive stability provokes several impressions. One is that cognitive stability measures a focused set of skills and attitudes, but I am uncertain how to label the constellation. It must have something to do with thinking clearly and accurately. Note the results that were confirmed or strongly confirmed: thinks clearly, decisive, accurate and allocentric self-concepts (this means accuracy in predicting the viewpoints of others about one's self), and the Rorschach measures of accuracy and control. Cognitive stability seems to mean clear and accurate reality resting. Of course, this central secondary process skill is what we sought to measure in the first place when we started out to validate Freud's hypothesis. But it is striking to find confirmation from the few other indices available that measured similar processes.

A second impression is that cognitive stability is not generally related to the men's self-ratings of maturity, either for the PSQ,[1] the SIQ mature and immature traits of maturity, the Valuator Test, and not very notably for the MMPI as well. Now these results do not mean that the more cognitively stable person is not more mature. He is, as judged in several different ways by his close friends and the selection judges. But it is clear from the results that Barron's measure labelled "ego strength," for example, certainly does not measure how well a person masters disturbing information, or how resilient he is in recovering his cognitive stability once he has been disorganized.

This nonfinding raises a related and troubling issue. The PSQ had been designed to provide an alternate measure of cognitive maturity. But its cognitive skill measure was not related to the cognitive stability scores. It predicted a different pattern of relationships,[2] primarily one measured by self-reports. So we have

1 Quite ironically, only the retrospective PSQ ratings made by the Haverford men of their maturity ten years earlier very significantly and consistently were associated as predicted with all of the cognitive stability scores. These results were not included in the *weakly* confirmed listing, because the Haverford PSQ ratings were not methodologically similar to the PSQ ratings of the Italians and Turks.

2 To illustrate the tenor of the PSQ's findings, I cite only the *confirmed* PSQ Cognitive Skill correlates. *Very strongly confirmed:* cognitively mature persons are more independent (MMPI), have more mature values (Valuator), stable self-concepts, as well as positive self- and social self-esteem (SIQ); *Strongly Confirmed:* are more well-adjusted, defensively reflective, assertive, have greater ego strength, are less anxious, compulsively rigid, moody, socially

two indices designed to test a similar hypothesis, each unrelated to the other but each predicting a plausible set of findings. While not an unusual dilemma in personality research, further theoretical clarification and efforts to establish convergent validation are obviously necessary (Campbell and Fiske, 1959).

A third observation is that for one of the few times in the research, Holt's Rorschach scores have been consistently validated across several cultures. Of significance is that it was the scores measuring cognitive control and defense effectiveness rather than the primary process content of a person's memories and images that were related to cognitive stability. Apparently, what is critical is not that a person has highly bizarre, perverse wishes or memories, but that he retains the clarity of his thought while operating on his memories when in awareness. This result makes sense. After all, the tests measuring cognitive stability were designed to assess just this skill. As an aside, these results provide another clue about our idiosyncratic Istanbul men. Of all the men, they most consistently supported the direct relation between the effectiveness of a person's defenses and controls, and the ability to reason with disturbing information. This finding and others of the Istanbul group suggest that its men were able to be very "loose" with seemingly morbid intense wishes and primitively organized memories, but able to reassert their control over such primary process content when necessary.

The measures of cognitive stability are cumbersome and complex to administer and score. But they may be reasonably valid for assessing cognitive efficiency in diverse cultures.

Integration and stability of the self-concept. The magnitude and diversity of the research on the self-concept is enormous, though I have found much of it to be fragmented, conceptually disordered, and impossible to recall and communicate sensibly to others. Psychologists just have no convincing systematic model that clarifies and orders what is now known and not known about the self-concept. The model of maturing helped to organize the research about the self-concept by suggesting what aspects of the self-concept might most powerfully predict a person's maturity. The model's

---

aloof, and intolerant (MMPI); and have more stable and symbolizable values (Valuator). *Confirmed:* are more intellectually efficient, socially responsible, have better control of their impulses, and are less guarded in their relationships (MMPI); have more integrated and allocentric self-concepts (SIQ), more allocentric and autonomous values (Valuator), and are judged to be more mature by the selection judges.

hypotheses about the self-concept were strongly confirmed. The four most powerful predictors of the maturity of men in three different cultures were measures of the self-concept: its integration, stability, allocentricism, and accuracy. Furthermore, as I demonstrated in Chapters 5 and 7, measures of how maturely a person thinks of himself and believes others think of him are also very powerful predictors of a host of other personality traits. Of all the concluding statements that can be made from the research, the most decisive and positive will be those about the dimensional maturity of the self-concept and the attitude one takes towards one's self.

Organizing the study in terms of the model of maturing also provided a rationale for systematically relating the attributes of the self-concept to other aspects of the personality. Given the assumptions of the model, we can predict that persons with more rather than with less well-integrated self-concepts will have more controlled access to primary process, or more socialized values, or more symbolizable personal relations. While not intuitively implausible hypotheses, neither self-theories nor psychoanalytic theory can make such predictions without considerable contortions and *ad hoc* assumptions.

If we included the SIQ measures of integration and stability of the self-concept in a maturity detector, whom might they identify for us in Hong Kong and Jakarta? The increasingly well-integrated passers-by would

Trait
Very Strongly Confirmed
Be more well-adjusted, calm, consistent, intellectually efficient and independent, but not socially aloof and withdrawn from others (MMPI Tot, At, F, Ie, Dy, Sc).

Have higher self-esteem and believe that others think more highly of them[1] (SIQ Priv, Soc).

Be more mature in terms of the model of maturing (PSQ Tot).

Have more allocentric and stable self-concepts (SIQ Alloc Friend, Judg, Stab).

1 Because some of the SIQ dimensional scores are not independent of each other, significance tests were technically not appropriate. I include the scores, however, in the category they would have been assigned if such tests had been appropriate. Because both the integrated and more stable persons so consistently and significantly rated themselves, and were so rated by their friends and selection judges, to be more mature on so many SIQ traits, I do not report the SIQ traits that were only *weakly confirmed*.

Strongly Confirmed

Be judged to be more mature by the selection judges and be rated to be more mature on traits typical of mature persons (Sel Judg, SIQ Judg).

Be dimensionally more mature in their values, self-concepts, and in the integration of their personalities (PSQ Val, Self-con, Integ).

Be better able to defensively reflect about issues, and have greater ego strength; be less moody, self-preoccupied and compulsively doubting; act in socially responsible ways, and be tolerant and trusting in their relations with others (MMPI K, Es, D, Hs, Pt, Pd, Rer, To, Pa).

Judge themselves to be energetic and other-centered persons (SIQ trait differences).

Confirmed

Appear to others to be socially well-adjusted, possibly because they control their emotions more appropriately and are not withdrawn from social activities (MMPI Sr, Hy, Nu, Im, Si).

Be more allocentric and better able to symbolize their experience; describe their intellectual skills and relations with males to be more mature (PSQ Alloc, Symb, CgSk, Rel M).

Have more mature values which are better integrated (Val Tot, Integ).

Have more accurate and autonomous self-concepts (SIQ Symb Friend, Aut).

Rate themselves, believe others rate them, and be rated in fact by independent judges to be more energetic, purposeful persons of high aspirations; be rated by judges to be more ordered persons possessing strong convictions (SIQ trait differences).

Weakly Confirmed

Be more inclined to think and try to integrate ideas and theories than to rely on their feelings in making judgments (SV Theo, Aes).

Be more stable and autonomous, and mature in their relations with females (PSQ Stab, Aut, Rel F).

Be less erratically impulsive and driven as well as less repressed; be more assertive (MMPI Ma, R, Do).

Have more allocentric and autonomous values (Val Alloc, Aut).

Be more cognitively efficient after prior experience with disturbing information (CgEff T2).

Be more imaginally productive to disturbing information as well as be more accessible, with good control, to more regressed types of thinking (TAJ No. St; Ror Con%, DDxDE%).

If we put the SIQ measure of the stability of a person's self-concept in the maturity detector, we would identify from the clicks somewhat similar passersby. Those whose self-concepts were increasingly more stable would

Trait
Very Strongly Confirmed

Be more well-adjusted and less anxious (MMPI Tot, At).

Be more mature generally, and more specifically so in their cognitive skills; be more well-integrated (PSQ Tot, CgSk, Integ).

Have high self-esteem and believe others think highly of them as well (SIQ Priv, Soc).

Have more integrated self-concepts and think of themselves as trusting others; be judged by their friends to be more realistic, and by other judges to be less easily upset (SIQ Integ, Trait differences).

Strongly Confirmed

Be judged to be more mature on traits typical of mature persons; be more accurate in predicting what others think of them (SIQ Judg, Alloc Friend).

Be more mature in their values and be more stable generally (PSQ Val, Stab).

Be more consistent, intellectually efficient, and have greater ego strength and resilience; not be intolerant, socially aloof, or socially introversive (MMPI F, Ie, Es, Sc, Si).

Describe their values as more mature and stable (Val Tot, Stab).

Judge themselves to anticipate consequences better, be more other-centered, and have stronger convictions; and be judged by their friends to be more imaginative and by others to be self-insightful (SIQ trait differences).

Confirmed

Be more allocentric and have more dimensionally mature self-concepts as well as more mature relations with men (PSQ Alloc, Self-con, Rel M).

Be rated psychologically healthier (Ror Clin Rtg).

Appear to be socially well-adjusted, in part due to their better defensive and reflective control of their impulses, social assertiveness, more trusting and socially responsible relationships; be less dependent and dominated by impulses, moods, and obsessional thoughts of self-doubts (MMPI Sr, K, Do, Pa, Rer, Dy, Im, D, Pt).

Have more autonomous values (Val Aut).

Have more accurate self-concepts, and be rated by their friends to be clearer thinkers, more energetic, and understanding of others. Other judges rated them to be clearer thinkers, more ordered, and understanding of others, as well as having greater aspirations. They would say of themselves that they think more clearly, have higher aspirations, and are more energetic, calm, predictable, and reflective (SIQ Symb Friend, Trait differences).

Weakly Confirmed

Be judged mature (Sel Judg).

Not be as preoccupied by libidinal and aggressive images, or swayed by primary process modes of thinking; use defenses more effectively to control such images and modes when they do occur (Ror Form%, L1%, Mean DE, DD × DE%).

Have controls that are neither overly rigid nor repressive so that they do not act out emotional displays or behave anti-socially; appear to be socially well-adjusted, independent, and responsible (MMPI Eo, Rgm, R, Hy, Ma, Pd, Sr, Dy, Rer).

Be aware of their values (Val Symb).

Be more able to symbolize their experiences, and more mature in their relations with females (PSQ Symb, Rel F).

Tend to be more cognitively efficient in mastering disturbing information (CgEff T1, T2, Th, Nt).

Have a more autonomous self-concept (SIQ Aut).

What impressively consistent results! When findings can be replicated significantly in four and sometimes five of five different cultural groups, then we can quite confidently insist that the SIQ measures of integration and stability should be in a maturity detector. Both measures predicted a variety of procedures, including the judgments of different types of judges. These results from several diverse cultures amply confirm the original findings with other American groups that the integration and stability of the self-concept are central to any transcultural definition of maturity.

I have only a few brief reflections. The indices of integration and stability seem to assess just what they were designed to measure. Persons whose beliefs about themselves coincide with those they believe that others have of them are well-adjusted, consistent, integrated, as measured by different types of procedures, and have more integrated values. Persons with more stable self-concepts are less anxious and less easily upset, are more stable on different tests, and have more stable values. The patterns are congruent with those expected. In contrast to the failure of the alternate PSQ measure of cognitive maturity to be related to the performance measures of cognitive stability, both the PSQ and the Valuator indices of integration and stability were consistently related to the corresponding SIQ measures.

What of the two other potential self-concept components for a maturity detector? The SIQ measures of symbolization and allocentricism predicted as broadly independent judgments, performance, and other self-report tests. Their validity correlates were not as powerfully confirmed, primarily because of the Haverford group whose judges, that is, those who selected the men, may not have known the men as well. Actually, the Italians and Turks were more supportive than the Americans of the symbolization, allocentricism, and autonomy hypotheses. The SIQ indices of symbolization and allocentricism may be useful to other researchers if considerable care is taken to secure reliable independent ratings of the men's maturity.

Stability and autonomy of values. The issue of whose motives, preferences, and values are better or correct, true or right, healthy or mature has caused much conflict throughout history. Psychologists are no better equipped than others to decide which values are more true, correct, or right. They may some day be better qualified to suggest which of several alternative values should be selected to further an individual's maturing or healthiness. It is not an idle or frivolous question to ask if we can determine the maturity of a person's values. Personality psychologists have been preoccupied with this issue, particularly since Freud proposed his psychosexual theory of development. Anal preferences have been considered to be more "mature" than oral ones, though Fromm talks of a hoarding preference as being less mature than a receptive one. Maslow has a hierarchical model of motives. For Freud, the mature person is genitally organized; for Fromm, he is productive; for Maslow, he is self-actualized.

More recently, others have directly assessed the maturity of a person's values. Kohlberg measures if one person's ethical choices are developmentally more mature than another's (1968). Others have queried whether certain religious values are more mature than others, and if they have maturing or immaturing effects on their members (Becker, 1971; Spilka and Werme, 1971).

The basic questions are, what do we mean by mature values? and how do we measure them? The model of maturing provides one theoretical rationale for answering the first question. More mature values are more symbolizable, allocentric, integrated, stable, and autonomous. The cultural studies support the hypothesis that more mature persons have more mature values. The stability and autonomy of a person's values have been found to mark a mature person. The judges of the three cultures also agreed very consistently that the mature person had stronger convictions, was more purposeful and decisive.

The Valuator Test was our answer to the question about how to measure the maturity of a person's values.[1] It is not a very adequate test psychometrically. It measures *only* how a person rates himself on scales describing the dimensional maturity of his values. Kohlberg's test, on the other hand, measures more directly the maturity of a person's ethical choices as he imagines how certain dilemmas could be solved. To assess the Valuator Test, I report the validity of its total score, not of the stability and autonomy scales which were highly correlated with it. I will comment about the Valuator sub scales later.

What kind of person would the Valuator Test identify for us? Those who have more mature values in constrast to those with less mature values will

Trait

Very Strongly Confirmed

Be more tolerant and intellectually efficient (MMPI To, Ie).

Have greater self-esteem and believe others also have high regard for them (SIQ Priv, Soc).

Be more mature in their intellectual skills, values, concepts of themselves, personal relationships, particularly on the dimensions of stability and symbolization (PSQ CgSk, Val, Self-con, Rel M, Rel F, Stab, Symb).

1 Test items available from NAPS.

Rate themselves to be more energetic, reflective, and have stronger convictions (SIQ trait differences).

Strongly Confirmed

Be less maladjusted, compulsively organized, anxious, dependent, and impulsive; be more socially concerned and responsible, capable of forming close relationships in which they are probably assertive (MMPI Tot, Pt, At, Dy, Im, Rer, Sc, Do).

Have stable self-concepts (SIQ Stab).

Rate themselves to think more clearly, be more other-centered, purposeful, trusting and understanding; be rated by judges to be more purposeful (SIQ trait differences).

Confirmed

Be more intellectually consistent and have greater strength to control and direct the expression of their impulses in socially acceptable ways; be less anxious about their health, moody, and socially introversive (MMPI F, Es, Pd, Hs, D, Si).

Have more integrated self-concepts; be rated by friends to be more mature on traits typical of mature persons (SIQ Integ, Friend Judg).

Rate themselves to be objective, realistic, and fulfilling their potentials as well as to have high aspirations; be rated by judges to be highly controlled (SIQ trait differences).

Weakly Confirmed

Be more defensively reflective and have greater contol over the expression of their feelings and drives; be more trusting in their relationships (MMPI K, Hy, Ma, Nu, Pa).

Have more allocentric and autonomous self-concepts (SIQ Alloc Friend, Aut).

Prefer a way of life that emphasizes caring about the welfare of others (SV Soc).

Be more imaginative to disturbing information (TAJ No. St).

Be rated by friends, occasionally by other judges, and also by themselves, to be self-acceptant, decisive, objective, placid, realistic, warm, trusting, understanding, and to have strong convictions (SIQ trait differences).

The Valuator Test does not break out of the pattern of results that we have noted earlier between the PSQ, MMPI, and SIQ. It was designed to supplement the PSQ score measuring the maturity of a person's values. Not surprisingly, it did; for the rationale and structure of the PSQ and Valuator Test were identical. That the two tests' scores correlated as highly as they did at least confirms that they are consistently reliable. Value maturity was not related to the more cognitively oriented performance tasks. Persons mature or not so mature in their values do not differ in their anxiety thresholds, have neither more nor less primary process available, and are neither more nor less cognitively efficient with disturbing information.

The scores for stability and autonomy (as well as for integration) were the most powerfully predictive of the Valuator Test's subscores. Their pattern of correlates was similar to that of the total score. The Valuator subscores illumined some new facets about our puzzling Sicilian and Istanbul men. The value autonomy score was the most powerfully discriminating measure of any of the more than one hundred measures used with the Sicilians. Forty percent, for example, of its correlations with the MMPI and the SIQ were significant beyond the .005 p level. It was the most powerfully predictive test score of the friends' SIQ ratings of the maturity of the Sicilian men. Clearly, to set high value on independence, self-assertion, and autonomy is a cardinal defining trait of a Sicilian's maturity. It made no difference whether a person valued socially caring, altruistic, or understanding relations with others. Such values were not related to maturity. The data apparently confirm the depth of the *machismo* value for Sicilians.

What of the quixotic Istanbul men? Interestingly, in contrast to the men of the other four cultural groups, the integration of their values did *not* predict their maturity. This is a provocative nonfinding. One of the most pressing conflicts of the Istanbul men was their hyperawareness of the urgency to fashion an identity that reconciled their Turkish values and background with the American style and values of their college. If most of the men had not resolved this immediate conflict in their values, the measure of the integration of their values would not be related to maturity in that setting.

Is there any relation between the maturity of a person's values and the specific content of his values? The Study of Values portrays value preferences; it does not assess their maturity. But we can ask if certain preferences or styles of life are more mature than others. Persons who preferred a social, more other-centered, caring way of life on the SV were more mature in their values—that is, had more stable, allocentric, and integrated values—than those who preferred the aesthetic way of life. Too much development of aesthetic values in late adolescence is associated with instability, maladjustment (Heath, 1965), and a less well-integrated value stance.

Some Reflections About Factorial Patterning

I have talked of "patterns of findings" throughout the book. The phrase "patterns of findings" has at least four different referents: consistency with which a relationship recurs among the five groups; consistency with which different types of scores covary with each other, *e.g.*, the PSQ, SIQ, and MMPI scores versus the cognitive efficiency and PT scores; the consistency with which the intertest pattern of relationships of a cultural group's scores hold for the four remaining cultural groups; and the consistency with which particular individuals maintain their relative ranking on the principal measures of maturing. These different meanings are related. We have examined, for example, the consistency of individual rankings in the pair-wise correlational relationships for each of the cultural groups. We have not examined systematically the consistency of the intertest patterns among the three cultures.

The analysis of intertest patterns is theoretically important. I have made a number of assumptions about the model of maturing that I claim hold for different cultures. One of the assumptions is that a person is a multidimensional system. Maturing on one dimension affects or is dependent upon maturing on the other dimensions. This assumption has more the status of a logical assertion than of an empirically verified fact at this point. In Chapter 1 I made explicit some of the dimensional dependencies that fragmentary evidence suggests exist. I have also assumed that there are five principal dimensions. Operationally, I have assumed that the psychological meanings of the indices of each dimension are stable across different cultures, an assumption supported to some extent by the material in Chapter 4, and actually tested in the remaining chapters. I have also assumed that the pattern of relationships associated with the indices of a particular dimension are identical in the three cultures.

The specific testable predictions that follow would be, in factor analytic terms: 1) five factors should account for a large proportion of the total variance of the measures for each culture; 2) the five factors should be moderately correlated with each other; and 3) the five principal factors should be identical for each culture.

However, research about concepts like maturity and psychological health, and about their transcultural measures, in particular, is only in its infancy. The research and the measures I have reported are only a first step. So I believe it is premature to test with any confidence hypotheses about the underlying factor structure of maturing.[1] Unfortunately, what Campbell and Fiske said in 1959 still applies to research on maturity today. They presciently warned against making too sophisticated analyses of exploratory methods: "We believe such summary statistics (like factor analysis) are neither necessary nor appropriate at this time. Psychologists today should be concerned not with evaluating tests as if the tests were fixed and definitive, but rather with developing better tests" (1959, 103).

The Transcultural Assessment of Maturing

That a common factor structure for affective meaning has been found for twenty-three diverse cultures (Osgood, May and Miron, 1975) provides hope that one may also be found for a transcultural model of maturity. We have made a beginning step toward that goal by demonstrating that small groups of mature and immature men from three diverse cultures differ similarly from each other. But just as Osgood found subuniversal and unique factors among his cultural groups, so we may expect that some components of the model of maturing will be differentially affected by a culture's particular pattern of values. I now return to the two groups whose cultural values seem to have had the greatest "distorting" impact on the results, the men of Istanbul and Sicily. Each provides the opportunity to examine in greater depth the relation of cultural

1 Like the proverbial cat, my curiosity got the better of my common sense, however. An exploratory principal components analysis was made of the thirty-one most useful and theoretically relevant scores for the most reliable group of each culture. Both the orthogonal and oblique varimax rotations made such little psychological sense that I could not interpret the principal factors. Five factors for each group accounted for between 75 and 84 percent of the total amount of variance of the correlational matrices: the five factors of each group were only minimally correlated with each other; and, with only a few exceptions, the factors for one cultural group were not similar to those of the other two groups. Too few participants, too many measures, too few valid "marker" variables make the playful factorial exploration too unreliable to take seriously.

values to autonomy, the one dimension whose hypotheses have been the most difficult to confirm. My purpose is not to "explain" the specific Istanbul or Sicilian culture, but to illustrate how the contextual pattern of a culture's values affects the assessment of a person's maturity.

The data to which I refer are *all of the unpredicted markedly divergent findings*, the deviant intratest patterns (see Appendix B), and the other information that violated our expectations. For argumentative purposes, I take the stance that these inconsistent and nonpredicted significant findings forge a meaningful psychological pattern, are not random, and are not due just to the experimenter errors and other methodological limitations that characterized the data of the Istanbul and Sicilian groups in particular. I have no way to separate out the variance contributed by inadequate test administration. Let us try to make some sense of the findings that may help illumine other issues about personality and cultural values.

The Istanbul group was the most deviant and inconsistent of the five cultural groups. It is, therefore, the critical group for determining what sociocultural limits there may be to the validity of the model of maturing. Three themes organize its deviant results: defensiveness that reduced the relation of self-esteem to the measures of maturity; ambivalence about the control of impulses; and conflicts with men and women.

The Istanbul men thought very highly of themselves; their friends called them self-centered. They were students from the elite families attending the elite college of Turkey from which many of the country's leaders had come. That their self-esteem may have been more defensively based than that of any other group is suggested by several other "deviant" findings. It was the one group whose values were least well-integrated and not predictive of the dimensional maturity of their other values, thus suggesting that their high self-esteem was not the result of having achieved a stable identity. Another clue was the failure of the self-report scales to predict to many other types of measures for this group. Recall that the men's ratings of their maturity on the SIQ traits were not powerfully related to their close friends' ratings of them.

We can understand the defensive quality of their self-reports better by examining their attitude toward controlling their impulses. On the one hand, the MMPI was generally useless for the Istanbul men. When confronted with its blatant demand to reveal weaknesses, foibles, and pathology, the men reacted quite defensively. The pattern of their scores that measured domination by moods, self-depreciation, and femininity were highly deviant. Furthermore, their score for reflective control was the highest of any cultural group, and its pattern of correlates deviated from that of every other group I have studied. Ordinarily, the ability to be consciously selective about what one describes about one's self is highly predictive of measures of maturity. But if one becomes too self-consciously and rigidly selective, then one is defensive. Only for the Istanbul group did reflective control significantly correlate with rigid overcontrol, thus suggesting defensiveness. This result helps to illuminate another deviant finding. The group's initial response to the disturbing phrases of the Phrase Association Test did not predict its subsequent responses to the same phrases, the first time that this has ever occurred for any of many groups ever tested. The PT gets around the conscious control of a person, puts him off guard, so to speak, and may have elicited such great anxiety that the normal intertest patterning of PT scores was disrupted.

On the other hand, we confront the paradox of the Rorschach in which these seemingly defensive, overcontrolled men seeking to maintain the appearance of being strong, powerful, and autonomously self-sufficient gave very "loose," bizarre, and particularly indiscriminate sexual and other primary process responses. Highly defensive persons are frequently threatened by unstructured tasks, like the PT and Rorschach, since they cannot control their responses to them as readily. One way defensively intellectual persons secure control in threatening situations is to flood an experimenter, particularly a conscientious one laboriously taking down every word they say, with a torrent of words ("rubbish" in the words of the Turkish supervisor). When the Istanbul group confirms a prediction, particularly one involving the Rorschach and one that no other group confirmed, then that finding may have special significance for that group. For the Istanbul men, the ability to defensively control the emergence of threatening images on the Rorschach significantly predicted their cognitive efficiency in solving the disturbing problems of the *highly structured* tests.

Efforts to control one's impulses, to appear powerful and strong, contribute to the growth of autonomy. But when increasing autonomy becomes defensively exaggerated and is nonintegrative with allocentric development, autonomy has a distorting immaturing effect. Excessive autonomy becomes narcissistic self-sufficiency. Interestingly, the PSQ score of autonomy had a different meaning for the Istanbul men than for any other group that I have ever tested. It did not predict the PSQ Total score very well. Instead, increasing autonomy was directly and significantly related to decreasing intellectual efficiency, poor ego strength, compulsive self-doubts, decreasing social adaptability, and increasing suspiciousness in relations with others.

Why this puzzling and complicated pattern of defensive self-esteem and exaggerated autonomy that undercut many of the predicted relations about maturity? One clue comes from the third pattern of deviant results. The *immature* Istanbul men were significantly more mature in their allocentric relations with men and women, and reported having more integrative relations with men. They also had greater access to images reflecting a more varied range of personal relationships, and showed better judgment in dealing with disturbing interpersonal themes in their first encounter with them. But the Istanbul group is the only one in which more mature relationships with other males is *significantly* associated with increased accessibility to passive, dependent, feminine, possibly homosexual, inclinations. And unabashedly reporting penises and sexual relations in the Rorschach is one way to impress another (and one's self) about one's own virility for a person defensively insecure about his own potency, sexual role, and presumed autonomy.

What sense can be made out of these strands of evidence and conjecture? They may reflect, in part, efforts to adapt to and integrate the conflicting values of the Turkish and American cultures. The Istanbul Turks were very well aware of the American way of life; they had been drawn to their American-founded college partially because of its values; they encountered while there numerous representatives of the American culture. Coming from a strongly authoritarian culture to a setting that valued the assertion of independence, criticism, and individualism must have reinforced the rebellious spirit of late adolescents. The LeComptes' study of the perception of American and Turkish youths of their fathers' approval of traditional and individualistic actions clearly demonstrated that the Turkish youth significantly rated their fathers to be more disapproving of individualism (LeCompte and LeCompte, 1973). Exaggerated autonomy, including defiance, may be necessary to break one's excessively dependent ties with one's family and with the "old traditional ways." Excessive autonomy means distrusting potentially disruptive uncontrollable impulses as well as unstructured situations in which one risks the loss of self-control or of becoming dependent. Asserting one's autonomy leads to an exaggerated posture of self-esteem about one's own power and potency. The Istanbul males may have been denying those impulses, particularly ones associated with "weakness," that challenged their virility. Contact with the American repressive values about emotional expression, passion, dependency, and sexuality as well as with its more equalitarian views of the role and rights of women may have accentuated the need to secure control over one's own impulses, particularly affectional and sexual. Interpersonal relations become more complicated and ambivalent, particularly for the more mature person seeking to integrate the diverse cultural expectations. Exaggerated autonomy is nonintegrative, however; it limits interpersonal maturing, particularly for young male adults who need to learn how to be emotionally dependent to be able to love. It was the less mature, and probably not so autonomous, men who described their relations with both men and women to be more mature, possibly because they were not compensatorily denying more "feminine" needs in such relations.

That the basis of the Istanbul group's deviant results may be largely cultural is suggested by an interesting pattern in its results. The *markedly disconfirming* results occurred with the *socially judged mature and immature but not with the psychologically defined mature* (PSQ) *and healthy* (Rorschach) *groups* of Istanbul men. Could it be that the judges selected as mature those whose autonomy was most manifest, like the political leaders of the college, and that their autonomy was not fully integrative for a number of them?

A similar though not as exaggerated pattern was found to describe the maturing of American men in college (Heath, 1968, 150–55). Exaggerated intellectual and familial autonomy inhibited interpersonal maturing in males for whom continued maturing required, at a different level of maturity, openness to emotional dependence on their peers. Maturing in Turkey for its youthful elites may exaggerate such problems, for in contrast to American males, the young Turks must establish their identity and autonomy from a strongly paternalistic and authoritarian culture. Contact with a contrasting culture just at the time the issue of autonomy becomes psychologically most critical aggravates conscious as well as defensive efforts to keep one's self together while searching for some more enduring integrative solution.

The Sicilian group's results also illuminate how the assessment of maturity must take account of the *pattern* of a culture's values. Despite the group's greater homogeneity, the questionable reliability of some of its tests, and my consequent expectation that its results would not be too useful, the Sicilians were generally as supportive of the predictions as the more reliable Haverford, and occasionally more so, Ankara, and Pisa men. The Sicilians also came from a strongly authoritarian culture. But in contrast to the Istanbul men, their culture, particularly its linkage to Mafiosian elements, although under attack from the Italian north, was not as questioned by the men themselves. They were not living in an "alien" cultural environment, as the Istanbul young men certainly were (and the Ankarans to a lesser extent). There is no evidence that the Sicilians were challenging their culture's values as severely as the Turks were. As a consequence, evidence of conflict, anxiety, inner tumult, and intense introspective efforts to master the eruption of primary processes was minimal. Defensive efforts to hold one's self together while refashioning an autonomous identity were not as necessary in a culture whose values were stably organized and not being internally challenged. The culturally patterned identity was assimilated, not rebelliously rejected, in other words.

One might say that the cultural stimulus to further maturing— that is, challenge to and disorganization in traditional cultural values—was much less for the Sicilians than for the other groups. The imaginal constrictedness, seeming inner flatness, and the remarkable sameness of the men's Rorschachs may reflect in part the absence of inner turmoil, and, conversely, perhaps the presence of highly stable, rigidly structured patterns of values and expectations.

In contrast to the Istanbul men whose autonomy was rebelliously defensive, the Sicilian men's autonomy was integrative with their culture's values. The autonomy of the Istanbul men's values did not predict maturity; the autonomy of the Sicilian's values was the most powerful predictor of every measure of maturity used with the group. The Sicilian *machismo* value, an integral part of its masculinely authoritarian culture, provides the stable organizing core of values around which a Sicilian male shapes his identity. To be an independent assertive, masculine male is essential to a man's self-esteem.

While both the Turkish and Sicilian cultures are male-dominated and authoritarian, their response to femininity, acceptance of emotional dependency, and sensitivity to their feelings, particularly the expression of affectionate and dependency ones, radically diverged. For the Istanbul men, increasing femininity was significantly and directly associated with increasing maturity in male, but not female, relationships. Otherwise, femininity in males was not related to either maturity or immaturity. For the Sicilian men (and only for them), increasing femininity was inversely related to increasing interpersonal intimacy with males. More striking, femininity very consistently, and powerfully so statistically, predicted immaturity, low self-esteem, low esteem from others, lack of autonomy, immaturity in one's values, particularly in their integration and autonomy, anxiety, dependency, impulsiveness, and limited resilience. The *machismo* complex with a psychological vengeance! For Sicilians, interpersonal autonomy means being a "real" male; dependent needs are satisfied, as Chapter 3 suggests, in prolonged and close familial relationships. For the Istanbul men, autonomy means self-control, and independence of familial and cultural patterns; dependency needs may be satisfied in their peer relations with other males.

No independent means are available to check the validity of this synthesis of the significantly disconfirming results. If valid, then the Istanbul group's discrepant results do not in fact disconfirm the model; they reflect, instead, the complexity of the relation between the dimensions of maturing and cultural values.

What do the Istanbul and Sicilian men teach us about the problems of assessing maturity transculturally? First, they confirm an earlier hunch that different hypotheses of the model will be more readily confirmed in some cultural settings than in others. If we had initiated the research only in Sicily, the autonomy hypotheses might well have been confirmed more readily than the symbolization and allocentric ones. It is an important point to understand that no one culture can provide a definitive test of the validity of the model.

Second, the Istanbul results suggest, though they do not confirm, that conflict in cultural values is a potent source of personality disruption that may spark maturing. Gordon Allport once chided me about underrating the maturing effect of adolescent disorganization and confusion. The Istanbul and Sicilian Rorschachs were like night and day. The Istanbul men were letting everything hang out; the Sicilians seemingly had little to show. As overtly disorganized and strange as were the Istanbul men's inner lives, the men were actually less maladjusted (MMPI), more mature (PSQ), and more psychologically healthy (Rorschach) than the Sicilian men, if we can make reliable direct crosscultural comparisons of specific scores. A dose of anxiety, a dash of perplexity, and a pinch of madness may give life the spice that whets the appetite for continued maturing. But conflict in cultural values can severely test a person's integrative capacity and distort development, as occurred for some Istanbul men. Longitudinal studies of maturing have suggested that those determinants that have potentially powerful maturing effects also have as potentially powerful immaturing effects, depending upon how adaptively the person copes in response (Heath, 1968, 1977b).

Third, a culture's values affect maturing quantitatively *and* qualitatively. The rate of maturing is affected by many complex determinants, one of which is the opportunity to confront new demands that challenge one's stabilized and autonomous habits and values. A rigidly suppressive culture that prescribes role relationships very tightly, and limits access to contradictory types of information may enhance the overstabilization and thus the rigidity of its members. On the other hand, too rapid cultural change that results in the abandonment of integrative cultural myths and values may provoke much inner turmoil, introspection, and searching. The absence of cultural models of integrative values limits the stabilization of a youth's identity and distorts the nature of his autonomy. The contrast between the Istanbul and Sicilian "meaning" of autonomy and its different patterns of personality correlates tell us that the specific content of a culture's values may have a more decisive effect on the patterning of maturing than I have recognized to date. I would still argue, however, that there is an *optimal* patterning which the model describes, and that over time it will be confirmed from the combined results of many diverse cultures. One consequence of this argument is, of course, that a person may be *culturally* defined to be immature (or psychologically unhealthy), but may not be so in terms of the model.

Fourth, does the model provide any criteria of maturity independent of culturally-defined standards by which to assess the maturity of its members? Szasz claims that mental illness, and presumably mental health, or maturity, are culturally bounded. On what basis can we claim that the Sicilian *machismo* value that seems to be central to its definition of maturity is any more or less mature than some other culture's values? This issue is troubling and complex, one with which cultural anthropologists are wrestling (Naroll, 1969). If the generality of the model of maturing can be confirmed further, then its *systemic* organismic assumption becomes the touchstone for making such an evaluation. If the excessive autonomy of a male limits his self-insight about his dependency needs, blocks the integration of his emotional needs, and fosters a rigid cultural identity, then his adaptive potential is being adversely limited. Although he may be well-adjusted to his traditional culture, I would predict his potential for adapting either to change in his culture or to the expectations of other cultures would be restricted. As I have already suggested, I assume that a psychologically healthy system is educable, resilient, adaptable, and has freed affect.

Summary

We have taken some small beginning steps toward constructing a "culture-free" maturity detector. We can now suggest what some of its key components might be, and make some educated guesses about the types of instruments that could be included in it. The measures of cognitive stability are quite reliable and valid, and should be in a maturity detector. But they are uneconomical and too bulky; they need to be miniaturized and simplified. Certainly the SIQ dimensional procedures could be included as well. They are economical, quite reliable and valid, and easily portable. The Valuator Test is a reasonable first approximation of an economical and possibly valid measure of the maturity of a person's values; it needs much more refinement and validation, however. The similar but more extensively validated PSQ is promising, and could well be included as an alternate back-up system.

At this point, we do not know how the components should be fitted together inside the maturity detector. We cannot yet specify how the contributions of each are to be combined to produce the rate of clicking that most validly identifies who is and who is not mature.

Finally, the meaning of the rate and pattern of the "clicks," the results of our different measures of maturity, cannot be understood in isolation from a richly differentiated understanding of a culture's expectations and values, as the lives of the Istanbul and Sicilian men told us about their autonomy and its relation to their maturing. The assessment of transcultural maturity is a much more complexly holistic task than my fanciful image of a maturity detector suggests. It requires sensitivity to and understanding of the *patterned* psychological meanings of a culture's values, a stance similar to that taken by those seeking to understand the relation of mental illness to sociocultural values (Kiev, 1969; Opler, 1969; Wallace, 1961).

CHAPTER 9

The Transcultural Model of Maturing: An Assessment

Research on maturity has the disconcerting effect of provoking challenging but not readily answerable questions. To resist the temptation to wander speculatively far beyond the focus of this book and its supporting data, I shall tether myself to the issues about which the research has generated some data. I will first summarize the evolving argument, and then the response the results enable us to make. After that, we will be prepared to turn back to the issues discussed in Chapters 1 and 2 about the relation of maturing to other related concepts, particularly competence, and to the grander but more elusive issue of cultural values and their relation to a culture-free model of healthy development.

The argument

1 A developmentally based dimensional model of maturing relatively independent of personal and cultural values can be formed. Such a model may clarify, if not make redundant, related terms such as *psychological healthiness* and *self-actualization*.

2 In contrast to immature persons, mature persons are better able to symbolize their experiences; they are also more allocentric, integrated, stable, and autonomous in their cognitive skills, concepts of themselves, values, and personal relationships.

3 The model describes how any person matures, when he is maturing, regardless of his ethnic, socioeconomic status, and

cultural values. Different cultures may inhibit or facilitate maturing in some ways rather than others.

4 Concepts like adjustment, normality, and competence, which refer to effectiveness in relating to the demands of specific environmental situations, are basically defined by the requirements of the environment and/or by societal values.

5 When competence refers to general personality traits associated with effectiveness in adapting to many complex environmental demands, its core traits are those described by the model of maturing.

6 Research on maturity necessarily begins with the judgments of judges about who is and who is not a maturely organized person. Such judgments are influenced by the competence with which a person adjusts to institutional and cultural expectations. Hence, the values of judges affect the initial selection of mature and immature persons.

7 When different procedures, like judge ratings, performance measures, self-report and imaginal tests, produce converging and confirmatory results, that which is being measured becomes progressively objectified or "freed" from determination by the assumptions, biases, and values of any particular method being used.

8 The study of effectively functioning or competent and mature persons in diverse cultures will lead to the distillation and identification of a universal or recurring set of core traits that further adaptation generally. The model of maturing predicts what those traits will be.

9 To identify such a recurring set of traits descriptive of mature persons selected by numerous and diverse types of judges in diverse cultural areas begins to "free" the concept of maturity from idiosyncratic personal and cultural values. A scientifically validated developmental conception of maturing becomes possible.

The findings

1 We did study mature and immature men from *diverse* cultures. Their diversity was measured in exploratory studies by the judgments of nationals of each culture. The American, Italian, and Turkish cultures were perceived to differ in the patterns of personal relationships that they rewarded and punished.

2 The five small cultural groups selected from the three cultures to be studied were more similar than dissimilar to each other

in intellectual level, educational and socioeconomic background, as well as in personality traits. The groups from the same culture were more similar to each other than either was to groups from other cultures. The groups shared the basic religious identification of their culture, the criterion on which the cultures were initially defined to differ from each other.

3 Different judges from the five cultural areas studied agreed upon who was and who was not a very competent and maturely organized person in the populations being assessed.

4 When such judged mature and immature persons were actually compared, the mature persons from the five cultural areas were consistently found to differ similarly from the immature men. A common core set of traits define maturity in the three cultures: ability to anticipate consequences; calm, clear thinking; fulfilling potential; ordered; predictable; purposeful; realistic; reflective; strong convictions; and unshakable.

5 The social judgments of maturity (and/or competence) validly predicted a variety of test indices of maturity in the three cultures, particularly the self- and the social-esteem of the mature and immature men.

6 The hypothesized differences between the *socially judged* mature and immature men were generally supported. They were specifically confirmed for the symbolization, allocentricism, integration, and stability of the self-concept, and for the symbolization and stability of cognitive skills.

7 Test indices of maturity – self- and social-esteem, psychological adjustment, and dimensionally defined maturity— generally predicted each other within each of the three cultures.

8 The model's predictions about differences between *psychological test-defined* mature and immature men of the three cultures were generally supported; they were specifically confirmed for the allocentricism, integration, and stability of the self-concept, and for the symbolization, stability, and autonomy of values.

9 The social judgments and the psychological test indices of maturity, when combined, confirmed 40 percent, weakly confirmed 50 percent, and neither confirmed nor disconfirmed 10 percent of the model's hypotheses.

10 Social judgments of maturity and/or competence, when combined with the Perceived Self Questionnaire, a summary measure of the model's hypotheses (or with the Self-Image Questionnaire's Self-esteem score), probably would be the most

economical and valid scre_ning procedure to use in future research for identifying groups of mature and immature persons.

11 Future validation of a transcultural model of maturity depends upon the development of more adequate measures, particularly of the dimensional maturity of interpersonal relationships. Measures of cognitive stability as well as self-concept and value dimensional maturing were validated by convergent measures and may be useful in future transcultural research. However, it is premature to determine if the concept of maturity has a common factorial structure across diverse cultures.

Evaluation of Findings

Just how credible are the findings? Can we account for them in terms of factors other than hypothesized culture-free universal dimensions of maturing? Two general points must be kept clearly in mind when evaluating their reliability. First, the transcultural study of maturing is *not* methodologically typical of most cross-cultural studies. We did not *directly* compare the behavior of Sicilians with that of Pisans, or of Americans with that of Ankarans. I did not ask if mature Sicilians had more stable self-concepts than mature Ankarans. Instead, I compared the similarity of *patterns of significant differences* found between mature and immature men from five cultural groups. The implications of this distinction are easily misunderstood. Many of the typical methodological problems that obscure the meaning of crosscultural findings just do not apply as forcefully to our research strategy. While it was important that our procedures be kept constant from one cultural group to another, of greater importance was that they be kept identical for the mature and immature men *within* each group. The research, for example, was *not* necessarily crippled by the fact that Americans were more test-wise than the Italians and Turks, or that precisely equivalent translations of the five word-phrases of the Phrase Association Test were impossible to create among the three cultures, or that the experimenters differed in their styles of relating. I do not suggest that such departures from exact procedural comparability did not hurt the study. They probably did. Differences in experimental style may have affected the findings of the individually administered tests. As sources of error, they worked *against* confirming some hypotheses. But what was critical for assessing the reliability of the cultural similarities was that we did find, despite numerous sources of error, that the mature and immature persons *within* each culture were equally test-wise, perceived the translated materials, and were related to by the group's experimenter similarly. There is no evidence whatsoever that the mature and immature persons of each group did not receive precisely the same treatment.

The second general point to keep in mind is one made by Osgood and Triandis that "... studies designed to prove crosscultural generalities are not as dependent upon methodological details as those designed to reveal cultural differences" Osgood, May and Miron, 1975, 411), "[since] if one obtains similarities among cultures in spite of differences in language, instrument administration, etc., the phenomenon must be reasonably robust" (Triandis, Malpass and Davidson, 1973, 357). I have made the same point earlier. If we find that mature and immature persons differ similarly from one cultural group to the next, *in spite* of translation inequivalences, experimenter errors, unknown test reliabilities, and other sources of error typical of personality research, *then* the fact that such consistent differences, particularly among several, sometimes even five, cultural groups occur, must mean they are indeed quite marked to overcome the attenuating effects of so many possible sources of error.

What are some specific ethnocentric biases and sources of error that typically limit the reliability and validity of crosscultural research? It might be argued that the model of maturing is typically Western, specifically American, and rationalistically Apollonian in flavor. Some may say that I have forced other persons, particularly Turks, to accommodate themselves to this Procrustean bed at the expense of their cultural uniqueness. However, the test of the model was really not as imperious as this stereotypical argument suggests. The local psychologists of each country generated, by means of native translators, their own consensually agreed upon test phrasings and meanings; no local psychologist or participant mentioned that the tests and their items were foreign to their experience. More importantly, a very wide range of different procedures was used, including unstructured imaginative procedures like the TAJ and Rorschach, as well as judge ratings, that permitted cultural uniqueness to emerge. Such a large variety of relatively independent indices measuring diverse behaviors provides a culture the opportunity, so to speak, to mold and sculpture its own patterned mosaic of relationships, as we saw happen with the indices of autonomy for the Sicilians and Italians. What is impressive is that the general pattern of the mosaic that the five cultural groups formed was so very similar in so many predicted ways.

I have discussed at length the problem of translation equivalency. Recommended preferred translation procedures and bilingual bicultural translators were used. Translation-free types of tests like the Thematic Concept, Thematic Judgment, and the Rorschach tests were used. However, the translation of the Italian and Turkish imaginative responses back into English, made by expert bicultural bilingual translators, were potential sources of error, given the sensitivity of Holt's Rorschach scores to linguistic styles and content subtleties. Since the effect of such semantic inequivalences actually worked against establishing cultural similarities, our confirmed findings cannot be explained by translation difficulties. Some failures to confirm hypotheses may be so explained.

Another potential factor limiting the reliability of the results is the intensiveness of the study itself, necessary to deal with the systemic complexity of the model of maturing. No previous as intensive personality study of either Italians or Turks had been done to provide guidance about possible pitfalls. The necessary use of small nonrandom samples in exploratory research of course raises serious doubts about the generality of the findings. But there was no other reasonable way to begin, given our dependence on the judgments of judges in the beginning phases of research on a topic not heretofore explored transculturally. One methodological purist unthinkingly said mature and immature samples should have been randomly drawn to represent the mature and immature populations of each cultural area! Another impractically said randomly representative samples (of what?) should have been selected from the populations of each cultural area. Although they seriously misunderstand the theoretical strategy of research on maturity, and impose a stereotypical bias about how exploratory research should proceed, these comments remind us that we must be very circumspect in our claims about testing the generality of the model—an issue to which I return shortly.

Critics will suggest other factors that may have produced the similarities found among the mature and among the immature men. The argument that the three cultures were *not* very dissimilar in their values and socialization patterns is not persuasive, given the findings reported in Chapter 3 and Appendix A. Nor is the argument persuasive that the vague criteria given the selection judges so biased their judgments as to override culturally internalized conceptions of what a maturely organized person was like, as was argued in Chapter 3. The argument is too feeble to account for the full sweep of the very consistent findings, particularly those not even remotely related to the selection criteria, among three, four, and sometimes five cultural groups. Another explanation might be that the mature and immature men as well as the selection judges were not very "American," "Turkish," or "Italian" in their character and values. Even if both my impressionistic sketch of the three cultures (given in Chapter 3) and my more disciplined hunches (given in Appendix A) were correct, they may not adequately describe the men and the judges. Certainly the men and possibly the judges of Istanbul were probably "deviants" within their own culture with respect to some of its values. To have checked the validity of this explanation would have plunged us into cultural and personality issues more deeply than the immediate focus of the study would warrant. Yet, there were clues to show that the American, Turkish, and Italian men of the study differed in their values and personalities.

I have no data with which to assess the degree of identification of the judges with their culture. But the student judges, both those who selected the participants and those who were close friends, were drawn from the same population as the students who rated the dimensional maturity of their cultures' attributes and interpersonal reinforcement hierarchies to differ. Presumably the students who served as selection judges would have rated their culture's attributes and interpersonal patterns similarly. Presumably their assessment of the maturity of the men they selected was based on an intimate association with, if not internalization of, the values and interpersonal patterns reinforced by their cultures. It is not a compelling argument that any significant number of selection judges were "national-less" persons, psychologically freed of their cultural history and values.

Assessment of Model of Maturing

The criteria I use to assess the adequacy of the model are its comprehensiveness, validity, generativity, and usefulness. I shall postpone the evaluation of its generality until later.

Comprehensiveness. The model of maturing (psychological health and self-actualization) is the most systematically comprehensive one of which I am aware. Its comprehensiveness has been assessed in a variety of ways. The model comprehended and coherently organized the principal goals of educational philosophers who traditionally have been preoccupied with the direction of healthy growth (Heath, 1968, Appendix A). Analyses of probing interviews with freshmen and seniors about how they had changed in college, and with adult men in their early thirties about how they had changed since college did not reveal any consistent changes that could not be classified reliably by independent judges as examples of the hypotheses of the model. If the model is to be altered to be more comprehensive, it may need a category indexing the affective release of energy that results in increased enthusiasm, joy, humor, and sense of power that occur following a successful adaptation or achievement of a new level of maturity. With respect to testing the model, every cross-sectional and longitudinal study has cast a very large psychological net, including the use of two of psychology's most wide-ranging tests, the MMPI and Rorschach, to identify nonpredicted differences between mature and immature men. Remarkably few nonpredicted marked differences have been found; in the cultural studies, fewer than three percent. When they were found, as between the Istanbul mature and immature men, they were not strongly supported by any other cultural group. The model ordered a large number of varied personality measures in a way that did not violate what was found empirically.

To establish the comprehensiveness of the model incurred two heavy costs. The assessment of comprehensiveness was bought at the cost of depth and possibly generality. We explored broadly, though we disciplined that search by rigorously studying in depth one of the twenty hypotheses, cognitive stability. To have initiated a narrowly focused study might have meant examining with precision and impeccable procedures hypotheses that may not have been fruitful to pursue. Our more exploratory cultural foray has now identified which hypotheses might most profitably and economically be tested in a more focused way with larger numbers of persons in the future. Testing as many hypotheses as we did necessarily required intensive work with small groups, which limited the generality of the findings. However, confirming a number of hypotheses with several, occasionally all five, culturally diverse groups provides confidence that their results may be stable and replicable.

The model may also buy its comprehensiveness at the heavy cost of precision and specificity. The model is abstract; its dimensions are probably factorially complex; its categories are vaguely classificatory. Furthermore, many standard test indices did not precisely "fit" the dimensional hypotheses. Though such abstractness is necessary to identify similarities that may underly culturally specific behaviors (Triandis, 1972a), one risks creating hypotheses so elastic that they are incapable of disconfirmation. Hopefully, more focused measures of the dimensional hypotheses, like those reported in Chapter 8, will be available in the future to serve as valid marker tests by which to confirm, for example, our interpretation of MMPI or Rorschach scores.

Validity. The validity of the model has been not only generally confirmed, but also more sharply etched than previously. The results reported in Chapters 5 through 8 consistently support many of its hypotheses. About two-thirds of them were supported, though not statistically confirmed, when different tests and judgmental procedures were used to define mature and immature groups. The number of *significantly* confirmed findings ranged from 10 percent for the MMPI, 11 percent for Rorschach clinical ratings, 21 percent for the PSQ definition of maturity, and 18 percent for social judgments of maturity. Tables 7-2 and 7-3, which summarize the hypotheses in terms of their degree of confirmation, clearly indicate that: 1) instead of talking about the validity of the model, we should more precisely talk about the validity of its specific dimensional hypotheses; 2) the hypotheses about the dimensional maturity of the self-concept have been *strongly confirmed*; and 3) further studies should focus particularly on validating the hypotheses about the maturity of interpersonal relationships.

Although inadequate measures of interpersonal maturity may have accounted for the failure to confirm hypotheses about it, another theoretically provocative cause may also have been involved. In their study of modernity, Inkeles and Smith (1974) found that items about interpersonal relations and expressive qualities did not predict modernity; only instrumental adaptive qualities did. Our results were similar. Temperamentally expressive and interpersonal traits were not as consistently related to maturity as were instrumental ones. Inkeles studied modernity primarily with factory workers; I studied maturity with college students. Both situations do not require interpersonal competences as much as they require problem-solving and organizing qualities. Have the personality demands of the impersonal task-oriented situations in which modern and mature persons were studied biased the meaning of effectiveness, the assessment of which has been our initial route into the study of maturing? Future validation studies might well seek out settings that demand interpersonal effectiveness in which to identify mature and immature persons.

We also have had difficulty establishing the dimensional hypotheses about autonomy. Why? Not only may autonomy have diverse cultural meanings, as the analysis of the Istanbul and Sicilian men suggests, but also autonomy is a pressing conflict for late adolescents. Hypotheses about the relation of autonomy to maturity may not be unequivocally confirmed during critical transitional periods of adaptation. If this explanation has merit, then we may have stumbled upon an important principle. Erikson (1963), Loevinger (1976), and other "stage" theorists propose that invariant psychological tasks are associated with different phases of development or "levels" of maturity. Such tasks disrupt previously stabilized patterns and so initiate the adaptive sequence. In the early phases of adapting, behavior is typically more chaotic, mercurial, frequently compensatory, and exaggerated, as parents of adolescents ambivalent about leaving home are wearily aware. To test the dimensional maturity of behavior, particularly of that which is a focal developmental conflict, while a person is in the midst of such disorganization, risks misidentifying transitional compensatory and defensive behaviors as immature. If there are such invariant psychosocial stages (and I am not persuaded that there are, at least for adults) that provoke anew the maturing process, then perhaps we would confirm more readily hypotheses about maturing once the behavior most involved with a particular dimension had become stabilized.

Generativity. Another criterion for evaluating a model's adequacy is its *generativity*. The model has provided the rationale for and spur to the development of new tests—for example, the PSQ, SIQ procedures, Valuator Test, and measures of cognitive efficiency—and has guided the formulation of hypotheses that might not otherwise have been framed, like those about the dimensional maturity of a person's self-concept and values. It also suggests ideas about the characteristics of mature in contrast to immature forms of coping, the distinction between educable and noneducable forms of disorganization (Heath, 1968, Ch. 9) and educational change (Heath, 1971, 1974, 1976e). The study may provide the conceptual means by which to coordinate certain types of questions about personality and cultural values. One intriguing possibility is the Cultural Value Test (see Appendix A), which offers a detailed map of a culture's perceived reinforcement hierarchies for different interactions with varied persons. To be able to plot which types of relationships are more or less culturally approved may provide the means for exploring the relation of personality socialization to cultural values. For example, is there a relation between the timing of a culture's shift in expectations with respect to independence and autonomy in personal relationships, subsequent achievement strivings, and its definition of maturity? The American culture demands independence significantly earlier in the life span; its definition of maturing emphasizes achievement; and its mature and immature men seem to have been selected more frequently than the Italians and Turks in terms of their achievement. Are there consistent relationships between different cultural patterns of expectations about appropriate and inappropriate types of personal relationships and subsequent dimensional maturing?

Utility. The model of maturing also has considerable *utility.* It offered a way to organize a host of disparate test indicators, thus facilitating the presentation of a mass of results in a coherent way. By categorizing the different indices of tests like the MMPI and Rorschach as we did (see Appendix C), we are actually creating hypotheses about their potential meaning for understanding maturing. The material presented in Chapters 5 through 8 could alternatively be viewed as studies of the validity of such test scores.

The availability of a potentially comprehensive map of the maturing process may help to evaluate the adequacy of work on personality change in other fields. Consider studies of the effects of higher education on students. If we believe their results, we may conclude that higher education has relatively meager effects: increased integrated and allocentric cognitive skills, accurately symbolized self-concepts, and allocentric values (Newcomb and Feldman, 1969). The glaring weaknesses of such studies, and of much evaluational research like that of the effects of Sesame Street or Headstart, is that effects may have occurred not tested by experimenters. Typically, experimenters have either tested for narrowly focused effects, and/or atheoretically selected tests to administer to college students that psychologists had developed for other purposes, like the Study of Values or MMPI. I know of no systematic effort to analyze what educational philosophers, even teachers, claim happens as the result of becoming educated in order to construct tests specifically measuring such effects. When the model, which does comprehend most educational philosophers' ideas about liberal education, was used to organize the study of effects of higher education, numerous effects were found never reported in the research literature (Heath, 1968, 1976e).

If Chickering's dimensions of educational maturing are compared to those of the model, we note that he tends to ignore cognitive maturation, like symbolization, allocentric self-concept, and value development, the symbolization of personal relationships, and the stabilization of personal relationships—effects that both educational philosophers and my studies identify as occurring (1968). Similarly hit-or-miss atheoretical studies on the comparative effects of vocation (Kohn and Schooler, 1973), parenting (Biller, 1974), and marriage (Kreitman, Collins, Wilson and Troop, 1970) report findings difficult to interpret because none used a systematic model of healthy development for assessing all the principal effects that could have occurred. The model is one systematic, partially validated classification that those studying the effects of different educational, psychotherapeutic, or institutional interventions or changes upon healthy growth might find useful.

The transcultural study of the model may also be useful in clarifying definitional issues. I have already suggested that concepts like psychological health or self-actualization may not be necessary. But what about competence?

Reassessment of the Concept of Competence

The theoretical status of competence and its relation to the model of maturing remain murky because competence is defined by several referents, none of which has yet been operationally defined. A new test of personal effectiveness may be useful (Poe, 1973), but it has not yet been independently validated (Jagede, 1976). Competence has been used as a *motive* by Robert White to refer to the desire to be efficacious and create effects on the environment. Our research included no direct measure of the strength of this motive; we cannot claim that mature persons have stronger desires to be efficacious than less mature persons.

Competence has also been used as a *behaviorally evaluative* term referring to the effectiveness with which a person functions. The criteria of effectiveness, as Chapter 2 suggests, may vary from judge to judge, from one task setting to the next, and from time to time. Research on this referent could become primarily a taxonomic task that might not have much generality, unless effectiveness were evaluated over a wide range of adaptive situations. Different situational demands require different patterns of attributes for their successful fulfillment. As the range of complexity of demands for effective functioning increase, as well as the frequency with which such demands change and create new adaptive problems, generalized personality traits, particularly those that facilitate adaptation, become more critical to effectiveness. By providing a theory of the adaptive process, the model of maturing identifies the traits that most generally facilitate adaptation. Therefore, the more broadly competent is a person, the more likely he is to be maturely organized. Competence as an evaluative term becomes useful to a scientific theory of personality only as it becomes determined less by situational and more by stable personality traits.

Competence has also been used structurally as a self-evaluative *attitude*. White speaks of "sense of efficacy or competence." Smith prefers "self-respect as a significant and efficacious person" (1974a), an attitude that provides the necessary self-confidence to risk initiating active efforts to cope. Both agree that achieving, coping, and adapting successfully enhance self-esteem. We did not directly measure the beliefs of the mature and immature men about how efficacious they were. Although the Total SIQ score was labeled "self-esteem," it may have been more appropriately labeled "sense of competence." Why? I have claimed that the core general traits defining competency are those predicted by the model of maturing because they are the traits necessary for making successful adaptations. The SIQ self-esteem score is *not* a traditional self-esteem score; rather, it is a global score based on a person's assessment of the degree to which he possesses specified traits that describe competent and mature persons. The research unequivocally supports the thesis that effectiveness is associated not only with a private sense of competence or self-esteem, but also with a belief that others also judge one's self to be able to cope successfully (social self-esteem).

Competence has also been used as a *higher order personality structure* by Smith to refer to the pattern of traits that define "the competent self." The research also unequivocally demonstrates that effective and ineffective persons differ on a core group of traits like anticipating consequences, clarity of thought, and so on. This core group differentiates the effective from the ineffective men *of every cultural group*. Smith's assumption, and ours, that there may be a transculturally universal group of traits defining the competent self was supported.

To use "competence" in four different ways is confusing. I suggest that White's initial term, "effectance," be used to describe the motive to create effects on the environment. *Competence* should be restricted to mean effectiveness of functioning, its most frequent usage among researchers. *Sense of competence* can be retained to refer to the attitude, belief, feeling that one is able to adapt successfully, that one has the potency to act and produce effects on the environment. The SIQ self-esteem score may be found to be an adequate measure of "sense of competence" and may therefore need to be relabeled. Finally, since the traits that define the "competent self" are derivable from the model of maturing, I suggest this phrase be replaced by the concept of mature personality organization. It is the stable attributes associated with mature personality organization that, in contrast to what is meant by *competence*, make it possible to induce generalizable and testable ideas about adaptation, irrespective of the personal or cultural values specific to the demands of the setting involved. A mature person may be incompetent in relation to such demands, but he has the potential to become more competent because of the adaptive potential associated with the traits that define his maturity.

Do we need both terms, competence and maturity? The research suggests that we do. Judged effectiveness only moderately predicted a variety of measures of adjustment, healthiness, and maturity. Several men of the Haverford and Istanbul groups judged to be highly effective were known independently by others or later discovered to be psychologically unhealthy and maladjusted. Judgments about effectiveness are complexly determined; maturity is only one determinant. Overt behavioral adjustment is not an infallible clue to internal organizing and motivating processes. At its root, this issue will remain unresolved until both terms are clarified further, and more adequate objective procedures developed to identify competent-incompetent and mature-immature men. Then we can empirically determine the degree of their overlap. The word *competence* remains fuzzy and has yet to be adequately operationalized. *Maturity* seems to be more precisely specified, and is gradually becoming more empirically defined by objective procedures.

In Chapter 2 I pointed out that when the research on maturity began, the only practical route to its study was by way of the judgments of others about effectiveness in adaptation— the route used by many investigators studying other concepts. Binet, for example, began his study of intelligence similarly. Now we use objective tests rather than subjective judgments to measure intelligence. In Chapters 7 and 8 I have taken some small steps toward identifying possible components and measures that might define maturity in the future *independently* of local social judgments and hence of knowledge of competency. The results suggest that it may be possible to separate the defining operations of the two terms, and so provide an independent way to resolve the need for both the concept of competence and that of maturity.

The Transcultural Universality of the Model of Maturing

Two general approaches have been used to test the generality of the model of maturity. Since it is a developmentally based model, it should validly describe the *process* of maturing. Accordingly, two major longitudinal studies, one of college men changing from their freshman through their senior year (Heath, 1968), and one of adult men changing during their twenties and early thirties (Heath, 1976a, c, e; 1977a, b), have confirmed that development from 17 through 33 can be validly organized by the dimensional hypotheses of the model.

The second method of testing the model's generality is to study different kinds of persons cross-sectionally. The model has proved to be useful with children (Lowry, 1967). A serious vacuum in research concerns the maturity of women. The recent research on male-female differences (J. H. Block, 1976; Maccoby & Jacklin, 1974; Sherman, 1971) suggests that the patterning of dimensional maturity may differ between the sexes. I reject the implication of some that we need one set of mental health criteria for men and another for women (Garai, 1970; Smith, 1974). We need general criteria that comprehend different patterns of maturing if they exist. Women may be more maturely developed in allocentric and integrative personal relationships, for example. Sex role differences, whether biologically and/or societally shaped, should, in principle, have the same theoretical status as cultural values, that is facilitating or limiting dimensional maturing. Preliminary studies of college women suggest that the inter and intra test patterns of the maturity of their self-concepts are similar to those of men. Even if differences are found, however, they would not invalidate the model's hypotheses; they would set limits to the patterning and possibly level of maturing, as I illustrated by an analysis of the effect that the *machismo* value had on the maturing of Sicilian men.

The transcultural studies are the principal test of the model's generality. Osgood has clarified the meaning of "transcultural universality." Anthropologists, he says, use the term in an absolute sense to mean no exceptions, regardless of degree of literateness, socioeconomic development, or political-societal complexity. The statistical meaning of universality refers to the nonchance occurrence of findings within a sample of world communities. If a significantly large enough number of different cultural groups tested support a hypothesis, we can say it is a transcultural universal. We also can talk of subuniversals, the commonalities that hold for only a few cultures. While I make the powerful assumption that the model of maturing is transculturally general, I do not expect all twenty of its hypotheses to be confirmed in all cultures. As the Sicilian and Istanbul results suggested, some hypotheses are more likely to be supported in some cultures rather than others. The transcultural results do not dispute the potential generality of the model. A number of its hypotheses hold for highly educated, middle and upperclass young male adults in three diverse cultures. We cannot strictly generalize beyond these limits; yet, none of the results suggest that such limits are impassable. Many hypotheses were supported by the Sicilians, many of whom were from lower socio economic peasant classes, for example.

As evidence accumulates that supports the generality of the model, the burden of demonstrating its limits falls increasingly upon the skeptic. To empirically establish the limits of its generality, particularly for Oriental cultures, is beyond my resources. But we can *theoretically* compare the model with Eastern and other religious views of healthy adult development to determine if mature and immature persons in Eastern cultures might differ as the model predicts. Campbell has provocatively hypothesized that if a detailed analysis were made of the religious ideals of ancient and modern complex societies, universal moral precepts would be discovered. Such precepts have adaptive survival value for the society because they counter the evolutionary biological competitive tendency toward selfishness, which, if unchecked, would destroy a society (1975). Such universals of the ideal person should be, if our hypothesis is correct, predicted by the model of maturing.

I do not have the expertise to make a detailed reliable comparison between religious ideals of the good life of some of the world's major religions. Fortunately, however, several psychological analyses of the mental health principles and views of healthy adult development (Bellah, *et al.*, 1976; Pedersen, 1977; Tart, 1975) have been made of the Indian Sikh scriptures (Neki, 1975), Confucianism (Tseng, 1973; Wei-Ming, 1976), Zen Buddhism (Goleman, 1975, 1976; Owens, 1975; Rohlen, 1976), the Sunni Muslim religious tradition (Lapidus, 1976), and Christianity (Bouwsma, 1976). These religious traditions agree in most of their basic assumptions about healthy adult growth; they disagree in their emphases on others.

They agree that 1) there are universal commonalities among all people, for instance, the brotherhood of man; 2) man is a complex system that functions best when in "balance," "harmony," or "moderation"; in other words, excessive development of one virtue results in systemic distortion; 3) healthy growth continues throughout the life span, and maturity is not an achievable endpoint; 4) development is a holistic process that results in the alteration of a person and relations with others and himself; 5) growth is multidimensional, and may progress through phases or stages, a progression most elaborately described in Zen. Such assumptions match those of the model of maturing.

But are the specific dimensional traits hypothesized by historic religions to describe Enlightenment, *Sahaja*, and self-realization comprehended by the model of maturing? I coded every trait mentioned in the principal commentaries with suggestive but *very unreliable* results. All of the great religions claim that the mature person is *well-integrated*, particularly in his *values* and *self*, and as a consequence is spontaneous and acts with integrity. The mature person also has *autonomous self*-control and *values*; he is a self-regulating person who has conquered if not abolished desire and so can act with courage independently of self-interest. He also has *allocentric values* and *personal relationships*; he shows loving compassion for others. Maturing involves persistent, disciplined commitment (*stable values*) that brings inner certitude, serenity, calm, repose, and self-confidence (*stability* of the *self*). As a person matures, he becomes more alive, joyful, and spontaneous, and transcends (or becomes more autonomous of) the reality of his body and surrounding world. Mentioned less frequently or universally in the commentaries were gaining understanding and knowledge of the self (*symbolization* of *self-concept*); expanding the self beyond family and nationality to be "at one with universal reality" (*allocentric* and *integrative self-concept*); controlling emotions so that they do not interfere with logical and judgmental abilities (*autonomy* of *cognitive skills*); cultivating interpersonal harmony (*integration personal relations*); developing more and more differentiated levels of meditative awareness (*symbolization* of *cognitive skills*); increasing detachment from and dependence upon but not declining interest in others (*autonomy personal relations*), and other traits of maturity. Finally, different religious traditions emphasize different dimensional pathways of growth more than others: Zen meditation values the increasing differentiation of and growth through different states of consciousness, rather than nurturing allocentric cognitive skills for testing and manipulating external reality. Confucianism emphasizes harmony in interpersonal relationships, frequently at the expense, in its cultural applications to filial piety, of autonomy. *Sajaha* emphasizes self-management or autonomy and integration, possibly, like Zen, at the expense of developing allocentric adaptive cognitive skills. Christianity emphasizes allocentric values and personal relationships at the expense of the integration of bodily, particularly sexual, needs. Some forms of Islam emphasize allocentric surrender and submission to God at the expense, for some variants of the Muslim faith, of developing autonomy. The commentaries also mentioned traits that I could not code with the categories of the model: transcendence, perfect knowledge, renunciation of will, nonattachment, formless self, *Samadhi*.

More dispassionate, expert, and reliable textual analyses are obviously required, but this cursory survey does suggest that a transculturally universal model of maturing remains a reasonable possibility.

Maturity, Adaptation, and the Good Life

Why do the great religious traditions of the world seem to agree about the core universals that define a "good" person? Why did we find some transcultural similarities in maturity?

One clue comes from cultural anthropological studies of psychopathology which show that

> there is a greater degree of convergence in the modes of external manifestations of psychopathology between relatively complex, large, differentiated societies, whether Western or non-Western in character, than between simple and complex societies (Draguns and Phillips, 1972, 7).

Advancing technology and modern communications are homogenizing most human societies. To be competent in modern societies, as Inkeles has shown (Inkeles and Smith, 1974), a person must be logically ordered in his thought, have the capacity to deal with abstract relationships, schedule his time, anticipate consequences, and so on. Increasingly, the fact that societies have culturally similar problems to solve is producing a universal "human nature" (Boulding, 1964; Doob, 1960; M. B. Smith, 1969a; Vernon, 1969). But this hypothesis does not account for the similarity in mental health principles among the world's religions, which evolved out of rural and simply organized cultures. Nor does it account for the differences *between* similarly educated mature and immature men who have had comparable cultural experiences with technology and the mass media.

A more speculative reason for the transcultural and religious similarities in defining maturity and the self-realized Enlightened person may be the universal personality requirements of the adaptive sequence. Men's responses to challenges, whether they be crop failure, death, advent of a new tool, or education, may vary in their adaptive value. Religious insight about "psychological survival," as well as our results, suggest that some ways of living, seen in certain personality traits, are more effective, more psychologically adaptive, than others. The good life and the model of maturing may identify the personality traits that historically have proved to be adaptive; one reason, perhaps, why diverse cultures may respond similarly on social desirability measures (Ghei, 1973). The model of maturing may not be just a twentieth-century emergent!

If only we had the necessary data from history. My hunch would be that the mature Babylonian, Periclean Greek, Dravidian Indian, and Mayan would have, in contrast to his immature brother and sister, differed similarly on the dimensions of maturing. Man learns from the consequences of his adaptations. Why some men learn more from their experience than others, in spite of similar school, work, or other societal experience, is not yet known. But the dimensions of the adaptive process are universal. Out of the hundreds and thousands of bits and chunks of man's adaptive experiences develop the intellectual skills, ideas about one's self, values, and personal relationships that become increasingly more symbolizable, allocentric, integrative, stable, and autonomous. Cultures recognize the potential adaptive consequence of these types of growth by idealizing them in similar ideas of maturity, wholeness or self-realization.

Philosophers and scientists have long disputed that the values defining the "good life" can be naturalistically derived by science (Maslow, 1959, 1963). Tillich believed that values are derivable from the "essential structures of being" (1959); Fromm asserts that the "source of norms for ethical conduct are to be found in man's nature itself . . . [that] moral norms are based upon man's inherent qualities" (1947, 7). Cattell suggests that a "firm ethics" can be derived from a scientific understanding of adaptation (1973, 17). Maslow claims that man's highest values are "instinctoid" (1963). Campbell says

> Moralizing systems . . . make complex social systems adapt better. They are present because they have contributed in the past to the survival and reproduction of certain social systems in competition with others (1976, 382).

What are those transculturally universal core adaptive values that may be derived from a scientifically validated model of maturing? Increasing ability to symbolize one's experience enhances one's potential honesty for representing one's internal and external world. Allocentricism provides the potential basis for compassion and loving kindness. Integration encourages integrity that results in spontaneity. Stability nurtures the potential of steadfastness and commitment. Autonomy leads to courage. Are these some of the core adaptive values that universally define the "good life"—honesty, compassion, integrity, commitment, and courage?

Similarities and Dissimilarities Among the American, Turkish, and Italian Cultures

At the time the research was initiated, the field of "culture and personality" had no accepted comprehensive theoretical rationale, systematic accumulative body of knowledge, or generally accepted methodologies (De Vos and Hippler, 1969). The past decade has brought many new promising developments: Triandis' work on subjective culture (1972a, b); Dawson's biosocial model, as summarized in Brislin, Lonner and Thorndike (1973); studies on modernization (Inkeles and Smith, 1974); and theoretical and methodological revaluations (Abel, 1974; Dragun, 1973; Levine, 1973). Certainly a perplexing problem in studying "culture and personality" is how to coordinate operationally the different levels of abstraction to which each term applies. Since I was working within the framework of a personality model of maturing, I asked if it was possible to describe significant attributes of a culture using the same categories describing the maturing of a person.

What do I mean? Let us take the Turkish father. He is perceived (LeCompte and LeCompte, 1973), and was similarly described in interviews, to be an authoritarian traditionalist with such decisive power over his children that he controls their decisions even as adults. The roles of the Italian and American father are quite different. As Triandis argued, a culture's expectations of its fathers may be one very important determinant of how fathers act. Presumably different types of paternal behavior have differential effects on the maturing of children. Research has suggested that authoritarian fathers may distort the maturing of autonomy in male children, for example. Could we evaluate how "mature" a culture's valuation of the role of the father is in the same terms used to describe the maturing of the children? We are asking how we might assess the subjective culture, "a cultural group's characteristic way of perceiving the man-made part of its environment" (Triandis, 1972b, 4).

Unfortunately, practical methods to assess cultural differences in ethos, values, or patterns of relationships were not available at the time the research was initiated.[1] New methods had to be developed. They are unabashedly exploratory, and should be considered as such.

Cultural Semantic Test (CST). A Cultural Semantic Test (CST), modeled on the Semantic Differential Test (Osgood, Suci and Tannenbaum, 1957) was developed. Judges rated each of eleven attributes of their culture—Turks, Turkish mothers, Turkish fathers, and so on—on eighteen scales defined at each end by contrasting adjectives that defined a dimension of maturing. Each dimension as well as the general concept of maturity was represented by three pairs of adjectivally defined scales.

Maturity: mature-immature, healthy-unhealthy; active-passive.

Symbolization: reflective-unreflective; imaginative-unimaginative; vague-clear.

Allocentricism: realistic-unrealistic; altruistic-egoistic; social-unsocial.

Integration: integrated-unintegrated; simple-complex; consistent-inconsistent.

Stability: stable-unstable; flexible-rigid; excitable-calm.

Autonomy: independent-dependent; conformist-individualist; impulsive-controlled.

A sample of the form and an example of how one Turk rated his country on three of the scales is:

---

1 Gillespie's and Allport's measures on attitudes seemed tangential (1955); Kluckhohn's and Strodtbeck's cultural interview method and questions inappropriate (1961); and Cantril's Self-Anchoring Striving Scale was too focused (1965). Morris's method of assessing a culture's paths of life seemed too diffuse and abstract, as well as methodologically complex (1956), but my gaze was too focused for his work was more applicable than I realized. I had not been aware at the time of the research of the Role Differential Test as used by Foa, Triandis, and Katz (1966) to compare familial role patterns.

Turkey Today

	X								
Unstable		— : — : — : — : — : — : —							Stable
Integrated					X				— : — : — : — : — : — : —	Unintegrated
Realistic						X			— : — : — : — : — : — : —	Unrealistic

The adjectives for each dimension were randomly ordered through the list as were the mature and immature ends of each scale. Each concept and its eighteen scales was printed separately on a page; the eleven concepts were randomly mixed for each judge. Each judge marked one of the seven scale positions for each pair of adjectives that best described the concept. To score the test, the scale position was weighted according to its degree of maturity. By adding the scores for the three adjectives defining each dimension of maturing, a map of the differential maturity of the components of the culture was secured, as judged by members of that culture themselves.

Translated copies of the CST were given to seventy students in university psychology courses of each culture. Approximately half of the judges were from eastern and half from western Turkey; half were from northern and half from southern Italy. All of the American judges were students from mid-Atlantic states. With the exception of twenty-six of the thirty-seven Sicilians who completed the CST, none of the judges knew of or participated in any phase of the research. Since the CST was used only for exploratory purposes, I will not report its specific test findings.

The CST's findings suggest some tentative ideas about the similarities and dissimilarities among the three cultures. In interpreting the results we must keep in mind that they describe what the most critically aware group—university students—of each culture *believes* about its culture. The results may or may not describe the culture accurately. The American students rated their culture and country to be more mature on the scales defining maturity than did the Italians and Turks. The Turks rated their culture to be least mature on every one of the eleven attributes. They rated themselves as least mature on 57 percent, the Italians on 26 percent, and the Americans on 17 percent of the total number of dimensions defining the maturity of the eleven attributes. More specifically, the Turks rated different aspects of their culture as being unstable and autocentric. These ratings probably reflect in part the turmoil and restlessness that modern Turkey has been going through as it has been wrenching itself away from the socially fatalistic grip of its Islamic tradition. The Italians judged their culture to be the best integrated and autonomous, though like Barzini, the Italians rated their country in contrast as the most conformist, dependent, and impulsive. The Americans rated their culture as least reflective and imaginative. The American pragmatic activist stance may not foster these qualities. Generally, the Americans rated their culture more favorably because they judged it to be more complex, active, social, and independent.

Interestingly, for each country its most economically backward or least "modern" geographical region was also rated consistently to be less developed on each of the dimensions. This result may support applying scales measuring "maturity" to institutional and societal categories. The more socially and economically advanced sector of each country (northern United States, northern Italy, and western Turkey) was judged to be more maturely developed on 95 percent of the scales. The judges from Sicily and Anatolia did not disagree in their ratings of the backwardness or immaturity of their own regions. When the ratings of the different regions were compared with the ratings of the country as a whole, the intriguing result was that the Turks and Italians, but not the Americans, judged the dimensional maturity of their country to be more similar to that of their backward than to their advanced regions. Apparently, the idea of "Italy" to Italians, and of "Turkey" to Turks, does not conjure up images of that part of their country which is more modern, vigorous, and healthy. One might say that northern Italy and western Turkey are deviants, not in harmony with the ethos and character that connote the nation as a nation to its members. Perhaps because the differences between the American north and south were not judged to be as polarized, America was rated as the most integrated of the three countries.

The three cultures' fathers and mothers were very favorably judged by the students. They were rated to be more mature than the typical American, Turk, or Italian, as well as more mature than the typical young man or woman of the culture. Consistent with the cultural differences already noted, the American, Italian, and Turkish fathers and mothers were judged to be progressively less mature in that order. The Turkish fathers (but not the Turkish mothers) were rated to be the most immature fathers on every dimension of maturity. This finding supported my impression that young Turks were harshly critical of their fathers. The fathers of every culture were rated to be the least maturely developed in their autonomy. They were judged to be impulsive and conformist, certainly not independent individualists. One of the clearest similarities among the three cultures was the outstanding caring allocentricism of their mothers. Not unexpectedly, the American, Turkish, and Italian mothers were seen as being very dependent and conformist, even more so than their husbands. The quality of the relationships among the families was rated to be less healthy and mature than the mothers and fathers were individually rated. Again, the Turks were most and the Americans the least critical with respect to the dimensional maturity of their family relationships. The Italian family was rated as being the most self-centered, dependent, and conformist; the Turkish as most rigid and unintegrated; and the American as most unreflective.

With respect to the maturity of specific customs, such as those related to sex and religion, the Italians and, particularly, the Turks, were most dissatisfied with their sexual customs. Actually, the category of sexual customs tended to be rated as the most dimensionally immature in all three cultures—perhaps an archetypal complaint of any young adult.

One of the few departures from the general cultural trends was found in the ratings of the maturity of religious customs. The Italian judges rated their religious tradition to be more mature generally than the American and Turkish judges rated their own religious customs, a result congruent with the greater identification with and participation in religious activities of the Pisan and Sicilian groups. Young Turks viewed Islam to be less healthy, active, and mature, rating it to be less socially concerned and realistic. These findings mirror the view of many young Turks I interviewed who were rejecting the hold that Mohammedism had had on their country for centuries.

Judgments about adjectives reflecting the maturity of one's country, people, and customs reveal what judges *believe* a culture's ethos *may* be like. They do not tell us much about the specific patterns of relationships that also produce differences in personality organization. Information about such patterns would establish more precisely how similarly and dissimilarly the three cultures rewarded and punished different ways of relating to others. In one sense, a method was needed that measured each culture's interpersonal reinforcement hierarchy.

The Cultural Valuator Test (CVT). The Cultural Valuator Test

(CVT) required a judge to rate on a seven-point scale the degree to which his culture approved, expected, and encouraged each of eight types of interactions between different kinds of persons.

What are the important interpersonal relationships to assess in different cultures? Previous studies had shown that twenty-eight different modes of relationships satisfactorily comprehended all the varied interactions that occurred in fantasied stories about other persons (Heath, 1965, Ch. 11). These modes could be classified by type of affect (positive to negative) and degree of self- or other-involvement in the interaction. Eight of the twenty-eight modes were selected to represent different combinations of positive and negative involvement with one's self and other persons. The eight modes of relatedness, ordered roughly in terms of decreasing positive affect through neutral to increasing negative affect were:

1 Flirting with, making advances toward, seducing, having sexual relations with;

2 Having an affectionate, loyal, devoted, close, confiding, non-sexual friendship with another;

3 Depending upon another for advice, guidance, support, love, security, and protection; preferring to follow another's leadership, obeying another's decisions, enjoying having people do things for oneself;

4 Playing and relaxing, having fun with, playing games or sports, talking or joking (no sexual implications);

5 Keeping away from, retreating, withdrawing, avoiding contact with, and not speaking to others;

6 Maintaining one's independence, making, asserting, and defending one's own decisions; defying or disobeying or rebelling against, if necessary;

7 Controlling, commanding, dominating, persuading, and making others obey;

8 Arguing, criticizing, ridiculing, injuring, attacking, fighting, and aggressing toward others.

Cultures approve or disapprove, that is, value or disvalue, relating in each of these ways to different persons, depending on the age, sex, marital status, socioeconomic and other characteristics of the persons involved in the relationship. Obviously, to measure how a culture values the ways each type of person should relate to every other type of person was forbiddingly complex. To simplify the judging task, I restricted the attributes to be assessed to age, sex, familial, and nonfamilial relationships, and marital status. The ages selected were spaced to include prepubertal, adolescent, young adult, and middle-aged persons. Twelve attributes were used: father, mother, brother, sister, boy of 11, girl of 11, boy of 17, girl of 17, unmarried man of 22, unmarried woman of 22, married man of 45 with family, and married woman of 45 with family.[1]

Appropriate types of persons were paired together to produce ninety-six different relationships to assess for each mode of relatedness. The judge rated the degree to which the culture approved, expected, or encouraged each mode of relating for each of the ninety-six paired relationships. For example, as the following illustrative example of part of one CVT rating sheet indicates, the judge rated the extent to which the Turkish culture approved a boy of 11 arguing, criticizing, or ridiculing his father, his mother, his brother, and so on.

The Turkish Culture

3 strongly approves, expects, encourages
2 moderately approves, expects, encourages
1 mildly approves, expects, encourages
0 is indifferent to, or neither approves nor disapproves
−1 mildly disapproves, prohibits, discourages
−2 moderately disapproves, prohibits, discourages
−3 strongly disapproves, prohibits, discourages
    arguing, criticizing, ridiculing,
    injuring, attacking, fighting or aggressing

By

Toward	Boy of 11	Girl of 11	Boy of 17	Girl of 17	Unmarried Man of 22	Unmarried Woman of 22	Married Man of 45 with Family	Married Woman of 45 with Family
Father	−3	−3	−3	−3	−3	−3	−3	−3
Mother	−3	−2	−1	−2	−3	−3	−3	−2
Brother	−1	−3	−1	−3	0	−3	−1	−3
Sister	−3	−2	0	−2	−3	−3	2	−2
11-year-old boy	1	−2	1	−2	1	−3	2	0
11-year-old girl	0	−1	−3	−2	−3	0	−1	−1

1 The CVT, while similar in idea to the Role Differential Test, differs by examining the appropriateness of different modes, *e.g.*, avoiding, rather than of specific behaviors, *e.g.*, who goes through an open doorway first, in nonfamilial as well as familial role relations (Foa, Triandis, Katz, 1966).

The format of the CVT was similar to that of the Cultural Semantic Test. Each of the eight modes of relatedness was placed on a separate sheet containing the grid of different relationships. The eight sheets, including an instructional sheet and a practice set of ratings, were collated to form a booklet. The order in which each mode was rated was randomized among the judges.

Psychologists in each of the five cultural areas administered the CVT to male and female students. No judges, except the Sicilians who took the CVT at the conclusion of their testing program, had any knowledge of the larger study or participated in it. Fifty American, fifty Turkish, and seventy Italian judges completed the CVT. These small samples provide hints, not definitive conclusions, about how the cultures are perceived to be different.

What did the CVT suggest might be some similarities and dissimilarities among the three cultures? I will abstract out of the data only the most salient general findings.

Table A–1 provides an overall picture of the three cultures' stances toward different modes of relatedness as rated by our judges. It reports the mean degree of approval of each culture for each mode of relatedness *irrespective* of whom that relationship is with. I must emphasize the latter qualification; obviously, American judges do not so strongly disapprove sexual relationships between adolescents or young adults as the Table suggests the American culture does generally. Table A–1 highlights some striking similarities and dissimilarities among the three cultures as rated by our small groups of judges. The cultures simply do not vary very much from each other in the pattern of their approval of different modes of relatedness. If we rank the relationships in terms of their degree of approval for each culture, their reinforcement hierarchies

Table A–1
Degree of Cultural Approval of Different Interpersonal Modes of Relatedness

CULTURE	MODES OF RELATEDNESS							
	Flirt-ing	Affect-ion	Depend-ing	Play-ing	Avoid-ing	Independ-ence	Control-ling	Aggress-ing
America	1.37[1]	4.66	3.63	5.10	2.98	4.78	2.85	2.16
Turkey	1.92	5.14	4.65	4.89	3.41	4.10	3.49	2.64
Italy	1.52	5.25	4.00	4.78	3.20	4.10	3.30	2.69

1 Score of 7 means culture strongly approves, expects, encourages; score of 4 means culture is indifferent to, neither approves nor disapproves; score of 1 means culture strongly disapproves, prohibits, discourages.

are significantly similar; that is, *rho* .98 between Italy and Turkey, .86 between Turkey and America, and .90 between America and Italy. The three cultures are rated to agree in disapproving the expression of sexual and aggressive impulses in most relationships. Their intensity is probably such as to be potentially very disruptive to other relationships. The cultures must channel their expression very prescriptively, which may be why Freud identified sexual and aggressive impulses as those most generative of psychopathology. The cultures also agree in encouraging their members to be independent and autonomous, as well as affectionate and playful. But the cultures were judged to differ in how they reward the remaining modes of relatedness. Italians and Turks are more approving of persons who seek support and guidance, and are not as disapproving as the Americans of those who seek to avoid or even to control and dominate others.

The generalization that the three cultures value different modes of relatedness similarly is strengthened by the remarkable similarity in their *degree* of approval of the modes of relatedness. The three cultures do not vary from each other in the extent of their approval by more than one score value on seven of the eight relationships. Only the American culture deviated notably, and in only one relationship at that. Americans apparently discourage or at least frown upon those who seek advice, support, and create dependent relationships.

Another dramatic finding was that of the three cultures, the American was clearly the most restrictive and punitive. Table A–1 demonstrates this generally; Table A–2 gives more specific confirming evidence about how the cultures differed. Table A–2 summarizes the number of statistically significant differences found between the ratings of the judges of each culture for each mode of relatedness for each of the ninety-six paired relationships being rated. For example, of the ninety-six different pairs of persons whose affectionate mode of relatedness was rated for the degree of the culture's approval—boy of 11 being affectionate with his father, his mother, his brother, and so on—fifty-two of the paired interactions differed significantly between the American and Turkish cultures. Table A–2 shows that the American culture was significantly more approving of affection being expressed in eleven and the Turkish culture more approving in forty-one of the ninety-six relationships.

Tables A–1 and A–2 allow us to say that the Turkish, Italian, and American cultures, in that order, were *decreasingly* approving of

Table A–2
Cultural Differences in Values About
Modes of Relatedness

MODE OF RELATEDNESS	NUMBER OF RELATIONSHIPS[1] EACH CULTURE SIGNIFICANTLY APPROVED IN COMPARISON TO REMAINING CULTURES					
	America compared to		Turkey compared to		Italy compared to	
	Turkey	Italy	America	Italy	America	Turkey
Flirting	2	5	62	55	21	0
Affection	11	5	41	8	65	20
Depending	4	2	62	50	41	12
Playing	28	41	10	10	7	2
Avoiding	0	0	29	17	14	0
Independence	61	71	2	16	0	6
Controlling	0	0	58	31	50	11
Aggressing	0	0	36	1	56	4

1 The table reports the number of significant differences between the ratings of the two cultures' judges for the ninety-six paired combinations of persons. Only differences significant at least at a two-tailed .05 *p* level are reported.

different modes of relating to others. Let us examine in detail the more disapproving and prohibiting American culture. In comparison with both the Turkish and Italian cultures, the Americans channel the expression of sexuality, affection, and dependency very narrowly. Table A–2 indicates that the American culture is significantly more approving of erotic flirtatious activity in *only* two and five of the ninety-six possible relationships, or conversely, that it is more disapproving than either the Italian or Turkish cultures of seductive relationships in twenty-one and sixty-two of the total number of relationships. In comparison with the Turks, the Americans more strongly approve sexual contact between seventeen-year-old males and females, and unmarried twenty-two-year-old men and women. In every one of the remaining sixty-two relationships, the Turks do not so strongly disapprove or discourage erotic relationships as much as the Americans do.

The American culture seems to have a polarized, accentuated attitude toward sexuality. It is more approving and encouraging of sexual relations among young adults of the same ages than are the other cultures; it is much more consistently discouraging and restrictive in most other types of relationships. The American culture provides its members with a much sharper, clearer set of acceptable options about whom to have sexual relations with. While disapproving, both Turks and Italians are significantly less disapproving than the Americans of pubertal and young adult homosexual, or extramarital relationships.

The American culture is also judged to be less approving of affectionate and emotionally dependent relations than are the other cultures. It is significantly more encouraging of affectionate and close friendships only among its adolescents, primarily with those pairs for whom sexual relationships are sanctioned. The expression of both sexuality and affection for Americans is much more regulated by age than it is in the other cultures. The data suggest the American culture does not distinguish as clearly as the other cultures do between sexual and affectionate friendships; close friendships seem to imply sexual relationships. With respect to seeking emotional support in a dependent relation, the American culture is significantly more approving than is the Turkish culture, for example, of prepubertal children being dependent. But once puberty is reached, the American culture no longer approves its adolescents or adults being dependent. Both the Turkish and Italian cultures are less disapproving of adults being dependent upon their families, for example. The data strongly suggest that in contrast to the development of Italians and Turks, the American adolescent must alter markedly his former dependency relationship to become progressively more independent of others.

Of interest are the two modes of relatedness in which the American culture is significantly judged to be more approving than the other cultures. Table A–2 emphatically says Americans value playfully jocular and independent, autonomous, self-sufficient relationships with many more people than do Italians and Turks. Americans expect their late adolescents to be independent, capable of standing by their own decisions, no longer dependent upon their families. This expectation is clearer for American males than for females. Finally, with respect to the more negative emotional relationships, like controlling and aggressing, the patterns are equally as clear. The Italian and Turkish cultures do not differ significantly in their disapproval of the expression of aggression and hostility, but both do differ from the American culture. Anyone who has ridden in an Italian taxicab, tried to cross the main thoroughfare of Istanbul, listened to an Italian family settle its dispute, or sensed the wrath of a Turkish student, can appreciate the finding that the Italian and Turkish cultures are consistently less disapproving of arguments, criticisms, and ridicule in a wider range of personal relationships than are the more self-controlled, independent, cool Americans. The strong anti-authoritarian, independent, individualistic emphasis in the American culture reflects its strong distrust of and repudiation of dominating, controlling, authoritarian types of relationships.

What sense can be made of these patterns? I do not attribute the markedly emotionally suppressive tone of the American culture, as illuminated by the ratings of the judges, to be due to moralistically-biased student ratings. The men and women judges were students of colleges that attract some of the most socially liberal, rebellious, and critical students of the country.[1] Rather, the results impressively reflect, I belive, how deeply engrained is the puritanistic stance toward the expression of emotion in America. Close affectionate, intimate, emotionally dependent, and expressive personal relationships are severely shunned by many Americans. Self-control, maintaining one's cool, pragmatic efficiency, and detachment are highly valued. Recall how widely praised was Jackie Kennedy's unemotional "performance" during the funeral of her husband. American students whom I interviewed in Italy and Turkey consistently remarked how "liberated" they felt emotionally with Italians and Turks, and how "deep" and reflective European friendships were in contrast to American ones. The data suggest that the American culture expects and rewards a friendly, bantering, gregarious, not withdrawing, type of sociability; it encourages individualistic self-sufficiency and independence at the expense of, perhaps even a defense against, too heavy personal emotional involvements. Americans may fear the potential sexual arousal that could occur in affectionate, intimate relationships; therefore, they confine their emotional needs almost exclusively to those of their own age with whom the culture does sanction sexuality as the means for more intense emotional gratification. To value self-sufficiency and independence is, of course, to disvalue any kind of relationship in which a person must submit the control of another.

I have not said much thus far about the Turkish and Italian cultures because their findings must be interpreted within the context of Table A–3. It reports the number of relationships in which the judges of each of the three cultures differed significantly among themselves, thus suggesting lack of judge agreement or

---

1 The American ratings on the CVT were secured after the massive collegiate disruptions and cohabitation movement. What is remarkable is that despite these surface movements, the American culture still emerges from the data so emotionally suppressive and controlled.

clarity about the degree to which the culture approved or disapproved the mode of relatedness being rated. To illustrate one way to interpret Table A–3, note that there was significantly more variability among the American than the Turkish judges on fourteen of the ninety-six different pairs of affectionate relationships—boy of 11 affectionate toward girl of 11, boy of 17, and so on. Apparently, the American judges were much less certain or clear about their own culture's attitude toward the expression of affection in more of their relationships than were the Turkish and Italian judges. The Italian judges agreed much more consistently among themselves about what their culture's expectations were about who could and could not have close, intimate, but nonsexual relations with whom. Perhaps the Americans could not agree because the culture confuses sexuality with affection, thus making close friendships more "dangerous" and so more ambiguous to rate.

Table A-3
Cultural Differences in Judge Agreement About the Approval of Their Culture About Modes of Relatedness

Number of Relationships in which Judges of Culture were Significantly More Variable than Judges of the Remaining Cultures

Mode of Relatedness	AMERICA COMPARED TO		TURKEY COMPARED TO		ITALY COMPARED TO	
	Turkey	Italy	America	Italy	America	Turkey
Flirting	2[1]	5	74	74	57	0
Affection	14	28	12	25	3	1
Depending	8	0	25	20	22	6
Playful	2	16	21	11	14	0
Avoiding	9	2	15	23	15	2
Independence	0	10	11	10	7	0
Controlling	0	0	44	16	37	0
Aggressing	0	0	32	16	7	0

1 Entries may total more than comparable totals in Table A–4 because they also include ratings whose variances, but not their means, differed significantly.

The most intriguing and puzzling finding in Table A–3 is that it was the Turkish judges who agreed least and the American judges who agreed the most among themselves about their culture's values. But it was the Americans who were least approving and the Turks most approving of the different modes of relating. The disagreement among the judges could have several roots: it can reflect cultural ambiguity about what its values are, and/or tolerance and acceptance of a wider range of "deviant" kinds of behavior. All three cultures have been going through major sociopsychological transitions in the past several decades that are challenging their traditional values. The significantly greater American consensus about its basic interpersonal values may suggest that the Turkish and Italian cultures have been experiencing a different and perhaps more pervasive transition than the American culture. Modern Turkey is struggling to free itself from some of its Anatolian traditions in areas where Islam is still deeply engrained in the values and character of its peasants; for example, a newspaper article reported an elementary school teacher was killed because he played soccer on a religious holiday. Italy also has yet to forge a national stance toward its own Sicilian traditions, such as the forcible rape of a woman as a man's declaration of his intention to marry her. Nor are the profound changes in the authoritarian parental-child relationships in modern Turkey, or the religious conflicts over Italian divorce laws comparable to the milder "permissive" changes in the American family or our arguments about abortion. The American tumult of the sixties apparently did not work very profound changes in the cultural consensus about what types of relationships are acceptable or not. Or, if very profound changes were occurring, at least they were not reflected in the judgments of youthful judges who were close to the forefront of whatever change was going on.

The disagreement among the judges about their cultural values may also say something about a culture's degree of acceptance and tolerance of diverse forms of emotional expression. Let us examine the two modes of relatedness in Table A–3 about which there was greatest disagreement among the judges. The Italian and Turkish judges were most in disagreement among themselves about their culture's sexual values, and then about who controlled and obeyed whom when their judgments were compared with those of the American judges. What is puzzling at first is that the Italians are models of consensual agreement when compared to the Turkish judges' ratings, but are models of disagreement when compared to the American judges' ratings. The American judges were in extraordinary agreement about their culture's attitudes; in some relationships the fifty judges agreed without exception about the culture's degree of disapproval. The American culture is known for being very restrictive and punitive about different forms of personal, particularly sexual, behavior. Its consistent judge agreement and the disapproving ratings given to erotic relationships reflect a very proscriptive and constricting sexual code. So in comparison, the Italian lack of judge agreement about sexuality may give the impression of cultural chaos. But Table A–3 indicated the Italians did not approve of indiscriminate sexual activity; they may just be a little more casual about their sexual relationships. The Turkish culture's attitudes about sexuality are more complex; more open and diverse forms of its expression are tolerated, at least for males, as the examples cited in Chapter 3 suggest.

A clue about the significant Turkish disagreement on who controls and obeys whom comes from the types of relationships about which the Turkish judges were in greatest disagreement. A disproportionate number of the total number of disagreements among the Turkish judges occurred in the ratings about familial relationships. The judges not only disagreed about the culture's values about who controls whom in the family, but also about the expression of playful, affectionate, aggressive, and avoidant tendencies within the Turkish family. The Turkish family seems to be under much more strain than the American or Italian family. Perhaps this is why a different group of Turkish judges who rated the CST were most critical of their culture's familial relationships, and why the culture was rated to be the least stable and integrated of the three in its familial relationships.

The exploratory study produced numerous other supplementary findings. Every culture was judged to restrict its women more than its men, though not as severely as I had anticipated. Intercultural differences could not be attributed to intra-cultural variability. For example, the Sicilians and Pisans did not disagree enough between each other for the judgments of either to account for the principal differences between the Italian and the other cultures. This does not mean the Sicilians did not view the Italian culture from a Southern perspective. They did. They rated, for example, the Italian culture as more acceptant and approving of sexual, playful, and dependent forms of relating, particularly for unmarried adolescents. The Sicilians also approved married adults being more dependent upon their parents than did the Pisans.[1] Generally, the Pisans and Sicilians agreed very consistently in interpreting the cultural values affecting familial relationships.

[1] These differences might also reflect social class differences in interpersonal expectations. More of the Sicilian CVT judges were from the lower socioeconomic classes. Pearlin has found that middle-class American and Italian families differ similarly from lower-class families in socialization attitudes (1971).

APPENDIX B

Test Procedures

Study of Values test (SV). Although it was not difficult to create linguistically equivalent translations of the SV test for the three cultures, we had no *a priori* basis for assuming that a scale composed of a number of items had the same psychological meaning in the three cultures. It may and probably does have. But we should be clear about the assumptions we make, assumptions that apply to all of the tests. Take the scale measuring religious preference. To assume that its items contribute in a similar way among the cultures to the total score is to assume that the meaning of each item is perfectly general and not influenced by different cultural values; that is, a high religious preference has the same components in the three cultures.

How might we check the equivalence of the meaning of the religious scale in the three cultures? We could restandardize each scale in each culture, and determine the similarity of the pattern of its correlates with some culturally defined criterion of religious preference. A less satisfactory and more indirect, but immeasurably more practicable, alternative is to determine the similarity among the three cultures of their pattern of intercorrelations between the different scales of the SV. Highly similar patterns presumably indicate that the cultural groups are responding to the different scales similarly. The intrascale correlates of the SV for the cultural groups were indeed remarkably similar, thus providing some confidence the scales may be similar in perceived meaning to the men.

Self-Image Questionnaire (SIQ). The translators had no difficulty creating equivalent linguistic forms. The cultural groups' patterns of correlates between the esteem and the dimensional scores, given in Tables B-1 and B-2, show considerable consistency among the groups. All of the scores are positively and similarly related to each other with the occasional exception of the Istanbul group. Persons who rate themselves mature believe others also judge them to be so, and, for the most part, are so judged by others. Also, social self-esteem generally predicts what others actually judge a person to be. The Istanbul men's ratings of their own maturity were not significantly related to similar ratings of them made by their friends—even though the Istanbul men had selected those friends who knew them best. Either the Istanbul men did not know themselves well, or were very defensive, or had friends who misunderstood them. The general results reassure us that the cultural groups responded similarly to the SIQ; the Istanbul results suggest that it is a deviant group.

Table B–1
Relationships Among the SIQ Esteem
(or Maturity) Scores for the
Cultural Groups

Private Self-esteem	Social Esteem	Judged Esteem
Haverford	.83**	.37[1]
Ankara	.71**	.60**
Istanbul	.76**	.17
Pisa	.74**	.46**
Sicily	.66**	.52**
Social Esteem		
Haverford		.69**
Ankara		.64**
Istanbul		.36
Pisa		.49**
Sicily		.39*

**$p < .01$, *$p < .05$.

1 Correlate not precisely comparable to others. It is based on four faculty-student judges who initially selected the men.

Rorschach. Of all of the tests used in the research, the Rorschach demanded the most clinical skill for its administration. Much research has shown that responses to the Rorschach may be influenced by the attitude 'of the administrator. Although each experimenter was trained to give the Rorschach similarly, subsequent evidence suggested the individual experimenters were a

Table B–2
SIQ IntraDimensional Correlates

Cultural Groups	DIMENSIONS OF MATURING			
	Allocentrisicm	Integration	Stability	Autonomy
Symbolization[1]				
Haverford	.83[2]	.46	.41	.10[3]
Ankara	.77	.49	.33	.41
Istanbul	.55	.19	.11	.34
Pisa	.62	−.04	.22	.22
Sicily	.56	.36	.57	.52
Allocentricism				
Haverford		.43	.56	.26
Ankara		.62	.43	.28
Istanbul		.35	.36	.38
Pisa		.39	.39	.23
Sicily		.80	.49	.48
Integration				
Haverford			.74	−.04
Ankara			.41	.15
Istanbul			.69	.58
Pisa			.32	.13
Sicily			.60	.48
Stability				
Haverford				.28
Ankara				.17
Istanbul				.67
Pisa				.22
Sicily				.23

1 Judges were two close friends for the Italian and Turkish groups; judges were four selection judges for Haverford group.

2 Tests of significance are not reported since some of the scores are not independent of each other. For those who wish to make their own interpretation, two-tailed .05 confidence levels are .40 for the Haverford and Ankara groups, .36 for the Istanbul and Pisa groups, and .37 for the Sicily group.

3 Haverford group's autonomy procedure differed from other groups.

major source of error. I misjudged how some would actually administer the test after the completion of the training.

The Pisan experimenter was the most accomplished clinician. He not only had considerable clinical skill but was also a gentle, patient, and nonauthoritarian person. I badly misjudged the effectiveness of the training given the Sicilian experimenter. His efficiency in initiating the research was such that by the time I returned to Palermo to monitor his first taped Rorschach protocols, he had completed the study of too many men to begin over again. His verbatim transcripts were imprecise and incomplete; he frequently failed to conduct an inquiry. The taped recordings indicated he related to the participants in an assertive and authoritatian way, as judged by the translators. Such traits had not emerged in the training sessions. Perhaps in playing the role of a psychologist he was fulfilling the Sicilian expectation that a male in a dominant position must be dominant. Maintaining one's *machismo* is essential to being respected in Sicily. Because I had no second Sicilian experimenter, it was not possible to determine how much of the imaginative constrictedness, almost impoverishment, of the Sicilian Rorschachs was due to the character of the cultural group or to the test conditions.

The Turkish experimenter created a different problem. Having had no prior clinical experience, he needed extensive training. He was initially the most anxious, detailed, and precise of the experimenters. The first protocols of the Istanbul group were excessively long, fragmented, and extraordinarily difficult to translate. The Turkish supervisor said they were atypical, and suggested that the experimenter, anxious to do a good job, defined a "good job" as securing great amounts of information from the men—a reaction not atypical of insecure fledgling Rorschachers. The supervisor described the Istanbul students to *not* be "inhibited, introverted, repressing creatures. On the contrary they are out to impress the other with their rich knowledge and verbosity . . . they show their hostility by making [the experimenter] . . . write all the 'rubbish' they say." Posttest interviews with the men revealed that the experimenter had put them on edge by his tenseness and demands to produce. The supervisor worked with him to be more relaxed.

How can we check if the reliability of the Rorschachs of the groups varied? Statistical comparisons were made of the data of those who participated early, and those who took part later in the research, after the experimenters had gained more experience and confidence. Since approximately equal numbers of mature and immature men were tested at similar time intervals, each group was divided into two subgroups differing only in terms of the time tested. Few significant differences were found between the early-and late-tested Italian groups. The Turkish differences were more interesting. Supporting the supervisor's hunches, those men studied early were more socially assertive but less intellectually disciplined, permitting dreamlike distortions to emerge more readily. The later participants monitored their thought more self-consciously; their judgments about problems like work and sex were more realistic, and they were more open to guidance and support in male relationships. The experimenter initiated the Ankara study about the time he had completed half of the Istanbul group. The Ankara men were more like the late-tested Istanbul men.

What does this add up to? Greater weight, I believe, should be placed on the results of the Rorschachs of the American, Pisa, and Ankara groups.

Reliability of index of psychological healthiness. I rated the Rorschachs of the cultural groups for degree of psychological healthiness, using Roy Schafer's criteria, five years after the completion of the cultural study. The Turkish and Italian protocols had been coded and randomly mixed, and were not identifiable in terms of their judged maturity. No ongoing record was kept of the number of men checked for their degree of psychological healthiness. To determine later, if necessary, the reasons for the discrepancies that might occur between my ratings and the other tests, a typed record was made of the analyses of each man's responses to each ink blot. The psychological health of each person was rated similarly on the same line scale that had been used for the American groups.

The critical question is, just how reliable are such ratings? Several factors reduce their reliability. Funds were not available to hire experts to rate 106 Rorschachs. I had become disillusioned about their potential usefulness due to the vagaries in test administration, difficulties in translating the Istanbul protocols, and the generally inconclusive results of the more objective methods of scoring the test. After I had written Chapter 3, however, I realized I had little feeling for what it meant to be a Turk or Italian. I had no personal contact with any men of the study; I felt like an outsider to their inner world. While my objectivity may have been enhanced by being an outsider, it became a personal necessity in order to be able to complete this book, to at least look at the men's Rorschachs, which I had never done. Since I did not anticipate my clinical ratings would be very useful, I allotted only a few days to analyzing 106 protocols. Fatigue alone must have accentuated the unreliability of the subtle judgments required by many of the Rorschachs.

Several different intrajudge reliability checks were made. Four weeks after making the initial ratings, another person identified those Rorschach ratings that deviated more than ten ranks from the ranked social indices of maturity. The twenty-six protocols were randomly mixed and reanalyzed. I had no knowledge of the previous ratings or analyses, or the direction in which the ratings deviated from the social index. Under these less-fatiguing judging conditions, I altered a number of my ratings. The reliability coefficient indexing the consistency of the ratings over a month interval was .61; it was .81 when three of the Rorschachs whose ratings were changed by more than ten ranks were excluded. Robert Holt, a distinguished Rorschach expert, subsequently independently evaluated the six Rorschachs on which I had altered my ratings the most, using Schafer's criteria. There was remarkable agreement between his and my second judgments, which suggest that the reliability of the final ratings may be acceptable. A second reliability check made a year later on twenty randomly selected protocols yielded a reliability coefficient of .74.

Reliability of Holt's primary process scores. Dr. L. Alston, trained by Holt, who had scored the Rorschachs of the original American groups, also scored the Turkish and Italian protocols. Comparability in the use of the scoring system, therefore, was maintained for the cultural groups. Interjudge reliability coefficients between his and my scores for the American groups were in the .90s. Holt has reported no stability coefficients. My own studies of the stability of his scores for four and ten year periods produce results comparable to those found for the traditional Klopfer scores, *i.e.*, median reliability coefficients in the .40s.

Since most of Holt's scores are based on an analysis of verbal content, we must examine the pattern of intercorrelations among Holt's scores for clues about differences in their psychological meaning. Given the differences in administration and the translation problems, the pattern of results for five different cultural groups was impressively consistent.[1] In fact, the patterns of the Italian and Turkish groups were more alike than those of the original American groups (Heath, 1965). The extraordinary length of the Istanbul Rorschachs, a factor known to produce higher primary process scores (Gray, 1969), combined with experimenter lack of expertise, suggests the Ankara group's results will be more reliable. The two Italian groups deviated consistently from the remaining groups in a puzzling way. The amount of primary process seemed to vary relatively independently of the men's effectiveness in integrating it adaptively. Their primary process products were much less intense and more socialized. Research has suggested that

1 Data available from NAPS.

moderately drive-organized images are not related to any indicators of immaturity (Heath, 1965). Since such "normal" emotionally fused thoughts do not demand defensive shielding or as much control, Holt's total primary process score, which includes such thoughts, would therefore not be as related to the effectiveness of a person's defenses. The Italian's dramatically colorful, mercurial, but refined, if indeed not staged, emotional outbursts may provide culturally sanctioned ways of expressing moderately intense primary processes. To identify such socialized expressions with immaturity or pathology, as I have done with Holt's primary process scores (Heath, 1965), would be false. So we may face interpretive problems with the scores of the Italian groups.

Perceived Self-Questionnaire (PSQ). How comparable were the translated editions of the PSQ for the cultural groups? The Italian and Turkish translators had no difficulty creating linguistically equivalent forms. Comparing the patterns of intrascale correlates of the groups revealed that they responded very similarly to the test scales. Only 12 percent of the total number of correlates of all of the groups deviated from the others by more than .30.[1] No group noticeably deviated from the others. The PSQ total maturity score is also very consistently correlated with its subscores for each cultural group with very few exceptions.[2] The scores for interpersonal maturity, autonomy, and possibly allocentricism are the least predictive of the total scores of maturity; the scores for the maturity of values and stability were most predictive. The Istanbul group's correlates were the most erratic, particularly for its measure of autonomy, which alerts us again that this group may differ from the others in the way it controls its impulses.

As the most systematically developed and comprehensive test of the model of maturing, the validity of the PSQ must be evaluated. A factorial study of White's idea of competence, using a large variety of measures including the PSQ, with both men and women, found the PSQ to be the most highly loaded test on the first factor, interpreted from other evidence to measure competence (Jensen, 1971). The test has also been useful for assessing maturing in college men and women (Erb, 1974; Fieselmann, 1973; Heath, 1968). It has also been used in longitudinal studies conducted ten years later on

1 Since the PSQ was developed after the completion of the research on the Haverford group, PSQ intrascale correlates on three other American groups of comparable age, background, and intelligence were included for this comparison. The patterns of correlates were remarkably similar among the seven different groups.

2 Data available from NAPS.

the American groups whose results originally supported the basic hypotheses of the model (Heath; 1976a). In all the principal studies using the PSQ, more than any other test, including the MMPI and Rorschach, it had proved to be the most consistent predictor of the widest range of personality traits associated with maturing. The test has some promise.

Minnesota Multiphasic Personality Inventory (MMPI). A published Italian edition of the MMPI was available. The Turkish team had little difficulty translating the test to be linguistically equivalent with the American edition. But just how psychologically "equivalent" were the three editions? Considerable research on MMPI items most predictive of the test's basic scales had demonstrated that the American and Italian editions were factorially similar, at least with respect to the principal factors (Comrey, 1960; Comrey and Nencini, 1961; Comrey, Meschieri, Misiti and Nencini, 1965). When the intrascale correlates of each culture group's tests were compared, the pattern of correlates was found to be very homogeneous. The groups apparently responded in similar ways to the items that made up the basic scales. However, the Istanbul group consistently deviated from the other groups in its correlates on the scales measuring depression and femininity. Since the Ankara group showed no such discrepancies, the problem is not with the translation, but is probably associated with the sample. We have another clue to substantiate our impression that the Istanbul group may cause us some interpretive embarrassments.

The Total MMPI score used to index psychological maladjustment was very consistently and similarly correlated with each of the basic scaled scores that composed it, suggesting that it too may have a similar psychological meaning for the different cultural groups.[1]

Phase Association Test (PT). It proved to be impossible to translate the items of the PT into exactly five-word phrases, particularly into Turkish. Neither the phrases' grammatical structure nor their pronounal references could be controlled as precisely.

The PT is highly reliable. Interjudge coefficients have been consistently in the 90s—as was the case for the cultural groups as well. The test is internally highly consistent. PT scores also tend to be highly stable over varying periods of time. To secure as stable thresholds as possible, the test was given twice in different sessions to

1 Data available from NAPS.

all of the groups except the Sicilians, for whom there wasn't time. Despite the high reliability coefficients obtained with the cultural groups, monitoring the taped recording of the Sicilian experimenter's test administration revealed that he tried to force quick responses by ceaselessly snapping his fingers and urging quicker responses. Situationally induced anxiety was probably much greater for his group, and may have masked the anxiety effects induced by the test's information. Also, analysis of the patterns of intratest correlates revealed that the American and Pisa PTs were the most internally consistent, and the Istanbul's most puzzlingly inconsistent. Its first and second anxiety scores for the threatening information were just not related, indicating there was no stability to the measures of anxiety. The American and Pisa groups are the most reliable; the Sicilian and Istanbul groups the least.

Thematic Concept Test (TCT). The TCT's objective scoring system did not require the judgments of judges. Low stability coefficients were expected, since differential improvement among the mature and immature men was predicted.[1]

Thematic Analysis-Synthesis Test (TAS). It proved to be impossible to translate the TAS and preserve all of the controls that had been built into the structure of the American sentences. The Turkish translators, in particular, were unable to produce a linguistically equivalent set of scrambled sentences. When a language does not possess pronouns like *he* and *she*, or definite articles like *the*, and frequently requires phrases to express the thought of one English word, major compromises in test structure have to be made. To preserve the format of ten units to be arranged, the Turkish translated sentences were divided into units of ten, some units possessing more than one or two words. Otherwise, order, format, test administration, and all other variables were held constant.

Trained Italian and Turkish judges scored the men's answers for each scrambled sentence before scoring the next sentence's answers to maintain comparable judging sets. As had been found in the American studies, high interjudge reliability coefficients in the .90s were obtained for all of the cultural groups. Disagreements in scoring, which were minimal, were resolved consensually.[2]

---

1 A summary of the personality traits associated with high conceptual efficiency to disturbing information is avaliable from NAPS.

2 A summary of the personality traits descriptive of analytic efficiency is available from NAPS.

Thematic Associative Judgment Test (TAJ). What modifications were made when using the TAJ in Italy and Turkey? Refreshingly, no translation problems plagued the interpretation of the results. But more than for the other tests, criteria that define a realistic or appropriate judgment are probably culturally determined. The type of personal relations Americans might describe as appropriate to the pictured interactions certainly might be assessed differently by Italians or Turks. So it was necessary to repeat exactly in Italy and Turkey the procedures used to determine the *degree of appropriateness* of each score category for each actor of each picture (Heath, 1965, 263–64). Analysis two years later of the judgments of the ten Italian judges revealed that some had been made quite casually, if not randomly. Because of the questionable reliability of these judgments, the Italian TAJs were reweighted using the Turkish weights; more internally consistent results were produced.

Two highly trained American judges independently scored the TAJ stories without any knowledge of the maturity status of the authors or of their cultural group. They scored all of the randomly mixed stories given to one picture before scoring the stories to another picture. The judges achieved quite satisfactory agreement: median $r = .80$ for the individual cards, .87 for the total score for the six types of information, and .99 for total TAJ score, the principal one used in the research. Disputed scores were consensually resolved. There is no evidence to suggest the TAJ scores for one group are more or less reliable than those of any other.[1]

Relationship of TCT, TAS, and TAJ. Of the total number of correlations between each of the pairs of basic scores of each of the tests for the Pisa, Istanbul, and Ankara groups (225), 73 percent in contrast to 70 percent for two American groups were positive. Forty-two percent of the Italian and Turkish correlations, in contrast to only 28 percent of the American groups, were more than $+.15$. However, 10 percent of the Italian and Turkish correlations were more than $-.15$ in contrast to only 5 percent for the Americans. Finally 14 percent of the Italian and Turkish correlations were significant (two-tailed) in contrast to only 2 percent of the American groups. No negative correlations were significant. As occurred in the American groups, conceptual and judgmental efficiency were unrelated. However, it was the

1 An example of the scoring of an Italian's stories, as well as a summary of the personality correlates of the TAJ are available from NAPS.

persistently significant relations between conceptual and analytic efficiency in the Pisa group that accounted for most of the significant correlations, a relation that was ambiguous for the American groups.

Valuator Test. The translators had no difficulty translating the Valuator Test. But its patterns of intratest correlates were not as consistently similar among the cultural groups.[1] The groups were most similar on the stability and integration dimensions defining the maturity of their values. The Sicilian and Istanbul intratest patterns were deviant. Given that almost 25 percent of the correlates between the PSQ Value score and the Valuator Test were not significant, I abandoned the idea of combining the two sets of items and report the results of each test separately later on.

Little research has been done with the Valuator test items. Validity data from the cultural groups, as well as from a ten-year longitudinal study of the three American groups on which the model of maturity was originally tested, suggest the test has some promise. Chapter 8 summarizes the extensive validity correlates the cultural study generated.

1 A copy of the Valuator Test items and its intratest and PSQ correlates are available from NAPS.

APPENDIX C

Abbreviations and Definitions of Scores Used in the Research

Abbreviation	Definition
CgEff Scores	Each Cognitive Efficiency score is a summary *standard* score that combines the appropriate converted test score of the TAJ, TAS, and TCT (see text and Heath, 1965, Ch. 12).
CgEff Agg	*Stability of cognitive skill*—Maintains cognitive efficiency solving problems of aggressive content.
CgEff Nt or Th	*Stability of cognitive skill*—Maintains cognitive efficiency solving problems of nonthreatening or threatening content.
CgEff Rel	*Stability of cognitive skill*—Maintains cognitive efficiency solving problems of relaxation-playful content.
CgEff Sex	*Stability of cognitive skill*—Maintains cognitive efficiency solving problems of sexual content.
CgEff Tot	*Stability of cognitive skill*—Maintains efficiency solving conceptual, analytic, and judgmental problems of disturbing content.
CgEff T1 or T2	*Stability of cognitive skill*—Maintains cognitive efficiency solving disturbing problems first or second time encountered.
CgEff Wk	*Stability of cognitive skill*—Maintains cognitive efficiency solving problems of cooperative work content.
MMPI Scores	Individual Minnesota Multiphasic Personality Inventory scores summarize responses of persons to different questionnaire items as defined by Dahlstrom and Welsh (1960).
MMPI At	*Instability of values*—Measure of anxiety, tension, and physiological disturbance.

MMPI D   *Lack of autonomy of self-concept*—Reports self ruled by moods, feelings of worthlessness, and depression.

MMPI Do   *Autonomy in personal relations*—Dominant, assertive control of relations with others.

MMPI Dy   *Lack of autonomy in personal relations*—Dependent upon others.

MMPI Eo   Overcontrols impulse. Score not used to index model of maturing because of its interpretive ambiguity.

MMPI Es   *Stability of cognitive skill*—Originally defined as ego strength, or capacity to be resilient and recover from personal disorganization. May more validly measure absence of gross pathological instability.

MMPI F   *Lack of integration of self-concept*—Extent to which responds inconsistently and illogically. Evidence indicates related to many indicators of maladjustment and unhealthiness.

MMPI Hs   *Autocentric self-concept*—Extent to which preoccupied about own body and its physical status; hypochondriacal self-centeredness.

MMPI Hy   *Inadequate symbolization of self-concept*—Extent to which hysterically expresses affect, instead of symbolizing impulses and dealing with conflicts ideationally

MMPI Ie   *Stability of cognitive skill*—Maintains intellectual efficiency.

MMPI Im   *Lack of autonomy of self-concept*—Impulsively unable to inhibit desires. Alternatively, could index inadequately autonomous cognitive skills. Included as self-concept measure because score based on conscious descriptions of own impulsivity.

MMPI K   *Symbolization of cognitive skill*—Uses reflection to control or suppress emergence of unacceptable ideas. Could be used alternatively as index of autonomy of cognitive skills.

MMPI Ma   *Lack of autonomy of self-concept*—Judgment and view of self may be grandoise and exaggerated because of uncontrollable aggressive energy that drives him into one action after another. Moody, with a predominance of uneasy highs.

MMPI Nu   *Lack of autonomy of self-concept*—Reports undercontrols impulses and acts out with little inhibition. Alternatively, could index lack of autonomy of cognitive skill.

MMPI Pa   *Autocentric personal relations*—Hypersensitive to and mistrustful of motives of others; guarded in relations with others whom he may believe wish him ill.

MMPI Pd   *Lack of autonomy in personal relations*—Acts out impulses in irresponsible and socially unacceptable ways.

MMPI Pt   *Instability in self-concept*—Highly obsessive, rigid, intellectualized way of handling stress. Self-doubting and lacks confidence in self.

MMPI R	*Inadequate symbolization of self-concept*—Extent uses repression.
MMPI Rer	*Allocentric personal relations*—Socially responsible with others.
MMPI Rgm	*Instability in self-concept*—Instability occurs as result of excessive rigidity. A too rigid person is more susceptible to sudden disorganization.
MMPI Sc	*Autocentric personal relations*—Socially and interpersonally distant, if not withdrawn; inadequate judgment in personal relations; schizoid.
MMPI Si	*Autocentric personal relations*—Socially introversive, and does not have a history of participating in group or other social activities.
MMPI Sr	*Allocentric personal relations*—Impresses others as socially well-adjusted.
MMPI To	*Allocentric personal relations*—Tolerant of others; not prejudiced.
MMPI Tot	*Maladjustment*—Summary measure of maladjustment as scored by the sum of the MMPI's basic psychopathological scales, that is, sum of D, Hs, Hy, Ma, Pd, Pa, Pt, Sc.
PSQ Scores	Each Perceived Self Questionnaire score is sum of scaled positions on ten bipolar questionnaire items indexing maturity on a dimension or personality structure (see text and Heath, 1968, Appendix B).
PSQ Alloc	*Allocentricism*—Allocentric cognitive skills (CgSk), self-concept (Self-con), values (Val), and relations with males (Rel M) and females (Rel F).
PSQ Aut	*Autonomy*—Autonomous cognitive skills (CgSk), concept of self (Self-con), values (Val), and relations with males (Rel M) and females (Rel F).
PSQ CgSk	*Maturity of cognitive skill*—Cognitive skills are symbolizable, logical and coherent, integrated, stabilized, and autonomous.
PSQ Integ	*Integration*—Thinks consistently and flexibly (CgSk), has integrated concept of self (Self-con), values (Val), and mutual relationships with males (Rel M) and females (Rel F).
PSQ Rel F	*Maturity of female relationships*—Aware of relations with females which are caring, integrative, enduring and autonomous.
PSQ Rel M	*Maturity of male relationships*—Aware of relations with males which are caring, integrative, enduring, and autonomous.
PSQ Self-con	*Maturity of self-concept*—Accurately aware of self, able to predict accurately others' views of self; integrative, stable, and autonomous identity.
PSQ Stab	*Stabilization*—Cognitive skills resilient to stress (CgSk), stable self-identity (Self-con), values (Val), and enduring male (Rel M) and female (Rel F) relationships.

PSQ Symb — *Symbolization*—Ability to reflect and symbolize (CgSk) ideas about self (Self-con), values (Val), and males (Rel M) and female (Rel F) relationships.

PSQ Tot — *Maturity*—Summary measure of dimensional maturity of person's cognitive skills, self-concept, values, and personal relationships.

PSQ Val — *Maturity of values*—Aware of values which are allocentric, integrated, stable, and less affected by other persons' viewpoints.

PT Scores — Each Phrase Association Test score is defined by the total number of anxiety signs given to examples of the PT's threatening and/or nonthreatening themes (see text and Heath, 1965, Ch. 8).

PT Agg — *Instability in personal relations*—High anxiety, that is, low anxiety threshold, when encounters information that arouses aggressive feelings toward father or mother.

PT Nt or Th — *Instability of values*—High anxiety, that is, low anxiety threshold, for nonthreatening information, like themes of receiving affection, relaxing, and working; or for threatening information, like themes of oral, sexual, and aggressive impulses.

PT Oral — *Instability in personal relations*—High anxiety, that is, low anxiety threshold, when encounters information that concerns loss of parental love.

PT RecAff — *Instability in personal relations*—High anxiety, that is, low anxiety threshold, when encounters information about parental affection.

PT Relax — *Instability in personal relations*—High anxiety, that is, low anxiety threshold, when encounters information concerned with relaxing and playing with other persons.

PT Sex — *Instability in personal relations*—High anxiety, that is, low anxiety threshold, when encounters information that arouses heterosexual and/or homosexual feelings.

PT T1 or T2 — *Instability of values*—Low anxiety threshold for disturbing information during first or second PT administration.

PT Work — *Instability in personal relations*—High anxiety, that is, low anxiety threshold, when encounters information about cooperative work with others.

Ror Scores — Rorschach scores are defined by either standard scoring conventions (Klopfer, Ainsworth, Klopfer and Holt, 1954), those established by Holt (1968), or modifications of Holt's scores for the purposes of the research. Source of score is indicated in parenthesis following definition of score.

Ror Agg DE — *Autonomy of cognitive skill*—Defensively controls in socially acceptable ways aggressive impulses (modified Holt).

Ror CF% — *Lack of autonomy in personal relations*—Lacks control of emotional impulsivity in response to other persons; acts childishly and impetuously at times (Klopfer).

Ror Clin Rtg
Psychological healthiness—Person judged on a line scale to be psychologically healthy using criteria established by Schafer. High scores mean greater healthiness (see text and Heath, 1965, Ch. 4).

Ror Con%
Lack of autonomy of cognitive skill—Percent of images organized and dominated by libidinal and aggressive drives (Holt).

Ror Con1%
Lack of autonomy of cognitive skill—Extent to which images determined by highly unacceptable libidinal and aggressive drives (modified Holt).

Ror Con2%
Lack of autonomy of cognitive skill—Degree to which content of images influenced by mildly unacceptable libidinal and aggressive drives (modified Holt).

Ror ConDD/ Form DD
Symbolization of cognitive skill—Controlled imaginative regression in which primary process ideas allowed in awareness without thought disorganization (modified Holt).

Ror Crea%
Symbolization of cognitive skill—Creative and original ideas (Holt).

Ror dd%
Symbolization of cognitive skill—Detailed and exact in use of cognitive skills (Klopfer).

Ror DDXDE%
Autonomy of cognitive skill—Ability to allow thinking to regress but under control that makes images and mode of thought socially acceptable. Could also be used to index allocentricism of cognitive skill (Holt).

Ror FAcc%
Allocentric cognitive skill—Accurately accommodates self to reality; perception and judgment are realistic (Holt).

Ror FC%
Allocentric personal relations—Ability to accommodate emotional reactions to social reality (Klopfer).

Ror Fc%
Allocentric personal relations— Affectionate and emotionally sensitive to others. Need for contact with other persons, but need under good control (Klopfer).

Ror FK+F+ Fc
Symbolization of cognitive skill—Intellectualized analytic mode of thinking (Klopfer).

Ror FK%
Symbolization of cognitive skill—Introspectiveness or ability to take·detached perspective (Klopfer).

Ror FM%
Lack of autonomy in personal relations—Dominated by infantile impulses in relations with others (Klopfer).

Ror Form%
Lack of integration in cognitive skill—Thinking is illogical, inconsistent, and fused with primary process types of condensations (Holt).

Ror Form1%
Lack of integration in cognitive skill— Severe, even pathological, types of bizarre and disorganized forms of thought (modified Holt).

Ror Form2% *Lack of integration in cognitive skill*—Socially acceptable form of unintegrated thought that does not have pathological implications (mod. Fied Holt).

Ror L1% *Autocentric cognitive skill*—Thought dominated by highly subjective, personal, and socially unacceptable images and modes of illogical organization (Holt).

Ror L2% *Autocentric cognitive skill*—Thought fused with more subjective, but not quite socially unacceptable kinds of images and modes of organization (Holt).

Ror M% *Symbolization of cognitive skill*—Depth of inner life and imaginal resources. Alternatively, could be interpreted as ability to symbolize personal relations or as empathy (Klopfer).

Ror m% *Instability of values*—Anxious and tense; ruled by vague feelings of foreboding and instability (Klopfer).

Ror Mean DE *Autonomy of cognitive skill*—Defensive accommodation or defense effectiveness indicating extent to which intellectually able to tame or defuse potentially anxiety-arousing quality of images (Holt).

Ror No. P *Allocentric cognitive skill*—Views world as others do; conventionality (Klopfer).

Ror No. R *Symbolization of cognitive skill*—Imaginative ability and productivity (Klopfer).

Ror Oral DE *Autonomy of cognitive skill*—Defensively controls in a socially acceptable way the emergence of oral drives (modified Holt).

Ror Pripro% *Lack of autonomy of cognitive skill*—Summary measure of extent to which thought dominated by uncontrollable impulses that result in strange and unacceptable ideas and modes of thought (Holt).

Ror Sex DE *Autonomy of cognitive skill*—Defensively controls in socially acceptable way the emergence of sexual drives (modified Holt).

Ror Sum DD *Lack of autonomy of values*—Imagination dominated by intense, socially unconventional, aggressive, and libidinal needs (modified Holt).

Sel Judg *Maturity-competence*—Men ordered in terms of number of judges selecting them to be mature and men to be immature. Order then re-ranked from low to high to indicate increasing ranked immaturity.

SIQ Scores Each Self-Image Questionnaire dimensional score is the sum of the differences between sets of two ratings of thirty traits each scale for eight positions. Each set of ratings defined by the procedures below. Low difference scores indicate greater dimensional maturity. Each SIQ maturity score is a weighted sum of the position of a person on twenty-six of the thirty items that describe maturity as rated by each participant and judge. High scores indicate greater judged maturity (see text and Heath, 1965, Ch. 5).

SIQ Alloc Friend *Allocentric self-concept*—Accuracy with which predicts ratings of close friend about self.

SIQ Alloc Judg *Allocentric self-concept*—Accuracy with which predicts ratings of selection judges about self.

SIQ Aut *Autonomy of self-concept*—Degree to which ratings of self remain unaffected when told information about self that contradicts ratings of self.

SIQ Integ *Integration of self-concept*—Degree to which rates self similarly on a variety of traits with how believes other persons would rate him on same traits.

SIQ Judg *Maturity*—Greater maturity as rated by the selection judges on the SIQ traits indexing maturity.

SIQ Friend Judg *Maturity*—Greater maturity as rated by close friend on SIQ traits indexing maturity.

SIQ Priv *Allocentric self-concept*—Degree to which rates self as more mature on variety of traits; indirect measure of self-esteem. High score indicates more self-esteem.

SIQ Soc *Allocentric self-concept*—Degree to which believes others rate him as more mature on variety of traits; indirect measure of one's social self-esteem. High score indicates more perceived social esteem for self.

SIQ Stab *Stability of self-concept*—Degree to which rates self similarly at two different time intervals on variety of traits.

SIQ Symb Friend *Symbolization of self-concept*—Accuracy of self-insight when measured against ratings of close friends.

SIQ Symb Sel Judg *Symbolization of self-concept*—Accuracy of self-insight whem measured against ratings of selection judges.

SV Scores Study of Values that measures relative preferences for different ways of life based on questionnaire items and scored following Allport, Vernon, and Lindzey (1960).

SV Aes *Lack of autonomy of values*—Prefers way of life based on subjective feelings; criteria of judgment are beauty, emotional fit, and harmony of idea with feelings. For adolescents, evidence indicates high aesthetic value reflects too strong subjective domination.

SV Rel Prefers way of life committed to basic religious principles and identification with orthodox beliefs.

SV Soc *Allocentric values*—Prefers way of life devoted to altruistic and philanthropic service to others.

SV Theor *Symbolization of values*—Prefers way of life organized around ideas, philosophical issues, scientific pursuit of truth.

TAJ Scores Each Thematic Associative Judgment score summarizes the weighted degree of judgmental realism of different ideas cited in

stories to pictures of the same interpersonal situations included in the PT, TAS, and TCT. Higher scores indicate greater judgmental realism or more of the dimensional quality being assessed as defined below (see text and Heath, 1965, Ch. 11).

TAJ +Aff Other *Allocentric personal relations*—Number of times uses positive affectively toned other-directed, e.g., loving, affiliating with others valuators to describe the relationship of two people in imaginative stories.

TAJ −Aff Other *Autocentric personal relations*—Number of times uses negative affectively toned, e.g., punishing, aggressing valuators to describe the relationship of two people in imaginative stories.

TAJ +Aff Self *Allocentric self-concept*—Number of times uses positive affectively toned self-referent, e.g., playing, enjoying valuators in imaginative stories.

TAJ −Aff Self *Autocentric self-concept*—Number of times uses negative affectively toned self-referent, e.g., submitting, health destroying valuators in imaginative stories.

TAJ No. Int *Symbolization of personal relations*—Number of different types of interactions imagined in response to pictures of two people relating to each other.

TAJ No. St *Symbolization of cognitive skill*—Imaginative breadth measured by number of different stories given to pictures portraying different types of relationships.

TAJ Nt or Th *Stability of cognitive skill*—Maintains realistic judgment when solving nonthreatening or threatening problems.

TAJ Tot *Stability of cognitive skill*—Maintains realistic judgment when solving disturbing problems.

TAJ T1 or T2 *Stability of cognitive skill*—Maintains realistic judgment when solving disturbing problems the first or second time encountered.

TAS Scores Each Thematic Analytic and Synthetic score summarizes the rapidity with which person recombines scrambled sentences in a grammatically correct and meaningful form. The content of the sentences is the same as that included in the PT, TAJ, and TCT. Higher scores indicate greater analytic-synthetic efficiency (see text and Heath, 1965, Ch. 10).

TAS Nt or Th *Stability of cognitive skill*—Maintains analytic and synthetic efficiency in solving nonthreatening or threatening problems.

TAS Tot *Stability of cognitive skill*—Maintains analytic and synthetic efficiency in solving disturbing problems.

TAS T1 or T2	*Stability of cognitive skill*—Maintains analytic and synthetic efficiency in solving disturbing problems the first or second time encountered.
TCT Scores	Each Thematic Concept Test score summarizes the rapidity and correctness of a person's identification of concepts portraying the same themes as used in the PT, TAJ, and TAS. Higher scores indicate greater conceptual efficiency (see text and Heath, 1965, Ch. 9).
TCT Nt or Th	*Stability of cognitive skill*—Maintains conceptual efficiency in solving nonthreatening or threatening problems.
TCT Tot	*Stability of cognitive skill*—Maintains conceptual efficiency in solving problems with disturbing content.
TCT T1 or T2	*Stability of cognitive skill*—Maintains conceptual efficiency in solving disturbing problems the first or second time encountered.
Val Scores	Each Valuator score is the sum of a person's responses to an eight point scale for bipolar questionnaire items about the dimensional maturity of his values. Higher scores mean more dimensionally mature values.
Val Alloc	*Allocentric values*—Values more other-centered and caring.
Val Aut	*Autonomy of values*—Values not readily influenced by opinions of others and by earlier childhood experiences.
Val Integ	*Integration of values*—Consistent values and philosophy of life.
Val Stab	*Stability of values*—Values persist and do not fluctuate over an extended period of time..
Val Symb	*Symbolization of values*—Able to reflect about and bring values into awareness.
Val Tot	*Maturity of values*—Summary score of the degree to which a person's values were symbolizable, allocentric, integrated, stable, and autonomous.

Mature and Immature Differences

Table D–1
Differences Between Mature and Immature Men
in Indices of Symbolization

Group	PSQ	TAJ		ROR		FK+F		ConnDD/		MMPI
					Cognitive Skills					
	CgSk	No.St	No.R	dd%	FK%	Fc%	M%	FormDD	Crea%	K
Haverford	—	05[1]	C C[2]	C	025	I	C	01	—	C
Ankara	C	C	05	C	,C	C	I	C	C	I
Istanbul	C	I	I[2]	C	C	C	C	I	I	C
Pisa	05	005	C	025	C	C	C	C	I	I
Sicily	C	—	C	C	I	C	I	C	I	C

Group	PSQ	SIQ		MMPI		PSQ	Val	SV
		Self-Concept					*Values*	
	Self-con	SymbJudg	SymbFriend	R	Hy	Val	Symb	Theo
Haverford	—	01	—	C	C	—	—	C
Ankara	C	005	025	I	I	C	C	C
Istanbul	C	005	05	C	C	C	I	C
Pisa	C	025	025	05	I	025	05	C
Sicily	C	C	I	C	C	I	I	I

Group	PSQ		TAJ
	Personal Relations		
	Rel M	Rel F	No. Int
Haverford	—	—	001
Ankara	I	C	C
Istanbul	C	I	I
Pisa	C	05	01
Sicily	C	I	—

1 One tailed significance tests for all predicted differences based on *t* tests.

2 C, I mean difference between mature and immature group for the test score was *consistent* or *inconsistent* with the predicted direction. When the groups did not differ, an S for same score is listed.

Table D–2
Differences Between Mature and Immature Men in Indices of Allocentricism

Group	PSQ CgSk	L1%	L2%	FAcc%	No.P
		Cognitive Skills			
		Ror			
Haverford	—	05	I	C	01
Ankara	C	C	01	C	I
Istanbul	C	C	C	C	I
Pisa	I	I	C	C	I
Sicily	C	C	I	C	C

	PSQ Self-con	Judg	SIQ Fr Judg	Priv	Soc	TAJ +Aff Self	TAJ −Aff Self	MMPI Hs	PSQ Val	Values Val Alloc	SV Soc
				Self-Concept						Values	
Haverford	—	05	—	025	01	I	I	025	—	—	C
Ankara	C	005	01	C	005	C	I	C	05	C	C
Istanbul	C	025	C	C	025	025	C	C	01	C	05
Pisa	I	05	05	C	025	C	C	I	C	05	I
Sicily	C	C	05	05	025	—	—	C	C	I	C

	PSQ RelM	PSQ RelF	Rer	Sr	Si	Sc	Pa	To	FC%	Fc%	TAJ +Aff Other	TAJ −Aff Other
			MMPI		Personal Relations				Ror			
Haverford	—	—	01	01	025	025	C	05	I	C	I	I
Ankara	I	I	C	C	I	C	C	C	C	01	I	I
Istanbul	I	I	C	C	C	I	C	I	I	C	I	C
Pisa	C	C	C	I	I	I	C	I	C	I	C	I
Sicily	C	C	C	C	C	C	005	C	1	C	—	—

Table D–3
Differences Between Mature and Immature Men in Integration

Group	PSQ CgSk	Form 1%	Form 2%	PSQ Self-con	SIQ Integ	MMPI F
		Cognitive Skills			Self-Concept	
		Ror				
Haverford	—	025	C	—	01	01
Ankara	C	C	C	I	025	C
Istanbul	025	C	C	C	C	C
Pisa	025	I	C	05	I	C
Sicily	C	C	C	C	025	05

	PSQ Val	Val Integ	PSQ RelM	RelF
	Values		Personal Relations	
Haverford	—	—	—	—
Ankara	I	C	C	I
Istanbul	C	C	I	I
Pisa	C	I	C	I
Sicily	C	C	C	I

Table D–4

Differences Between Mature and Immature Men in Indices of Stabilization

Group	PSQ CgSk	Tot	T1	T2	Th	CgEff Nt	Agg	Sex	Wk	Rel	MMPI le	Es
						Cognitive Skills						
Haverford	—	025	C	05	025	05	05	05	025	S	05	C
Ankara	C	C	C	C	C	C	C	C	C	C	C	I
Istanbul	C	C	I	C	I	C	S	I	C	I	C	C
Pisa	C	005	025	005	005	005	05	005	025	005	C	I
Sicily	C	—	—	—	—	—	—	—	—	—	C	C

	PSQ Self-con	SIQ Stab	MMPI Rgm	MMPI Pt	PSQ Val	Val Stab	Ror m%	MMPI At	PT T1	T2	Th	Nt
		Self-Concept						*Values*				
Haverford	—	01	I	05	—	—	I	C	C	C	C	I
Ankara	I	C	I	C	I	C	C	I	I	I	I	I
Istanbul	C	025	C	I	C	C	C	C	C	C	C	C
Pisa	C	C	C	I	C	C	C	I	025	C	05	C
Sicily	C	C	C	C	C	S	C	C	I	—	I	I

	PSQ RelM	RelF	Oral	Agg	Sex	PT RecAff	Work	Relax
				Personal Relations				
Haverford	—	—	I	I	C	C	C	I
Ankara	I	C	I	I	I	I	I	I
Istanbul	C	I	C	C	C	C	C	C
Pisa	C	C	C	025	C	C	05	C
Sicily	025	C	I	I	I	I	I	I

Table D-5
Differences Between Mature and Immature Men
in Indices of Autonomy

Group	PSQ CgSk	Con1%	Con2%	MeanDE	Ror OralDE	AggDE	SexDE	DD×DE%
				Cognitive Skills				
Haverford	—	I	I	C	C	C	01	C
Ankara	I	C	I	I	C	C	I	I
Istanbul	I	C	C	C	C	C	05	C
Pisa	I	C	I	C	05	C	C	C
Sicily	I	C	C	C	C	C	05	C

| | Self-Concept | | | | | | Values | | | |
Group	PSQ Self-con	SIQ Aut	MMPI D	Ma	Im	Nu	PSQ Val	Val Aut	SV Aes	Ror SumDD
Haverford	—	—	01	C	C	C	—	—	C	C
Ankara	I	C	I	005	I	I	I	C	I	I
Istanbul	C	C	C	C	C	I	I	C	C	C
Pisa	C	I	I	C	I	I	C	I	C	I
Sicily	025	C	C	C	C	C	C	05	I	I

| | Personal Relations | | | | | | |
Group	PSQ RelM	RelF	MMPI Dy	Do	Pd	Ror CF%	FM%
Harverford	—	—	05	C	025	I	I
Ankara	C	I	I	I	C	C	I
Istanbul	I	I	I	I	I	C	I
Pisa	C	01	C	I	C	05	C
Sicily	I	I	C	I	C	I	C

References

Abel, T. M. *Psychological testing in cultural contexts*. New Haven, Conn.: College and University Press Services, 1974.

Ackman, P. The effects of induced regression on thinking processes. Unpubl. Ph.D. thesis, University of Michigan, 1960.

Allinsmith, W. & Goethals, G. W. Cultural factors in mental health: an anthropological perspective. *Review of Educational Research*, 1956, *26*, 429–450.

Allport, G. W. Mental health: a generic attitude. *Journal of Religion and Health*, 1964, *4*, 7–21.

Allport, G. W. *Pattern and growth in personality*. New York: Holt, Rinehart, & Winston, 1961.

Allport, G. W., Vernon, P. E., & Lindzey, G. *Study of Values*, Manual 3rd ed. Boston: Houghton Mifflin, 1960.

Almond, G. A. & Verba, S. *The civic culture; political attitudes and democracy in five nations*. Princeton, N.J.: Princeton University Press, 1963.

Ancona, L., Carli, R., & Schwarz, E. Psychological and psychopathological aspects of migration. *Archivo di Psicologia Neurologia e Psychiatria*, 1971, *32*, 355–402.

Angyal, A. A theoretical model for personality studies. In C. E. Moustakas (Ed.), *The self: explorations in personal growth*. New York: Harpers, 1956, Ch. 4.

Ashton, P. T. Cross-cultural Piagetian research: an experimental perspective. *Harvard Educational Review*, 1975, *45*, 475–506.

Ausubel, D. P. Personality disorder *is* disease. *American Psychologist*, 1961, *16*, 69–74.

Barron, F. *Creativity and psychological health*. Princeton, N.J.: D. Van Nostrand Co., 1963.

Barzini, L. *The Italians*. New York: Atheneum, 1964.

Becker, R. J. Religion and psychological health. In M. P. Strommen (Ed.), *Research on religious development*. New York: Hawthorn Books, 1971, Ch. 10.

Beiser, M., Benfari, R. C., Collumb, H., & Ravel, J. L. Measuring psychoneurotic behavior in cross-cultural surveys. *The Journal of Nervous and Mental Disease*, 1976, *163*, 10–23.

Bellah, R. N. *et al*. Adulthood. *Daedalus*, 1976, *105*, No. 2.

Benedict, R. *Patterns of Culture*. Boston: Houghton Mifflin, 1934.

Berne, E. *Games people play*. New York: Grove Press, 1964.

Biller, H. B. *Paternal deprivation: family, school, sexuality and society*. Lexington, Mass.: Lexington Books, 1974.

Block, J. *Lives through time*. Berkeley, Calif.: Bancroft, 1971.

Block, J. *The Q-sort method in personality assessment and psychiatric research*. Springfield, Ill.: Charles C. Thomas, 1961.

Block, J. H. Issues, problems and pitfalls in assessing sex differences: A critical review of *The Psychology of Sex Differences*. *Merrill-Palmer Quarterly*, 1976, *22*, 283–308.

Bonney, M. E. A descriptive study of the normal personality. *Journal of Clinical Psychology*, 1962, *18*, 256–266.

Bonney, M. E. Some correlates of a social definition of normal personality. *Journal of Clinical Psychology*, 1964, *20*, 415–422.

Boulding, K. E. *The meaning of the twentieth century: the great transition*. New York: Harper & Row, 1964.

Bouwsma, W. J. Christian adulthood. Adulthood, *Daedalus*, 1976, 77–92.

Brislin, R. W., Lonner, W. J., & Thorndike, R. M. *Cross-cultural research methods*. New York: Wiley, 1973.

Broadhead, R. S. A theoretical critique of the societal reaction approach to deviance. *Pacific Sociological Review*, 1974, *17*, 287–312.

Brown, D. R. Non-intellective qualities and the perception of the ideal student by college faculty. *Journal of Educational Sociology*, 1960, *33*, 269–278.

Bruner, J. W., Goodnow, J. J., & Austin, G. A. *A study of thinking*. New York: Wiley, 1956.

Campbell, D. T. On the conflicts between biological and social evolution and between psychology and moral tradition. *American Psychologist*, 1975, *30*, 1103–1126.

Campbell, D. T. Reprise. *American Psychologist*, 1976, *31*, 381–384.

Campbell, D. T. & Fiske, D. W. Convergent and discriminant validation by the multitrait-multimethod matrix. *Psychological Bulletin*, 1959, *56*, 81–105.

Campbell, D. T. & Stanley, J. *Experimental and quasi-experimental design for research*. Chicago: Rand-McNally, 1966.

Campbell, J. D. Peer relations in childhood. In M. L. Hoffman & L. W. Hoffman (Eds.), *Review of child development research*. New York: Russell Sage Foundation. 1964, *1*, 289–322.

Cantril, H. *The pattern of human concerns*. New Brunswick, N.J.. Rutgers University Press, 1965.

Carpenter, W. T., Jr., Strauss, J. S., & Bartko, J. J. Flexible system for the diagnosis of schizophrenia: report from the WHO International Pilot Study of Schizophrenia. *Science*, 1973, *182*, 1275–1278.

Cattell, R. B. The measurement of the healthy personality and the healthy society. *The Counseling Psychologist*, 1973, *4*, 13–18.

Cattell, R. B., Schmidt, L. R. & Pawlik, K. Cross-cultural comparison (U.S.A., Japan, Austria) of the personality factor structures of 10 to 14 year olds in objective tests. *Social Behavior and Personality*, 1973, *1*, 182–211.

Caudill, W. Tiny dramas: vocal communication between mother and infant in Japanese and American families. In W. P. Lebra (Ed.), *Transcultural research in mental health*. Vol. II. Honolulu, Hawaii: University Press of Hawaii, 1972, Ch. 3.

Caudhill, W. & Frost, L. A comparison of maternal care and infant behavior in Japanese-American, American, and Japanese families. In W. P. Lebra (Ed.), *Youth, socialization, and mental health*. Vol. III. Honolulu, Hawaii: University Press of Hawaii, 1974.

Chickering, A. W. *Education and identity*. San Francisco, Calif.: Jossey-Bass, 1969.

Chodorkoff, B. Self-perception, perceptual defense, and adjustment. *Journal of Abnormal & Social Psychology*, 1954, *49*, 508–512.

Clausen, J. A. Values, norms, and the health called "mental": purposes and feasibility of assessment. In S. B. Sells (Ed.), *The definition and measurement of mental health*. National Center for Health Statistics, U.S. Public Health Service, 1968.

Clausen, J. A. & Huffine, C. L. Sociocultural and social-psychological factors affecting social responses to mental disorder. *Journal of Health and Social Behaviour*, 1975, *16*, 405–420.

Coelho, G. V., Hamburg, D. A., & Murphey, E. B. Coping strategies in a new learning environment. *Archives of General Psychiatry*, 1963, *9*, 433–443.

Coelho, G. V., Silber, E., & Hamburg, D. A. Use of the Student-TAT to assess coping behavior in hospitalized, normal, and exceptionally competent college freshmen. *Perceptual & Motor Skills*, 1962, *14*, 355–365.

Comrey, A. L. Comparison of certain personality variables in American and Italian groups, *Educational & Psychological Measurement*, 1960, *20*, 541–550.

Comrey, A. L., Meschieri, L., Misiti, R., & Nencini, R. A comparision of personality factor structure in American and Italian subjects. *Journal of Personality and Social Psychology*, 1965, *1*, 257–261.

Comrey, A. L. & Nencini, R. Factors in MMPI response of Italian students. *Educational & Psychological Measurement*, 1961, *21*, 657–662.

Cox, R. D. *Youth into maturity*. New York: Mental Health Materials Center, 1970.

Cross, K. P. *Beyond the open door*. San Francisco, Calif.: Jossey-Bass, 1971.

Crown, S. "On being sane in insane places": a comment from England. *Journal of Abnormal Psychology*, 1975, *84*, 453–455.

Crutchfield, R. S. Conformity and character. *American Psychologist*, 1955, *10*, 191–198.

Cummings, L. L., Harnett, D. L., & Schmidt, S. M. International cross-language factor stability of personality: an analysis of the Shure-Meeker Personality/Attitude Schedule. *Journal of Psychology*, 1972, *82*, 67–84.

D'Arcy, C. The contingencies and mental illness in societal reaction theory: a critique. *The Canadian Review of Sociology and Anthropology*, 1976, *13*, 43–54.

Dahlstrom, W. G. & Welsh, G. S. *An MMPI handbook; A guide to use in clinical practice and research*. Minneapolis; University of Minnesota Press, 1960.

Davis, J. A. *Education for positive mental health: a review of existing research and recommendations for future studies*. Chicago: Aldine, 1965.

Davis, K. Mental hygiene and the class structure. *Psychiatry*, 1938, *1*, 55–65.

De Charms, R. *Personal causation*. New York: Academic Press, 1968.

Devereux, G. "Normal and abnormal," the key problem of psychiatric anthropology. *Some uses of anthropology, theoretical and applied*. The Anthropological Society of Washington, D.C., 1956.

De Vos, G. A. & Hippler, A. A. Cultural psychology: comparative studies of human behavior. In G. Lindzey & E. Aronson (Eds.), *The handbook of social psychology*. Reading, Mass,: Addison-Wesley, 1969, Ch. 33.

Dewey, J. *Human nature and conduct*. New York: Henry Holt, 1922.

Dohrenwend, B. P. & Dohrenwend, B.S. Social and cultural influences on psychopathology. *Annual Review of Psychology*, 1974, *25*, 417–452.

Doob, L. W. *Becoming more civilized, a psychological exploration*. New Haven, Conn.: Yale University Press, 1960.

Doob, L. W. Scales for assaying psychological modernization in Africa. *Public Opinion Quarterly*, 1967, *31*, 414–421.

Doyle, J. A. Field-independence and self-actualization. *Psychological Reports*, 1975, *36*, 363–366.

Draguns, J. G. Comparisons of psychopathology across cultures. Issues, findings, directions. *Journal of Cross-Cultural Psychology*, 1973, *4*, 9–37.

Draguns, J. G. & Phillips, L. *Culture and psychopathology: the quest for a relationship.* Morristown, N.J.: General Learning Press, 1972.

Duncan, C. B. A reputation test of personality integration. *Journal of Personality and Social Psychology*, 1966, *3*, 516–524.

Dunham, W. W. Society, culture and mental disorder. *Archives of General Psychiatry*, 1976, *33*, 147–156.

Eaton, J. W. & Weil, R. J. The mental health of the Hutterites. *Scientific American*, 1953, *189*, 31–37.

Edgerton, R. B. On the "recognition" of mental illness. In S. C. Plog & R. B. Edgerton (Eds.), *Changing perspectives in mental illness.* New York: Holt, Rinehart, & Winston, 1969, 49–72.

Endicott, J., Spitzer, R. L., Fleiss, J. L., & Cohen, J. The Global Assessment Scale. A procedure for measuring overall severity of psychiatric disturbance. *Archives of General Psychiatry*, 1976, *33*, 766–771.

Erb, D. L. Research on college development. Personal communication, 1974.

Erickson, E. H. *Childhood and society*, 2nd ed. New York: Norton, 1963.

Ezekiel, R. S. The personal future and Peace Corps competence. *Journal of Personality and Social Psychology Monograph Supplement*, 1968, *8*, Part 2.

Farber, I. E. Sane and insane: constructions and misconstructions. *Journal of Abnormal Psychology*, 1975, *84*, 589–620.

Fawcett, J. T. An observer-evaluation method for the comparative study of modal personality: a cross-cultural investigation based upon Q-sort descriptions of students. Unpubl. Ph.D. thesis, University of California, Berkeley, 1965.

Fenichel, O. *The collected papers of Otto Fenichel.* (1938). New York: W. W. Norton, 1954, Ch. 5.

Fenichel, O. *The psychoanalytic theory of neurosis.* New York: W. W. Norton, 1945.

Fieselmann, A. The college environment as an affector of maturity. Unpubl. thesis, Hanover College, 1973.

Fineman, S. Maturity and homosexuality. Unpubl. thesis, Haverford College, 1976.

Fischer, R. A cartography of the ecstatic and meditative states. *Science*, 1971, *174*, 897–904.

Foa, U. G., Triandis, H. C., & Katz, E. W. Cross-cultural invariance in the differentiation and organization of family roles. *Journal of Personality* & *Social Psychology*, 1966, *4*, 316–327.

Foxman, P. Tolerance for ambiguity and self-actualization. *Journal of Personality Assessment*, 1976, *40*, 67–72.

Frank, G. H. A review of research with measures of ego strength derived from the MMPI and the Rorschach. *Journal of General Psychology*, 1967, *77*, 183–206.

Freud, S. *The ego and the id* (1923). New York: W. W Norton, 1960.

Freud, S. *The interpretation of dreams* (1900). New York: Basic Books, 1956.

Freud, S. The unconscious (1915). *Collected Papers*. London: The Hogarth Press and the Institute of Psycho-Analysis, IV, 1925.

Fromm, E. *Man for himself.* New York: Holt, Rinehart, & Winston, 1947.

Fromm, E. *The sane society.* New York: Holt, Rinehart, & Winston, 1955.

Funkenstein, D. H., King, S., & Drolette, M. E. *Mastery of stress.* Cambridge, Mass.: Harvard University Press, 1957.

Garai, J. E. Sex differences in mental health. *Genetic Psychological Monographs*, 1970, *81*, 123–143.

Ghei, S. N. A cross-cultural comparison of the social desirability variable. *Journal of Cross-Cultural Psychology*, 1973, *4*, 493–500.

Gillespie, J. M. & Allport, G. W. *Youth's outlook on the future. A cross-national study.* New York: Doubleday, 1955.

Ginzberg, E., Ginsburg, S. W., Axelrad, S., & Herma, J. L. *Occupational choice: an approach to a general theory.* New York: Columbia University Press, 1951.

Golden, J., Mandel, N., Glueck, B. C., Jr., & Feder, Z. A summary description of fifty "normal" white males. *American Journal of Psychiatry*, 1962, *119*, 48–56.

Goleman, D. The Buddha on meditation and states of consciousness. In C. T. Tart (Ed.), *Transpersonal psychologies*. New York: Harper & Row, 1975, Ch. 5.

Goleman, D. Meditation and consciousness: an Asian approach to mental health. *American Journal of Psychotherapy*, 1976, *30*, 41–54.

Gordon, L. V. Q-typing of Oriental and American youth: initial and clarifying studies. *Journal of Social Psychology*, 1967, *71*, 185–195.

Gough, H. G. A measure of individual modernity. *Journal of Personality Assessment*, 1976, *40*, 3–9.

Gough, H. G. Appraisal of social maturity by means of the CPI. *Journal of Abnormal Psychology*, 1966, *71*, 189–195.

Gough, H. G., De Vos, G., & Mizushima, K. Japanese validation of the CPI Social Maturity Index. *Psychological Reports*, 1968, *22*, 143–146.

Gough, H. G. & Quintard, G. A French application of the CPI social maturity index. *Journal of Cross-Cultural Psychology*, 1974, *5*, 247–252.

Gould, R. L. The phase of adult life: a study in developmental psychology. *American Journal of Psychiatry*, 1972, *129*, 521–531.

Gove, W. R. Labelling and mental illness: a critique. In W. R. Gove (Ed.), *The labelling of deviance*. New York: Halstead Press, Wiley, 1975a, Ch. 3.

Gove, W. R. The labelling perspective: an overview. In W. R. Gove (Ed.), *The labelling of deviance: evaluating a perspective*. New York: Halstead Press, Wiley, 1975b, Ch. 1.

Gray, J. J. The effect of productivity on primary process and creativity. *Journal of Projective Techniques and Personality Assessment*, 1969, *33*, 213–218.

Grinker, R. R. Sr. with the collaboration of Grinker, R. R., Jr. & Timberlake, J. "Mentally healthy" young males (homoclites). *Archives of General Psychiatry*, 1962, *6*, 405–453.

Grinker, R. R. Mentally healthy young men (homoclites) 14 years later. *Archives of General Psychiatry*, 1974, *30*, 701–704.

Gutmann, D. Parenthood: a key to the comparative study of the life cycle. In N. Datun & L. H. Ginsberg (Eds.), *Life-span developmental psychology*. New York: Academic Press, 1975, Ch. 10.

Haan, N. Coping and defense mechanisms related to personality inventories. *Journal of Consulting Psychology*, 1965, *29*, 373–378.

Haan, N. Proposed model of ego functioning: coping and defense mechanism in relationship to IQ change. *Psychological Monographs: General and Applied*, 1963, *77*, No. 8, 1–23.

Harmon, D. K., Masuda, M., & Holmes, T. H. The Social Readjustment Rating Scale: a cross-cultural study of Western Europeans and Americans. *Journal of Psychosomatic Research*, 1970, *14*, 391–400.

Harris, D. B. Problems in formulating a scientific concept of development. In D. B. Harris (Ed.), *The concept of development: an issue in the study of human behavior*. Minneapolis, Minn.: University of Minnesota Press, 1957, 3–14.

Harris, J. G. A science of the South Pacific. Analysis of the character structure of the Peace Corps volunteer. *American Psychologist*, 1973, *28*, 232–247.

Hartmann, H. *Ego psychology and the problem of adaptation* (1939). New York: International University Press, 1958.

Hartmann, H. Towards a concept of mental health. *British Journal of Medical Psychology*, 1960, *33*, 243–248.

Heath, C. W. *What people are; a study of normal young men*. Cambridge, Mass.: Harvard University Press, 1945.

Heath, D. H. Adolescent and adult predictors of vocational adaptation. *Journal of Vocational Behavior*, 1976a, *9*, 1–19.

Heath, D. H. The changing American character: How healthy? *Chautauqua, Publications*, Chautauqua, New York: 1976b.

Heath, D. H. Competent fathers: their personalities and marriages. *Human Development*, 1976c, *19*, 26–39.

Heath, D. H. Educating for maturity. *College & University Journal*, 1974, *13*, 15–22.

Heath, D. H. *Explorations of maturity*. New York: Appleton-Century-Crofts. 1965.

Heath, D. H. *Growing up in college: Liberal education and maturity*. San Francisco, Calif.: Jossey-Bass, 1968.

Heath, D. H. *Humanizing schools: New directions, new decisions*. New York: Hayden, 1971.

Heath, D. H. Individual anxiety thresholds and their effect on intellectual performance. *Journal of Abnormal and Social Psychology*, 1956, *52*, 403–408.

Heath, D. H. Maternal competence, expectation, and involvement. *Journal of Genetic Psychology*, 1977 (In press).

Heath, D. H. More healthy sexual roles for the future. *Monograph*, Boys Clubs of America, 1976d.

Heath, D. H. Secularization and maturity of religious beliefs. *Journal of Religion & Health*, 1969, *8*, 335–358.

Heath, D. H. Some possible effects of occupation on the maturing of professional men. *Journal of Vocational Behaviour*, 1977b, (In press).

Heath, D. H. What the enduring effects of higher education tell us about a liberal education. *Journal of Higher Education*, 1976e, *47*, 173–190.

Holt, R. R. *Manual for the scoring of primary process manifestations in Rorschach responses*. New York: Research Center for Mental Health, New York University, 1968, 10th draft.

Holt, R. R. Review of Loevinger, J. & *Wessler, R. Measuring ego development*. In *Journal of Nervous & Mental Disease*, 1974, *158*, 310–316.

Holt, R. R. & Havel, J. A method for assessing primary and secondary process in the Rorschach. In M. A. Rickers-Ovsiankina (Ed.), *Rorschach psychology*. New York: Wiley, 1960, Ch. 10.

Hsu, F. L. K. American core values and national character. In F. L. K. Hsu (Ed.), *Psychological anthropology. Approaches to culture and personality*. Homewood. Ill.: Dorsey Press, 1961, Ch. 7.

Inkeles, A. Making men modern: on the causes and consequences of individual change in six developing countries. *American Journal of Sociology*, 1969, *75*, 208–225.

Inkeles, A. The modernization of man. In M. Weiner (Ed.), *Modernization*. New York: Basic Books, 1966, Ch. 10.

Inkeles, A. & Levinson, D. J. National character: the study of modal personality and sociocultural systems. In G. Lindzey & E. Aronson (Eds.), *The handbook of social psychology*. Reading, Mass.: Addison-Wesley, 1969, *4*, Ch. 34.

Inkeles, A. & Smith, D. H. *Becoming modern. Individual change in six developing countries*. Cambridge, Mass.: Harvard University Press, 1974.

Inkeles, A. & Smith, D. H. The fate of personal adjustment in the process of modernization. *International Journal of Comparative Sociology*, 1970, *11*, 81–114.

Jagede, R. O. Psychometric attributes of the psychological effectiveness scale. *Journal of Psychology*, 1976, *92*, 155–159.

Jahoda, M. *Current concepts of positive mental health*. New York: Basic Books, 1958.

James, W. *The principles of psychology*. New York: Henry Holt, 1890, Vol. 1, Ch. 10.

Jensen, R. E. The concept of competence: a provisional attempt at construct validation. Unpubl. ms., 1971.

Jourard, S. *Healthy personality; an approach from the viewpoint of humanistic psychology*. New York: Macmillan Co., 1974.

Kahl, J. A. *The measurement of modernism: a study of values in Brazil and Mexico*. Austin, Texas: University of Texas Press, 1968.

Kiev, A. Transcultural psychiatry: research problems and perspectives. In S. C. Plog & R. B. Edgerton (Eds.), *Changing perspectives in mental illness*. New York: Holt, Rinehart, & Winston, 1969, 106–127.

King, S. H. *Five lives at Harvard: personality change during college*. Cambridge, Mass.: Harvard University Press, 1973.

Klein, D. C. Some concepts concerning the mental health of the individual. *Journal of Consulting Psychology*, 1960, *24*, 288–293.

Klein, M. H., Miller, M. H., & Alexander, A. A. When young people go out in the world. In W. P. Lebra (Ed.), *Youth, socialization, and mental health*. Honolulu, Hawaii: University Press of Hawaii, 1974, Ch. 16.

Klopfer, B., Ainsworth, M. D., Klopfer, W. G., & Holt, R. R. *Developments in the Rorschach technique. Vol. 1: Technique and theory*. Yonkers-on-the-Hudson: World Book, 1954.

Kluckhohn, F. R. & Strodtbeck, F. L. *Variations in value orientations* Evanston, Ill.: Row, Peterson, 1961.

Knapp, R. A. Relationship of a measure of self-actualization to neuroticism and extraversion. *Journal of Consulting Psychology*, 1965, *29*, 168–172.

Knapp, R. R. & Comrey, A. L. Further construct validation of a measure of self-actualization. *Educational & Psychological Measurement*, 1973, *33*, 419–425.

Kogan, W. S., Quinn, R., Ax, A., & Ripley, H. S. Some methodological problems in the quantification of clinical assessment by Q array. *Journal of Consulting Psychology*, 1957, *21*, 57–62.

Kohlberg, L. Moral development and the education of adolescents. In R. F. Purnell (Ed.), *Adolescents and the American high school*. New York: Holt, Rinehart, & Winston, 1970.

Kohlberg, L. The child as a moral philosopher. *Psychology Today*, 1968, *2*, 25–30.

Kohlberg, L. The development of moral character and ideology. In M. L. Hoffman & L. W. Hoffman (Eds.), *Review of child development research*. New York: Russell Sage Foundation, 1964, Vol. 1.

Kohlberg, L. The development of moral stages. Uses and abuses. *Proceedings of the Individual Conference on Testing Problems*, 1973, 1–8.

Kohn, *M. L.* & *Schooler, C.* (Occupational experience and psychological functioning: an assessment of reciprocal effects). *American Sociological Review*, 1973, *38*, 97–118.

Kreitman, N., Collins, J., Nelson, B., & Troop, J. Neurosis and marital interaction: I. Personality and symptoms. *British Journal of Psychiatry*, 1970, *110*, 683–697.

Laing, R. D. *The politics of experience*. New York: Ballantine, 1967.

Lanyon, R. I. Measurement of social competence in college males. *Journal of Consulting Psychology*, 1967, *31*, 495–498.

Lapidus, I. M. Adulthood in Islam: religious maturity in the Islamic tradition. In Adulthood. *Daedalus*, 1976, 93–108.

Lebra, W. P. (Ed.), *Transcultural research in mental health*. Honolulu, Hawaii: University Press of Hawaii, 1972.

Lecky, P. *Self-consistency: a theory of personality*. New York: Island Press, 1945.

LeCompte, W. F. & LeCompte, G. K. Generational attribution in Turkish and American youth: a study of social norms involving the family. *Journal of Cross-Cultural Psychology*, 1973, *4*, 175–191.

Leighton, A. H. A comparative study of psychiatric disorder in Nigeria and rural North America. In S. C. Plog & R. B. Edgerton (Eds.), *Changing perspectives in mental illness*. New York: Holt, Rinehart, & Winston, 1969, 179–199.

Leighton, A. H. Reflections of a tender-minded radical. In W. P. Lebra (Ed.), *Transcultural research in mental health*. Honolulu, Hawaii: University Press of Hawaii, 1972, Ch. 27.

Leighton, A. H. and others. *Psychiatric disorder among the Yoruba; a report*. Ithaca, N. Y.: Cornell University Press, 1963.

Lemert, E. *Human deviance, social problems and social control*. Englewood Cliffs, N.J.: Prentice Hall, 1967.

LeVine, R. A. *Culture, behavior, and personality*. Chicago: Aldine, 1973.

Levinson, D. J., Darrow, C. M., Klein, E. B., Levinson, M. H., & McKee, B. The psychosocial development of men in early adulthood and the mid-life transition. In D. F. Ricks, A. Thomas, & M. Roff, (Eds.), *Life history research in psychopathology*. Vol. 3. Minneapolis, Minn.: University of Minnesota Press, 1974, 243–258.

Lichtenberg, P. Emotional maturity as manifested ideational interaction. *Journal of Abnormal and Social Psychology*, 1955, *51*, 298–301.

Lichtenberg, P., Cassetta, R. K., & Scanlon, J. C. Mutual achievement strivings: a continuum for mental health. *Journal of Abnormal and Social Psychology*, 1961, *63*, 619–628.

Lindzey, G. *Projective techniques and cross-cultural research*. New York: Appleton-Century-Crofts, 1961.

Loevinger, J. *Ego development: conceptions and theories*. San Francisco, Calif.: Jossey-Bass, 1976.

Loevinger, J. The meaning and measurement of ego development. *American Psychologist*, 1966, *21*, 195–206.

Loevinger, J. & Wessler, R. *Measuring ego development: construction and use of a sentence completion test*. Vol. 1, San Francisco, Calif.: Jossey-Bass, 1970.

Lowry, D. Frustration reactions in 22 six year old boys. Unpubl. thesis, Haverford College, 1967.

Luborsky, L. Clinicians' judgments of mental health. *Archives of General Psychiatry*, 1962, *7*, 407–417.

Luborsky, L. & Bachrach, M. Factors influencing clinicians' judgments of mental health: eighteen experiences with the Health Sickness Rating Scale. *Archives of General Psychiatry*, 1974, *31*, 292–299.

Maas, H. S. & Kuypers, J. A. *From thirty to seventy*. San Francisco, Calif.: Jossey-Bass, 1974.

Maccoby, E. E. & Jacklin, C. N. *The psychology of sex differences*. Palo Alto, Calif.: Stanford University Press, 1974.

MacKinnon, D. W. The highly effective individual. *Teachers College Record*, 1960, *61*, 367–378.

Mahoney, J. & Hartnett, J. Self-actualization and self-ideal discrepancy. *Journal of Psychology*, 1973, *85*, 37–42.

Mandler, G., Mandler, J. M., Kremen, I., & Sholiton, R. D. The response to threat: relations among verbal and physiological indices. *Psychological Monographs*, 1961, *75*, No. 9.

Maslow, A. H. A theory of metamotivation: the biological rooting of the value-life. *Journal of Humanistic Psychology*, 1967a, *7*, 93–127.

Maslow, A. H. Fusions of facts and values. *American Journal of Psychoanalysis*, 1963, *23*, 117–131.

Maslow, A. H. *Motivation and personality*. New York: Harper & Row, 1954.

Maslow, A. H. (Ed.), *New knowledge in human values.* New York: Harper & Row, 1959.

Maslow, A. H. *The psychology of science: a reconnaissance.* New York: Harper & Row, 1966.

Maslow, A. H. Self-actualizing and beyond. In J. F. T. Bugental (Ed.), *Challenges of humanistic psychology.* New York: McGraw-Hill, 1967b, Ch. 29.

Maslow, A. H. *Toward a psychology of being.* Princeton, N.J.: D. Van Nostrand, 1962.

Masuda, M. & Holmes, T. H. The Social Readjustment Rating Scale; a cross-cultural study of Japanese and Americans. *Journal of Psychosomatic Research,* 1967, *11,* 227–237.

McClelland, D. C. Testing for competence rather than for "intelligence." *American Psychologist,* 1973, *28,* 1–14.

McGehee, T. P. The stability of the self-concept and self-esteem. *Dissert. Abstr.,* 1957, *17,* 1403–1404.

Mead, G. H. *Mind, self and society from the standpoint of a social behaviorist.* Chicago: University of Chicago Press, 1934.

Meade, R. D. & Brislin, R. W. Controls in cross-cultural experimentation. *International Journal of Psychology,* 1973. *8,* 231–238.

Moore, M. S. Some myths about "mental illness." *Archives of General Psychiatry,* 1975, *32,* 1483–1497.

Morris, C. *Varieties of human values.* Chicago: University of Chicago Press, 1956.

Mowrer, O. H. Commendation and a few questions. *The Counseling Psychologist,* 1973, *4,* 21–22.

Murphy, J. M. A cross-cultural comparison of psychiatric disorder: Eskimos of Alaska, Yorubas of Nigeria, and Nova Scotians of Canada. In W. P. Lebra (Ed.), *Transcultural research in mental health.* Honolulu, Hawaii: University Press of Hawaii, 1972, Ch. 14.

Murphy, J. M. Psychiatric labeling in cross-cultural perspective. *Science,* 1976, *191,* 1019–1028.

Murphy, L. B. The widening world of childhood. New York: Basic Books, 1962.

Naroll, R. Cultural determinants and the concept of the sick society. In S. C. Plog & R. B. Edgerton (Eds.), *Changing perspectives in mental illness.* New York: Holt, Rinehart, & Winston, 1969, 128–155.

Neill, A. S. *Summerhill.* New York: Hart, 1960.

Neki, J. S. *Sahaja*: An Indian ideal of mental health. *Psychiatry,* 1975, *38,* 1–10

Neugarten, B. L. Dynamics of transition of middle age to old age. Adaptation and the life cycle. *Journal of Geriatric Psychiatry,* 1970, *4,* 71–87.

Newcomb, T. M. & Feldman, K. A. *The impacts of colleges on students*. San Francisco, Calif.: Jossey-Bass, 1969.

Norbeck, E. & De Vos, G. Japan. In F. L. K. Hsu (Ed.), *Psychological anthropology*. Homewood, Ill: Dorsey Press, 1961, Ch. 2.

Offer, D. The concept of normality. *Psychiatric Annals*, 1973, *3*, 20–29.

Offer, D. & Sabshin, M. *Normality. Theoretical and clinical concepts of mental health*. Rev. Ed. New York: Basic Books, 1974.

Opler, M. K. Anthropological contributions to psychiatry and social psychiatry. In S. C. Plog & R. B. Edgerton (Eds.), *Changing perspectives in mental illness*. New York: Holt, Rinehart, & Winston, 1969, 88–105.

Osgood, C. E., May, W. H., & Miron, M. S. *Cross-cultural universals of affective meaning*. Urbana, Ill.: University of Illinois Press, 1975.

Osgood, C. E., Suci, G. J., & Tannenbaum, P. H. *The measurement of meaning*. Urbana, Ill.: University of Illinois Press, 1957.

Owens, C. M. Zen Buddhism. In C. T. Tart (Ed.), *Transpersonal psychologies*. New York: Harper & Row, 1975, Ch. 4.

Parsons, O. A. & Schneider, J. M. Locus of control in university students from Eastern and Western societies. *Journal of Consulting and Clinical Psychology*, 1974, *42*, 456–461.

Pearlin, L. I. *Class context and family relations. A cross-national study*. Boston, Mass.: Little, Brown, 1971.

Perls, F. S. *Gestalt therapy verbatim*. Lafayette, Calif.: Real People Press, 1969.

Pedersen, P. Asian personality theories. In R. Corsini (Ed.), *Current Personality Theories*. Itasca, Ill.: F. E. Peacock Publ., 1977.

Perry, W. G., Jr. *Forms of intellectual and ethical development during the college years*. New York: Holt, Rinehart, & Winston, 1970.

Phillips, L., Broverman, I. K., & Zigler, E. Social competence and psychiatric diagnosis. *Journal of Abnormal Psychology*, 1966, *71*, 209–214.

Piaget, J. *The origins of intelligence in children* (1936). New York: International Universities Press, 1952.

Piaget, J. *The psychology of intelligence* (1947). New York: Harcourt, Brace & Co., 1950.

Piaget, J. & Inhelder, B. *The psychology of the child* (1966). New York: Basic Books, 1969.

Plog, S. C. & Edgerton, R. B. (Eds.), *Changing perspectives in mental illness*. New York: Holt, Rinehart, & Winston, 1969.

Poe, C. A. Development of a psychological effectiveness scale *Journal of Psychology*, 1973, *85*, 81–85.

Raanan, S. L. Test review. *Journal of Counseling Psychology*, 1973, *20*, 477–478.

Rahe, R. H. Life change and subsequent illness reports. In E. K. E. Gunderson & R. H. Rahe (Eds.), *Life stress and illness.* Springfield, Ill.: Charles C. Thomas, 1974, Ch. 4.

Rasmussen, J. E. Relationship of ego identity to psychosocial effectiveness. *Psychological Reports*, 1964, *15*, 815–825.

Rogers, C. R. A theory of therapy, personality, and interpersonal relationships, as developed in the client-centered framework. In S. Koch (Ed.), *Psychology: a study of a science*, Vol. 3. *Formulations of the person and the social context.* New York: McGraw-Hill, 1959, 184–256.

Rogers, C. R. & Dymond, R. F. (Eds.), *Psychotherapy and personality change.* Chicago: University of Chicago Press, 1954.

Rohlen, T. P. The promise of adulthood in Japanese spiritualism. In Adulthood, *Daedalus*, 1976, 125–143.

Rosen, B. C. & LaRaia, A. L. Modernity in women: an index of social change in Brazil. *Journal of Marriage and the Family*, 1972, *38*, 198–212.

Rosenhan, D. L. On being sane in insane places. *Science*, 1973, *179*, 250–258.

Rosenwald, G. C. Conflict, functional disruption, and defense-effectiveness. *Journal of Personality Assessment*, 1972, *36*, 218–229.

Rotter, J. B. Generalized expectancies for internal versus external control of reinforcement. *Psychological Monographs*, 1966, *80*, 1.

Sagarin, E. & Kelly, R. J. Sexual deviance and labelling perspectives. In W. R. Gove (Ed.), *The labelling of deviance.* New York: Halsted Press, Wiley, 1975, Ch. 9.

Sanford, N. What is a normal personality? In J. Katz, *et al.* (Eds.), *Writers on ethics: classical and contemporary.* Princeton, N.J.: D. Van Nostrand, 1962.

Sarbin, T. R. The scientific status of the mental illness metaphor. In S. C. Plog & R. B. Edgerton (Eds.), *Changing perspectives in mental illness.* New York: Holt, Rinehart, & Winston, 1969.

Scheff, T. J. On reason and sanity: political dimensions of psychiatric thought. In W. P. Lebra (Ed.), *Transcultural research in mental health.* Honolulu, Hawaii: University Press of Hawaii, 1972, Ch. 26.

Scott, W. A. & Peterson, C. Adjustment, Pollyannaism, and attraction to close relationships. *Journal of Counseling and Clinical Psychology*, 1975, *43*, 872–880.

Seeman, J. Personality integration in college women. *Journal of Personality and Social Psychology*, 1966, *4*, 91–93.

Seeman, J. Toward a concept of personality integration. *American Psychologist*, 1959, *14*, 633–637.

Selman, R. L. A developmental approach to interpersonal and moral awareness in young children: some theoretical and educational perspectives. Paper given to American Montessori Society, 1974.

Shainess, N. Discussion of R. White, The concept of healthy personality. *The Counseling Psychologist*, 1973, *4*, 41–44.

Shapiro, D. H., Jr. & Zifferblatt, S. M. Zen meditation and behavioral self-control. Similarities, differences, and clinical applications. *American Psychologist*, 1976, *31*, 519–532.

Sherman, J. A. *On the psychology of women. A survey of empirical studies.* Springfield, Ill.: Charles C. Thomas, 1971.

Shoben, E. J., Jr. Toward a concept of the normal personality. *American Psychologist*, 1957, *12*, 183–189.

Shostrom, E. L. A test for the measurement of self-actualization. *Educational & Psychological Measurement*, 1964, *24*, 207–218.

Shostrom, E. L. Comment on a test review: the Personal Orientation Inventory. *Journal of Counseling Psychology*, 1973, *20*, 479–481.

Shostrom, E. L. & Knapp, R. R. The relationship of a measurement of self-actualization (POI) to a measure of pathology (MMPI) and to therapeutic growth. *American Journal of Psychotherapy*, 1966, *20*, 193–202.

Singer, J. L. Navigating the stream of consciousness. Research in daydreaming and related inner experiences. *American Psychologist*, 1975, *30*, 727–738.

Sinnott, E. W. The creativeness of life. In H. H. Anderson (Ed.), *Creativity and its cultivation*. New York: Harper & Row, 1959, Ch. 2.

Smith, D. H. & Inkeles, A. The OM Scale: a comparative socio-psychological measure of individual modernity. *Sociometry*, 1966, *29*, 353–377.

Smith, G. M. Six measures of self-concept discrepancy and instability: their interrelations, reliability, and relations to other personality measures. *Journal of Consulting Psychology*, 1958, *22*, 101–112.

Smith, M. B. Competence and adaptation. *The American Journal of Occupational Therapy*, 1974a, *28*, 11–15.

Smith, M. B. Competence and "mental health": problems in conceptualizing human effectiveness. In S. B. Sells (Ed.), *The definition and measurement of mental health*. U. S. Dept. of Health, Education and Welfare, Public Health Service, 1968.

Smith, M. B. Competence and socialization. *Social psychology and human values*. Chicago: Aldine, 1969a, Ch. 15.

Smith, M. B. Explorations in competence: a study of Peace Corps teachers in Ghana. *American Psychologist*, 1966, *21*, 555–566.

Smith, M. B. *Humanizing social psychology*. San Francisco, Calif.: Jossey-Bass, 1974b.

Smith, M. B. "Mental health" reconsidered: a special case of the problem of values in psychology. *American Psychologist*, 1961, *16*, 299–306.

Smith, M. B. Normality: for an abnormal age. In D. Offer & D. X. Freedman (Eds.), *Modern psychiatry and clinical research*. New York: Basic Books. 1972.

Smith, M. B. On self-actualization: a transambivalent examination of a focal theme in Maslow's psychology. *Journal of Humanistic Psychology*, 1973, *13*, 17–33.

Smith, M. B. Optima of mental health. *Psychiatry*, 1950, *13*, 503–510.

Smith, M. B. Research strategies toward a conception of positive mental health. *American Psychologist*, 1959, *14*, 673–681.

Smith, M. B. Some thoughts on the legitimation of evil. *Social psychology and human values*. Chicago: Aldine, 1969b, Ch. 28.

Soddy, K. (Ed.). *Cross-cultural studies in mental health: mental health and value systems*. London: Tavistock Publications, 1961.

Spilka, B. & Werme, P. H. Religion and mental disorder: a research perspective. In M. B. Strommen (Ed.), *Research on religious development*. New York: Hawthorn Books, 1971, Ch. 12.

Srole, L. Measurement and classification in socio-psychiatric epidemiology: Midtown Manhattan study (1954) and Midtown Manhattan restudy (1974). *Journal of Health and Social Behavior*, 1975, *16*, 347–364.

Stein, K. B. & Chu, C. L. Dimensionality of Barron's Ego-strength scale, *Journal of Consulting Psychology. 1967, 31*, 153–161.

Sullivan, H. S. *The interpersonal theory of psychiatry*. New York: W. W. Norton, 1953.

Szasz, T. S. *Ideology and insanity*. Garden City, New York: Anchor Books, Doubleday Co., 1970.

Szasz, T. S. The myth of mental illness. *American Psychologist*, 1960, *15*, 113–118.

Szasz, T. S. *The myth of mental illness. Foundations of a theory of personal conduct*. New York: Dell Publ., 1961.

Szasz, T. S. The myth of psychotherapy. *American Journal of Psychotherapy*, 1974, *28*, 517–526.

Tart, C. T. States of consciousness and state-specific sciences. *Science*, 1972, *176*, 1203–1210.

Tart, C. T. *Transpersonal psychologies*. New York: Harper & Row, 1975.

Tiedeman, D. V. Decision and vocational development: a paradigm and its implications. *Personnel & Guidance Journal*, 1961, *40*, 15–21.

Tillich, P. Is a science of human values possible? In A. H. Maslow (Ed.), *New knowledge in human values*. New York: Harper & Row, 1959, 189–196.

Tippett, J. S. & Silber, E. Autonomy of self-esteem. *Archives of General Psychiatry*, 1966, *14*, 372–385.

Tosi, D. J. & Lindamood, C. A. The measurement of self-actualization: a critical review of the personal orientation inventory. *Journal of Personality Assessment*, 1975, *39*, 215–224.

Triandis, H. C. An approach to the analysis of subjective culture. In W. P. Lebra (Ed.), *Transcultural research in mental health*. Honolulu, Hawaii: University Press of Hawaii, 1972a, Ch. 16.

Triandis, H. C., Malpass, R. S., & Davidson, A. R. Psychology and culture. *Annual Review of Psychology*, 1973, *24*, 355–378.

Triandis, H. C. and others. *The analysis of subjective culture*. New York: Wiley, 1972b.

Tseng, W. S. The concept of personality in Confucian thought. *Psychiatry*, 1973. *36*, 191–202.

Turner, R. H. & Vanderlippe, R. H. Self-ideal congruence as an index of adjustment. *Journal of Abnormal and Social Psychology*, 1958, *57*, 202–206.

Vaillant, G. E. Antecedents of healthy adult male adjustment. In D. F. Ricks, A. Thomas, & M. Roff (Eds.), *Life history research in psychopathology*. Vol. 3. Minneapolis, Minn.: University of Minnesota Press, 1974, 230–242.

Vaillant, G. E. Natural history of male psychological health. III. Empirical dimensions of mental health. *Archives of General Psychiatry*, 1975, *32*, 420–426.

Vaillant, G. E. Natural history of male psychological health. V. The relation of choice of ego mechanisms of defense to adult adjustment. *Archives of General Psychiatry*, 1976, *33*, 535–545.

Vaillant, G. E. Theoretical hierarchy of adaptive ego mechanisms. *Archives of General Psychiatry*, 1971, *24*, 107–118.

Vaillant, G. E. & McArthur, C. C. Natural history of male psychological health. I. The adult life cycle from 18–50. *Seminars in psychiatry*, 1972, *4*, No. 4.

Van Doren, M. *Liberal education*. New York: Henry Holt, 1943.

Vernon, P. E. *Intelligence and cultural environment*. London, Eng.: Methuen & Co., 1969.

Wallace, A. F. C. *Culture and personality*. New York: Random House, 1961.

Wallach, M. A. The psychology of talent and graduate education. Paper presented to Conference on Cognitive Styles and Creativity in Higher Education, Montreal, Nov. 1972.

Wechsler, D. Intelligence defined and undefined. A relativistic appraisal. *American Psychologist*, 1975, *30*, 135–139.

Wechsler, D. *The measurement and appraisal of adult intelligence*, 4th ed. Baltimore, Md.: Williams & Wilkins, 1958.

Wei-Ming, T. The Confucian perception of adulthood. In Adulthood, *Daedalus*, 1976, 109–123.

Werner, H. *Comparative psychology of mental development*. Chicago: Follett Publ. Co., 1948, Rev. ed.

Werner, O. & Campbell, D. Translating, working through interpreters, and the problem of decentering. In R. Naroll & R. Cohen (Eds.), *A handbook of method in cultural anthropology*. New York: American Museum of Natural History, 1970, 398–420.

Westley, W. A. & Epstein, N. B. *The silent majority*. San Francisco, Calif.: Jossey-Bass, 1969.

Wexler, D. A. Self-actualization and cognitive processes. *Journal of Consulting and Clinical Psychology*, 1974, *42*, 47–53.

White, B. L. Fundamental early environmental influences on the development of competence. Paper presented Third Western Symposium on Learning: Cognitive Learning, Washington State College, Bellingham, Washington, 1971.

White, R. W. Competence and the psychosexual stages of development. *Nebraska Symposium on Motivation*, 1960, 97–141.

White, R. W. Ego and reality in psychoanalytic theory. *Psychological Issues*, 1963, *3*.

White, R. W. *Lives in progress*. New York: Dryden Press, 1952.

White, R. W. Motivation reconsidered: the concept of competence. *Psychological Review*, 1959, *66*, 297–333.

White, R. W. Personal correspondence, 1974.

White, R. W. The concept of healthy personality: what do we really mean? *The Counseling Psychologist*, 1973, *4*, 3–13.

Whiting, B. B. & Whiting, J. W. M. *Children of six cultures. A psycho-cultural analysis*. Cambridge, Mass.: Harvard University Press, 1975.

Wills, B. J. Personality variables which discriminate between groups differing in level of self-actualization. *Journal of Counseling Psychology*, 1974, *21*, 222–227.

Witkin, H. A. & Berry, J. W. Psychological differentiation in cross-cultural perspective. *Journal of Cross-Cultural Psychology*, 1975, *6*, 4–87.

Witkin, H. A., Lewis, H. B., Hertzman, M., Machover, K., Meissner, P. B., & Wapner, S. *Personality through perception: an experimental and clinical study*. New York: Harper & Row, 1954.

Witkin, H. A., *et al.* Social conformity and psychological differentiation. *International Journal of Psychology*, 1974, *9*, 11–29.

Wittkower, E. D. & Fried, J. Some problems of transcultural psychiatry. In S. K. Weinberg (Ed.), *The sociology of mental disorders*. Chicago: Aldine, 1967, 324–329.

Wright, L. & Wyant, K. Factor structure of self-actualization as measured by Shostrom's SAV Scale. *Educational* & *Psychological Measurement,* 1974, *34,* 871–875.

Yeh, E. K. & Chu, H. M. The images of Chinese and American character: cross-cultural adaptation by Chinese students. In W. P. Lebra (Ed.), *Youth, socialization, and mental health.* Honolulu, Hawaii: University Press of Hawaii, 1974, Ch. 15.

Index